# THE SOURCES OF HISTORY:
## STUDIES IN THE USES OF HISTORICAL EVIDENCE

GENERAL EDITOR: G. R. ELTON

*The Sources of History:*
*Studies in the Uses of Historical Evidence*

# Medieval Wales

by
R. IAN JACK

CORNELL UNIVERSITY PRESS
Ithaca, New York

First published 1972 by Cornell University Press.
This edition is not for sale in the British Commonwealth (except Canada) or Europe.

International Standard Book Number 0–8014–0692–7
Library of Congress Catalog Card Number 79–37005
Printed in Great Britain

Et potest preter hoc haberi alia utilissima cautela que in his circumstantiis potest attendi, ut sciatur cuiusmodi penitentia cui persone sit iniungenda. Alia enim penitentia est iniungenda Walensi, alia Anglico, alia forti, alia debili, alia iuveni, alia seni, et ita de ceteris. Similiter in convictu alia penitentia iniungenda est agricole, alia mercatori, alia militi, alia histrioni sive meretrici qui in sordido questu versantur, alia oratori, alia sutori, et ita de ceteris. Nunquam igitur penitentiam bene iniunget qui predictas et etiam sequentes varietates personarum non attenderit.

*Thomae de Chobham Summa Confessorum*, ed. F. Broomfield, Analecta Mediaevalia Namurcensia xxv (Louvain 1968), 51–2.

# Contents

# Abbreviations

| | |
|---|---|
| *Arch. Camb.* | *Archaeologia Cambrensis* |
| *B.B.C.S.* | *Bulletin of the Board of Celtic Studies* |
| *Brit.Num.J.* | *British Numismatic Journal* |
| D.D. | Deposited Document (in Cardiff Central Library) |
| *D.K.R.* | *Report of the Deputy Keeper of the Public Records* |
| *D.N.B.* | *Dictionary of National Biography* |
| *D.W.B.* | *Dictionary of Welsh Biography* |
| H.M.C. | Historical Manuscripts Commission |
| Lloyd, *History* | J. E. Lloyd, *A History of Wales from the Earliest Times to the Edwardian Conquest* (3rd ed., London 1939) |
| N.L.W. | National Library of Wales |
| *N.L.W.J.* | *National Library of Wales Journal* |
| P.R.O. | Public Record Office |
| *Trans. Hon. Soc. Cymm.* | *Transactions of the Honourable Society of Cymmrodorion* |

# General Editor's Introduction

By what right do historians claim that their reconstructions of the past are true, or at least on the road to truth? How much of the past can they hope to recover: are there areas that will remain for ever dark, questions that will never receive an answer? These are problems which should and do engage not only the scholar and student but every serious reader of history. In the debates on the nature of history, however, attention commonly concentrates on philosophic doubts about the nature of historical knowledge and explanation, or on the progress that might be made by adopting supposedly new methods of analysis. The disputants hardly ever turn to consider the materials with which historians work and which must always lie at the foundation of their structures. Yet, whatever theories or methods the scholar may embrace, unless he knows his sources and rests upon them he will not deserve the name of historian. The bulk of historical evidence is much larger and more complex than most laymen and some professionals seem to know, and a proper acquaintance with it tends to prove both exhilarating and sobering—exhilarating because it opens the road to unending enquiry, and sobering because it reduces the inspiring theory and the new method to their proper subordinate place in the scheme of things. It is the purpose of this series to bring this fact to notice by showing what we have and how it may be used.

G. R. ELTON

# *Preface*

When Thomas de Chobham, the sub-dean of Salisbury, wrote his manual for confessors in the year of Magna Carta, he emphasised that a careful psychological appraisal of the penitent was an essential part of the priest's function: the confessor should remember that a Welshman was as different from an Englishman as a minstrel or a harlot from a knight. No less a contrast exists between the Welsh reluctance to write general surveys of their history and of its sources and the zealousness of the English. If this book has any theme at all, it is the nature and cause of this contrast.

The central, superficial contrast is between the bulk of the sources for English medieval history, narrative, archival and material, and the small remains for medieval Wales. The difficulty of the Welsh sources, their physical dispersal and the lack of existing finding-aids create massive problems, and in the course of compiling this survey I have been acutely aware of my own ignorance in too many aspects of these sources. Like John Speed, I have been obliged to 'put my sickle into other mens corne'. It is my hope, however, that this initial survey will prompt those qualified in the special fields on which I have trespassed to produce fuller and more authoritative introductions for students. I hope, too, that the questions which I have asked and the projects which I have urged will do more than arouse a nod of approval or a snort of contempt—that they will encourage some activity, whether the translation of ideas into reality or explanations why the ideas should be refuted or the projects discouraged.

# CHAPTER 1

# Literary Sources

The study is still unwritten which will range widely over the various elements in medieval historical writing and explore properly the basic questions of purpose and design. In the medieval context, it is wrong to look at the chronicles and annals written in one country alone: the significance of the historical activity, from the grandest to the most localised, within one area can only be assessed in a wider study. The number of people involved in historical writing, their degree of learning, their width of horizon, their attitude towards their sources, their awareness of the passage of time, basic issues such as these cannot be discussed adequately on English or French, much less Welsh, materials alone. My purpose, however, in this chapter is not to attempt this major study, but to bring together elementary suggestions for some of the ways in which the narrative sources for Welsh history may eventually be fitted into this European scene. At the same time, the practical purpose of this series has dominated the presentation, so that anyone unfamiliar with the present state of scholarship may have some straightforward introduction to the texts themselves and to appraisals of them.

The creation of Wales and the evidences for it are very much corollaries of the *adventus Saxonum*. As England was born, so was Wales, not quite by default, but rather by remainder. The slow end of Roman Britain and the gradual conquest of much of the island by Germanic tribes is attested in four principal early literary sources, which are essential also for the study of early Wales. The works of the British writers, Gildas and Nennius, and the purely Anglo-Saxon works of Bede and the *Anglo-Saxon Chronicle* must jointly take first place in any survey.

The works of Gildas and Nennius, especially Nennius, pose, however, grave critical problems, turning on argument of a very specialised kind. These shadowy men have been the object of much ingenious and learned argument among historians, archaeologists, philologists and Celticists generally, and, although a reasonable consensus of opinion about Gildas has emerged, as much cannot be said for Nennius.

In the case of Gildas, the value of the reasonably firm conclusion which has been reached can best be shown by the implications of the dubiety which it has replaced. The *De Excidio et Conquestu Britanniae* as it has descended to us is a short book of 110 chapters, containing, especially in its first twenty-six chapters, a substantial amount of obscure historical narrative.[1] The 'Ruin of Britain' is, as Ebert described it, a *Tendenzschrift*:[2] this is no sober set of annals, no dispassionate chronicle; it is certainly in part, probably in whole, a bitter, despairing outburst by a man who lived through some part of the confusion of the Anglo-Saxon conquest. But to use the *De Excidio*, it is necessary to know facts about the author with greater precision. It has been argued that the historical section of the book is separate from the denunciatory, homiletic section, that they are by two distinct authors. The most influential, vigorous and extreme exponent of the two Gildases was the Rev. A. W. Wade-Evans, who died in 1964 after sixty years of study and publications on problems involving the interpretation of Gildas.[3] Archbishop Ussher, in the seventeenth century, had popularised the view that there were two Gildases, one Gildas 'Albanius' of the fifth century, the other, Gildas 'Badonicus' of the sixth century. Ussher, however, regarded the *De Excidio* as the sole work of Gildas Badonicus.[4] Wade-Evans used the old concept of Albanius and Badonicus, but divided the *De Excidio*

[1] For a bibliography of Gildas studies, see W. F. Bolton, *A History of Anglo-Latin Literature, 597–1066*, i, *597–740* (Princeton 1967), 244–8.

[2] Quoted in the Cymmrodorion Society edition of *De Excidio Britanniae*, ed. H. Williams (Cymmrodorion Record Series iii, 1899), i, p. v.

[3] See, as well as the list of works by Wade-Evans in Bolton, *Anglo-Latin Literature*, H. D. Emanuel, 'The Rev. A. W. Wade-Evans: an Appreciation of his Contribution to the Study of Early Welsh History', *Trans. Hon. Soc. Cymm.* (1965), 266–71.

[4] J. Ussher, *Britannicarum Ecclesiarum Antiquitates* (Dublin 1639), 441–2.

between them and redated them drastically. Gildas Albanius was, to Wade-Evans, the early author of the denunciatory part of the book, now designated the *Epistola* (as the author himself called it in the opening words of the preface), while Gildas Badonicus completed the historical section, the real *De Excidio*, in 708. The style of this early eighth-century work was then touched up to become more akin to the rhetorical ebullience of the *Epistola* and interpolated before the first chapter of the earlier text. Thus, in the eyes of Wade-Evans, the text as Mommsen established it in 1898[1] was a composite one. The implications of such an assertion are serious, of course, and coloured Wade-Evans's interpretation of the fifth century.[2] This is not to say that others have not reached comparable conclusions, reducing the dramatic quality of the invasions and emphasising the gradualness of the process: as Dr H. D. Emanuel has very properly pointed out, H. M. Chadwick and Kenneth Jackson would support a similar general conclusion from archaeological and philological evidence respectively.[3] But the effect of transferring the more historical part of the *De Excidio* to the eighth century is to deprive us of a remarkable contemporary account, however obscure, however polemical. It implies moreover a sophisticated ability to manipulate Latin, to imitate a past style of great artificiality: if this ability had been proven, it would have been of interest in the intellectual and ecclesiastical history of Britain.

This late dating no longer, however, has influential defenders. Anyone venturing afresh on the study of the fifth and sixth centuries must, of course, make up his own mind about his attitude to the first twenty-six chapters of the *De Excidio*, but he will now do so in the knowledge that modern linguistic analysis lends no support to the idea of dual authorship. The

[1] *Monumenta Germaniae Historica, Auctores Antiquissimi*, xiii, *Chronica Minora Saec. IV, V, VI, VII*, iii, ed. T. Mommsen (Berlin 1898), 1–85. There are only four manuscripts, one each from the eleventh, twelfth, thirteenth and fourteenth centuries.

[2] See, in particular, A. W. Wade-Evans, *The Emergence of England and Wales* (Wetteren, Belgium, 1956; 2nd ed., Cambridge 1959).

[3] Emanuel, *Trans. Hon. Soc. Cymm.* (1965), 269.

text is throughout consistent with sixth-century Latinity.[1]

Beyond the celebrated allusions to the *superbus tyrannus* (identified plausibly with Vortigern) and to Ambrosius Aurelianus,[2] the evidence which it supplies of education and church life a century and more after the Romans finally left Britain is uniquely valuable. The purely denunciatory later parts of the book contain long groups of chapters (38–63, 76–105) which 'can be regarded as nothing more than anthologies of scriptural passages bearing on the subject at hand':[3] clearly the author could expect his readers to recognise the stream of allusions and to be able to extract their meaning: 'I could wish indeed that these testimonies of holy Scripture . . . should all be interpreted according to the historical or the moral sense.'[4] Moreover, the severe strictures which Gildas lays upon his fellow-churchmen, are themselves evidence:

> Britain has priests, but foolish ones; a great number of ministers, but shameless ones; clerics, but crafty plunderers; shepherds, as they say, but wolves ready for the slaughter of souls . . . They teach the people, but by furnishing the worst examples, teach vice and evil morals . . . With a shudder, indeed, at having to linger long at these things, I can with truth make one statement, that is, all these are changed into the contrary deeds, so that the clergy are . . . unchaste, double-tongued, drunk, greedy of filthy lucre, having faith and, to speak more truly, infidelity in an impure conscience.[5]

Gildas, in short, is very treacherous to use for specific acts, specific people, specific dates,[6] but as a general source for the atmosphere of Britain as it was becoming England and Wales he is unique.

Although Bede is next in time to Gildas, and uses the first

[1] F. Kerlouégan, 'Le Latin du *De Excidio Britanniae* de Gildas', *Christianity in Britain, 300–700*, ed. M. W. Barley and R. P. C. Hanson (Leicester 1968), 151–76.     [2] cc. 23, 25.     [3] Bolton, *Anglo-Latin Literature*, 37.     [4] c. 93.     [5] cc. 66, 109.

[6] Cf. the defence of Gildas by C. E. Stevens, 'Gildas Sapiens', *English Historical Review*, lvi (1941), 353–73, and the attack by F. Lot, 'De la valeur historique de *De Excidio et Conquestu Britanniae* de Gildas', *Mediaeval Studies in Memory of Gertrude Schoepperle Loomis* (Paris 1927), 229–64.

twenty-six chapters of the *De Excidio* extensively, Nennius is more conveniently taken in conjunction with Gildas. The *Historia Brittonum* which goes under the authorship of Nennius is still 'one of the most difficult and most controversial texts in the historiography of the middle ages'.[1] The textual history is not in itself of uncommon complexity,[2] but the method by which the text itself was compiled is very debatable indeed. As with the *De Excidio*, there is a basic question of authorship. The problem of the *Historia* is, however, much more complicated because it is itself an edition of earlier works; it owes much in its early sections to the ecclesiastical history of Eusebius, the chronicle of Prosper of Aquitaine, probably Bede, certain early Irish works and Gildas himself. It incorporates Anglo-Saxon genealogies of the sixth to eighth centuries. It includes a *Liber Sancti Germani* which Lot ascribed, unconvincingly, to the industry of Nennius himself.[3] It has ten chapters on the 'marvels of Britain', curiosities of the island, including Ireland and Anglesey, very Celtic specimens of a common literary genre.[4] And, most celebrated, the *Historia* has in chapter 56 the twelve victories of Arthur, 'dux bellorum': there is a whole international literary culture erected on the hints given in chapter 56.

Clearly the elements in this work come from a long period of time. All are not found in all manuscripts and the debate turns on the number of 'editions' and 'editors'. The *Historia* indeed appears to be 'an organism rather than a composition as we usually understand the latter term'.[5] But Nennius as an individual has survived, and the balance of probability is not only that he

[1] F. Lot, *Nennius et l'Historia Brittonum* (Bibliothèque de l'Ecole des Hautes Etudes, Sciences historiques et philologiques, cclxiii, Paris 1934), introduction.

[2] Cf. F. Liebermann, 'Nennius', *Essays in Medieval History presented to Thomas Frederick Tout*, ed. A. G. Little and F. M. Powicke (Manchester 1925), 33. The four manuscript groups were established by Mommsen.

[3] *Ibid.*, 80–6. Mrs Chadwick regards it as deriving from a life written before 700, 'Early Culture and Learning in North Wales', *Studies in the Early British Church* (Cambridge 1958), 113.

[4] Lot, *Nennius*, 106–14.

[5] Chadwick, 'Early Culture and Learning', *Studies in the Early British Church*, 42.

existed but that he did make the basic compilation himself late in the eighth or early in the ninth century. He was a Welshman, probably from South Wales, although Lot is contemptuous of Liebermann's suggestion that he may have 'held the post of official interpreter at his prince's court near the English frontier'.[1] He was certainly a cleric, writing Latin which Lot castigated as 'exécrable, rempli de "brittonismes"':[2] and 'he is generally regarded, rightly or wrongly, as a dim-witted and muddle-headed person'.[3] He had a sense of humour, if the Nemniuus of a Bodleian manuscript is indeed the same man, as seems plausible. In this Bodleian manuscript there is a copy of a faked alphabet, of general Runic aspect, with the note: 'Nemniuus invented these letters, when a certain Saxon scholar jeered at the Britons for not having an alphabet of their own. So he suddenly devised them out of his own head, in order to refute the charge of stupidity brought against his nation'.[4]

This pioneer spirit in historical compilation and in Celtic mystification, who faked an alphabet as a good antiquarian joke, belongs in a small way to the world of Geoffrey of Monmouth: but he enshrines more fact and less fancy in his *Historia* than Geoffrey was to do three hundred years later. Nennius vexes all his users: he had little power of historical discrimination, as his treatment of Bede demonstrates. But he realised the need to preserve some records of his country's past and recognised, unlike Gildas, that the Anglo-Saxons had something to offer Wales, however immoral their original conquest of Britain may have been. 'He approached very near the door of Anglo-Latin civilisation, and paved the way for his greater countryman, the biographer of Alfred.'[5] But most of all, he paved the way for the ineffable Geoffrey of Monmouth.

[1] Lot, *Nennius*, 115 n.4; Liebermann, *Essays presented to Tout*, 39.

[2] Lot, *Nennius*, 116.

[3] K. Jackson, 'On the Northern British Section in Nennius', *Celt and Saxon*, ed. N. K. Chadwick (Cambridge 1963), 57.

[4] Ifor Williams, 'Notes on Nennius', *B.B.C.S.*, vii (1933–35), 380–1; 'The Nennian Preface: a Possible Emendation', *ibid.*, ix (1937–39), 342.

[5] Liebermann, *Essays presented to Tout*, 44.

It is a relief to turn to Bede after facing the bitter critical dilemmas and indifferent prose presented by Gildas and Nennius. Bede's *Ecclesiastical History* is still read and enjoyed by thousands of non-specialists: since the *editio princeps* in 1475–80 there have been few decades in which a printed edition has not been easily available somewhere in Europe. Today there are at least four editions of the Latin and five English translations in print. It circulated widely in manuscript from Bede's own day until a century after the printing press was operating in Europe. Over 160 manuscripts are still in existence.[1] The Moore and the Leningrad manuscripts, probably both copied from Bede's own autograph, went abroad quite early; copies were in Germany by 800; and an early ninth-century Nonantola manuscript seems to be central to the dissemination of the text in Italy. There is little textual problem, for 'the scribes of our two oldest manuscripts might well have been among the disciples who gathered around the master's death-bed' in 735.[2] The Christian world, therefore, has had constant access to the historical work of this Northumbrian monk for over twelve hundred years. Very few writers have exercised so consistent an appeal over so long a period.

What is it that has made Bede a monk for all seasons? His scrupulousness; his flair for dealing with evidence; the sheer interest of the story which he has to tell; his common sense; his solid, straightforward, lucid Latin rising occasionally to heights of genuine eloquence; his literary architecture which did not fully solve the problems of organising a narrative of Christian life in many independent English kingdoms but which avoided the sprawling incoherence to which medieval chroniclers were prone and which constructed individual scenes with dramatic skill; his fair-mindedness, even towards the adherents of the Celtic Easter when, like Aidan, they displayed compensating virtues;[3]

[1] M. L. W. Laistner and H. H. King, *A Hand-List of Bede Manuscripts* (Ithaca 1943), 94–102; *Bede's Ecclesiastical History of the English People*, ed. B. Colgrave and R. A. B. Mynors (Oxford Medieval Texts, Oxford 1969), xvii.   [2] *Ibid.*, xxxix and Textual Introduction, *passim*.

[3] *Historia Ecclesiastica*, iii, 17.

his memorable stories, like Caedmon's gift of song,[1] or the con-
frontation and arbitration between the rival ecclesiastical usages
at Whitby in 664,[2] or the parable of the sparrow flying fleetly
through the Northumbrian hall, out of darkness into darkness,
with which a counsellor of Edwin argued for conversion from
paganism to Christianity—'if this new doctrine brings us more
certain information, it seems right that we should accept it'.[3]

As a result of all these virtues, Bede's work has endured not
just as a unique source to be quarried but also as a book to be read.
As much can be said for very few medieval histories. Bede sat in a
place of calm. He included enough miracles to satisfy a credulous
age, but few enough to disarm a more cynical age; he wrote with
sufficient moral intent to encourage good and discourage evil
as his period and calling expected,[4] but presented matter of such
interest with such fairness and truthfulness that readers anti-
pathetic to moral history are rarely alienated.[5] Moreover, he
was not, like many historians then and now, scraping the bottom
of the barrel to write his book. He discarded more than he put in,
his chapters on St Cuthbert are the distillation of his own and
others' full-scale biographies of Cuthbert, his excursus on the
Easter controversy is a masterly digest by one of the leading
chronological specialists of eighth-century Europe. All this gives
density to his work: like a medieval scholar reading Holy
Scripture, the modern reader can appreciate the *Ecclesiastical
History* on a number of levels.

The corollary to this selectivity and condensation is that much
which Bede knew but rejected is wholly lost to us. This is not so

[1] *Historia Ecclesiastica*, iv, 24.      [2] *Ibid.*, iii, 25.
[3] *Ibid.*, ii, 13.      [4] *Ibid.*, Preface.
[5] Cf. Bede's own rare statement of principle in the leading case of Aidan:
'I have written these things about the character and work of Aidan, not by any
means commending or praising his lack of knowledge in the matter of the
observance of Easter; indeed I heartily detest it, as I have clearly shown in the
book which I wrote called *De Temporibus*, but, as a truthful historian, I have
described in a straightforward manner those things which were done by him or
through him, praising such of his qualities as are worthy of praise and preserving their memory for the benefit of my readers' (iii, 17).

acute a problem with the English Church itself, but it is acute for the less central parts: secular history which had no ecclesiastical implication, and the geographical periphery. Thus Wales is treated only very incidentally: Edwin's conquest of Anglesey and the revolt of Caedwalla of Gwynedd, allied to Penda of Mercia, in 633,[1] or the state of the Welsh church when Augustine came in 597,[2] are rare examples of *pura Wallia* in Bede. But in the period covered by Bede, up to the early eighth century, the history of Northumbria, Mercia and Wessex, the fate of the Hwicce in Worcestershire and Gloucestershire, the progress of Roman missionary activity compared with Celtic Christianity in the island, are all part and parcel of the history and context of Wales. Historians of Wales cannot but regret that there was no monk at Bangor-is-Coed writing a history of worth comparable to that of the monk of Jarrow: but there was no such monk, and one must be grateful for Bede. As Bertram Colgrave remarked in his last tribute to the man who had dominated his scholarly interests for most of this century, 'one might contrast our knowledge of England in the seventh century with the history of Ireland and Wales for the same period. Here almost all that is known definitely depends on chance references in Bede; for the rest, vague tradition written down centuries later gives us a very uncertain foundation on which to build anything like a comprehensive account.'[3]

The form in which the literary sources are cast changes markedly for the remainder of the Anglo-Saxon period. It is the heyday of the annals, one English, basically West Saxon, the *Anglo-Saxon Chronicle*, the others the *Annales Cambriae* and the more literary *Bruts*. The origin of such 'year-notes' lies deep in calendar studies. Most civilisations from the Babylonians to the Christians had need of calendar calculations, whether it be Jewish passover-dates or Roman consul-lists or Christian Easter-dates: each in its turn, on clay tablet, on papyrus, on stone or on parchment, took the opportunity of noting beside a column of years significant happenings within each year. The format was very circumscribing

[1] *Ibid.*, ii, 9, 20; iii, 1. Cf. iv, 23.     [2] *Ibid.*, ii, 2.
[3] *Bede's Ecclesiastical History*, ed. Colgrave and Mynors, xviii.

and the historical 'annals' broke free from the tables to be expanded in an exciting year and to skimp a barren year.[1] Although such annals would ideally be constantly augmented and brought up to date, it is clear that this did not always happen and that, moreover, the form in which annals have been preserved is dependent on a series of consolidations. The most celebrated of such consolidations is that of the *Anglo-Saxon Chronicle*, probably in the reign and possibly at the instigation of King Alfred. Once the text was consolidated, it was maintained in various monastic centres, more or less independent of each other, and continued in some after the Norman Conquest. The last entry in any version of the *Anglo-Saxon Chronicle* is 1155 in the Peterborough copy. The relationship of the seven manuscripts which survive is intricate,[2] but there is no great difficulty in using the Chronicle: both the original Anglo-Saxon and the English translation are easily accessible in parallel-text editions.[3]

There is a much more substantial Welsh content in the Chronicle than in the *Ecclesiastical History*, particularly during the Welsh campaigns of Harold and William the Conqueror, and again it is the principal source for the history of Wales's neighbours. But like Bede's work, the Chronicle is still looking at Wales from the outside, and Wales only figures when it impinges on English policy. It is only with the *Annales Cambriae* and the *Bruts* that this process is reversed: there glimpses of English history are obtained only when, for example, William the Conqueror came to St David's;[4] although later sections of the Welsh annals incorporate more fully materials from English sources.

---

[1] Cf. C. W. Jones, *Saints' Lives and Chronicles in Early England* (Ithaca 1947), esp. chaps. 1 and 2.

[2] See *The Anglo-Saxon Chronicle*, revised trans., ed. D. Whitelock, D. C. Douglas and S. I. Tucker (London 1961), Introduction and Bibliography.

[3] The parallel texts of the Anglo-Saxon are by B. Thorpe in the Rolls Series (23, London 1861, six texts) and by C. Plummer (Oxford 1892–99, two texts): the best translations are the one cited in the previous note and the Everyman version by G. N. Garmonsway (London 1953).

[4] *Annales Cambriae*, ed. J. Williams ab Ithel (Rolls Series 20, London 1860), *sub* 1079.

It is only in recent years that the mysteries of the Welsh annals have been opened to students. Although the *Annales* and the *Brut y Tywysogion* were both edited for the Rolls Series in 1860 by the Rev. John Williams ab Ithel,[1] the subsequent discovery of the important *Cronica de Wallia* for the years 1190 to 1266 and 1254 to 1285, in the library of Exeter Cathedral,[2] and the realisation that the Rolls Series edition of the *Brut* conflated two independent texts quite unsatisfactorily prevented the rigorous use of the texts without recourse to the manuscripts. Despite the formidable achievements of Sir John Lloyd in elucidating the relationships of the manuscripts,[3] the texts of the two main manuscripts of the *Brut* were not printed satisfactorily, in Welsh with translation, until Thomas Jones published them for the Board of Celtic Studies in 1941, 1952 and 1955: in 1946, moreover, Professor Jones printed the Exeter fragments in the original Latin, with other extracts from the same composite manuscript, in the *Bulletin of the Board of Celtic Studies*. The foundations of all this complex of surviving annals, the Latin originals from which the various *Bruts* were translated and adapted, are now lost, although there must have been at least three copies in existence in the early Middle Ages: but the *Annales Cambriae* (in British Museum, Harley MS 3859), the Latin annals copied in the thirteenth century into the Public Record Office's Breviate of Domesday and the Cotton MS Domitian A.i, together with the new *Cronica de Wallia*, are four sets of annals closely related to these lost exemplars. The text of the *Cronica* is available in a good modern edition; but the Rolls Series edition of the three others does not make the relationship of the separate manuscripts clear and there

[1] For earlier printed editions of the Welsh annals, see *Brut y Tywysogyon or The Chronicle of the Princes: Peniarth MS. 20 Version*, ed. T. Jones (Board of Celtic Studies, History and Law Series xi, Cardiff 1952), xiv–xxxi.

[2] Printed by T. Jones, *B.B.C.S.*, xii (1946–48), 27–44. The major text is attributed to a Cistercian monk of Whitland in Carmarthenshire writing in 1277 (J. B. Smith, 'The "Cronica de Wallia" and the Dynasty of Dinefwr', *B.B.C.S.*, xx (1962–64), 261–82).

[3] J. E. Lloyd, 'The Welsh Chronicles', *Proceedings of the British Academy*, xiv (1928), 369–91.

are errors enough in the transcription. Fortunately (although the *Bibliography of Welsh History* fails to mention them in the obvious place) there are better texts of the Harley manuscript and parts of the others tucked away in the publications of the Honourable Society of Cymmrodorion.[1] Yet both Mrs Chadwick and Professor Carney still find it necessary to go separately to all three manuscripts and they both appeal with much reason for a proper critical edition.[2]

On Latin annals such as these, the vernacular chronicles were based. But the *Bruts* were not written until much later and between the original compilation of the annals and the vernacular transmutation, a new comet swam into the historical sky. Geoffrey of Monmouth's *History of the Kings of Britain* was in some ways the most influential book of the Middle Ages. This remarkable work of fiction about the history of Britain up to the late seventh century is well-known for its place in the Arthurian cycles and, like Bede's *Ecclesiastical History*, has retained its appeal over the centuries: it is available today in English, like the *Ecclesiastical History*, as a Penguin Classic, which would have gratified Geoffrey inordinately, and in a Folio Society edition (to which the more modest monk of Jarrow has not aspired). Like too many compilations which are mentioned in this book, however, Geoffrey's *History* has a textual history which has in no serious way been tackled. There is a very large number of manuscripts, some two hundred, in existence and, although Professor Hammer printed a variant version for the Mediaeval Academy of America in 1951, this was a misconceived project which has confused rather than clarified the scene. Essentially the problem is created by a large number of recensions, probably made by the author himself; and also by a series of variant dedications to prominent figures in the reign of Stephen. Despite the

[1] E. Phillimore, 'The *Annales Cambriae* and Old-Welsh Genealogies from Harleian MS 3859', *Y Cymmrodor*, ix (1888), 141–83; J. E. Lloyd, 'The Text of MSS. B and C of "Annales Cambriae" for the period 1035–93, in parallel columns', *Trans. Hon. Soc. Cymm.* (1899–1900), 165–79.

[2] Chadwick, 'Early Culture and Learning in North Wales', *Studies in the Early British Church*, 48 n. 5; J. Carney, *Studies in Irish Literature and History* (Dublin 1955), 371.

great merit of the critical edition, produced from a very few manuscripts, by M. Faral in 1929, there is still less known about the development of the text than is needful. Despite Professor van Hamel's firmly stated conviction thirty-five years ago that until all the manuscripts of Geoffrey have been properly examined and assessed 'an absolute reserve must be recommended in drawing conclusions from the Welsh Bruts',[1] the examination has not been made nor the reserve maintained.

The importance of Geoffrey's work is that it put early British history on a whole new footing of circumstantial evidence. Despite the cavilling of William of Newburgh in the same century at the 'absurd figments' of Geoffrey's imagination,[2] the stories of Trojan Britain, culminating in the achievements of Arthur, introducing Lear and his daughters and the prophecies of Merlin en route, had a profound effect on the reading habits and story-telling of later medieval Europe. His influence on Wales is three-fold. One, the least obvious, is the 'romantic curiosity' which he and subsequent Arthurian writers aroused about Wales among some foreigners: although it would be rash to think of the Edwardian conquerors as antiquarian tourists, there is some evidence that Flemish soldiers took back home stories of their exploration among the Welsh '*mirabilia* with which literary fashion had made them familiar' and that such stories are the source for the surprising (and historically valueless) Welsh information in the fourteenth-century continuation of the *Speculum Historiale*.[3]

Secondly, Geoffrey stimulated Welshmen to defend his fictions into very modern times. His *History* was not successfully challenged in general until the sixteenth century: and thereafter his supporters (not only Welsh) fought back for centuries. Sir John Price's *Historiae Brytannicae Defensio*, published posthumously

[1] A. G. van Hamel, 'The Old-Norse Version of the *Historia Regum Britanniae* and the Text of Geoffrey of Monmouth', *Etudes Celtiques*, i (1936), 247.

[2] William of Newburgh, 'Historia Rerum Anglicarum', *Chronicles of the Reigns of Stephen, Henry II and Richard I*, ed. R. Howlett (Rolls Series 82, London 1884), i, 11–13.

[3] T. M. Chotzen, 'Welsh History in the Continuation of the "Spiegel Historiale" by Lodewijk van Veltham', *B.B.C.S.*, vii (1933–35), 42–54.

in 1573, was still being copied and translated in the eighteenth century.¹ John Lewis of Llynwene around 1610 wrote a history of Britain which prudently allowed that Geoffrey was guilty of 'a powdring of the British History with Fables' but which strongly defended the general story, and Lewis's book found a publisher in 1729.² Iolo Morganwg was to forge an entire Brut at the end of the eighteenth century, including inventions to make Geoffrey a luminary of Gwent: and this forgery was not publicly exposed until Sir John Lloyd spoke out in his Rhŷs Lecture of 1928.³

It is ironic that Welshmen have long shown such partiality towards Geoffrey. His book favours the Bretons rather than the Welsh. He was not of Welsh blood; although born to an immigrant Breton family in Norman Monmouth, he lived much of his life in Oxford and, although bishop of St Asaph for the last two years of his life, he never visited his diocese.⁴ Even his associate Walter, who allegedly brought from Brittany the notorious 'book written in the British tongue', through which Geoffrey claimed to know what was denied to others, has no known association with either Wales or Brittany and was the archdeacon of Oxford who witnessed charters there along with Geoffrey. The citing of this 'very ancient' book *Britannici sermonis* smacks very much of an Oxford ploy: but although Welsh scholarship says categorically that no existing Welsh text can possibly be Walter's book and although no Breton vernacular literature at all survives from Geoffrey's time, the issue of this British source is not yet dead:⁵ the president of St John's, Oxford,

¹ E.g., Fenton's copies, now in Cardiff Central Library, MS 4.37.

² G. M. Griffith, 'John Lewis of Llynwene's Defence of Geoffrey of Monmouth's "Historia" ', *N.L.W.J.*, vii (1951–52), 228.

³ Iolo's forgery was printed, as genuine, by the Cambrian Archaeological Association in 1863, with a translation by Aneurin Owen. See J. E. Lloyd, 'The Welsh Chronicles', *Proceedings of the British Academy*, xiv (1928), 376–7.

⁴ J. E. Lloyd, 'Geoffrey of Monmouth', *English Historical Review*, lvii (1942), 460–8.

⁵ J. S. P. Tatlock, *The Legendary History of Britain* (Berkeley and Los Angeles 1950), 422–4; T. Jones, 'Historical Writing in Medieval Welsh', *Scottish Studies*, xii (1968), 16.

as president also of the Royal Historical Society, has just reaffirmed his belief that it existed.[1]

Despite the poor showing which the Welsh made in the *History* after the emigrations to Brittany, there can be no doubt of the warmth of the reception given to Geoffrey's work in Wales. The third, and for our purpose, the most important influence of Geoffrey was then felt, for the book stimulated Welsh antiquarian scholars of the succeeding century and more to produce works of historical literature, not plain and unadorned annals such as the *Annales Cambriae* and the related texts. Such activity took two principal forms: one was the dissemination both in Latin and then in Welsh translation of the actual contents of the *Historia Regum*. One of the Latin versions survives, for example, in a manuscript of *c.* 1300, probably from Metz, preserved at Cardiff, where

Frater Walensis Madocus Edeirnianensis

introduces in Leonine verse the work gathered 'ex libris densis' containing the sweets of the history written by

Monemutensis Galfridus, acutus ut ensis.[2]

Most Welshmen would have echoed the tribute of brother Madoc from Edeirnion to Geoffrey, as sharp as a sword.

The Welsh versions of the book cannot be completely disentangled (not least because the versions of the Latin have not yet been sorted out to any satisfaction), but there seem to be six more or less independent translations, surviving in upwards of fifty manuscripts of very various authority, from the thirteenth

---

[1] R. W. Southern, 'Aspects of the European Tradition of Historical Writing, I, The Classical Tradition from Einhard to Geoffrey of Monmouth', *Trans. Royal Historical Society*, 5th series, xx (1970), 194.

[2] *Geoffrey of Monmouth, Historia Regum Britanniae, A Variant Version edited from Manuscripts*, ed. J. Hammer (Mediaeval Academy of America Publication, lvii, Cambridge, Mass., 1951), 8, 18.

to the sixteenth century.[1] These pose largely literary problems and are much less significant sources (except, of course, for cultural history) than the second form of reaction to Geoffrey, the creation of the developed chronicles in the thirteenth century and in particular the *Brut y Tywysogion*.

The two main versions of the Brut of the Princes have been authoritatively edited and translated by Professor Thomas Jones. They derive from two separate copies of a single lost Latin archetype, itself abbreviated from lost annals of Strata Florida.[2] The more complete of the two Welsh versions, in Peniarth MS 20, gives a history from the 680s up to 1282, with a continuation up to 1332 deriving from a mixture of lost annals compiled at Valle Crucis and elsewhere.[3] The Red Book of Hergest version covers the same period, without the continuation after 1282, with different phraseology and some differences in substance: in particular only the Peniarth 20 has the elegiac poem in Latin in the death of the Lord Rhys and the Latin eulogy engraved on his sepulchre,[4] and in general Peniarth 20 has more high rhetoric than Hergest. It is this elevation of style which must be ascribed, at least in part, to the influence of Geoffrey of Monmouth. The concept of high history and hack history was enshrined in Cicero's *De Oratore* and translated into medieval terms in Gervase of Canterbury's contrast between the historian (high) and the chronicler (hack):

> The historian and the chronicler have one and the same intention and use the same materials, but their modes of treatment are different and so is the style of their writing. Both have the same object in

[1] E. Reiss, 'The Welsh Versions of Geoffrey of Monmouth's *Historia*', *Welsh History Review*, iv (1968–69), 92–127. Cf. *Brut y Brenhinedd, Cotton Cleopatra Version*, ed. J. J. Parry (Mediaeval Academy of America Publication xxvii, Cambridge, Mass., 1937), ix–xiii.

[2] J. G. Edwards, review of Jones's edition of the Peniarth MS 20 version of the *Brut*, *English Historical Review*, lvii (1942), 371–2. The four texts of the *Annales Cambriae* discussed above contain elements of the lost archetype.

[3] *Ibid.*, 373–5; *Brut y Tywysogion, Peniarth Version*, trans. T. Jones, lxii–lxiii.

[4] Ed. Jones, 140–1; trans. Jones, 77–8 (the Latin is not translated there).

view because both eagerly pursue truth. The style of treatment is different because the historian marches along with a copious and eloquent diction, while the chronicler steps simply and briefly.[1]

Whereas the *Annales Cambriae* step simply and briefly, the *Brut y Tywysogion* marches along with a copious and eloquent diction.[2] The *Brut* is, it is true, in the vernacular, which Gervase did not have in mind, and its principal example in high writing, Geoffrey of Monmouth, did not perhaps pursue truth as eagerly as one might wish, but the context is plain enough: the compilers of the Welsh *Brut* belong to a European style of elevated history. At the same time, within its limitations, the *Brut* 'succeeds in presenting not unfairly the development of the Welsh people and their vicissitudes during the years from 682 to 1282'.[3] It is the most important narrative source for pre-Conquest Wales.

The other principal work of this sort is the *Brenhinedd y Saesson*, the Kings of the Saxons, which is a composite work interlarding English annals with yet another version of the *Brut y Tywysogion*. In one of the two surviving manuscripts of importance (Cotton Cleopatra B v), the *Brenhinedd* ends in 1197 but in the other, the *Black Book of Basingwerk*, it is continued down to 1461. The publication of the critical edition and translation, which Professor Thomas Jones promised in 1952, is now imminent, so soon one need no longer go to the manuscripts in London and Aberystwyth or use the poor transcription of the Cleopatra manuscript published in 1801 in the *Myvyrian Archaiology of Wales*.[4]

The next category of native narratives is more restricted, either in time or in place, or in both. Standing in a class by itself is the only biography of any Welsh prince, the *Ancient History of Gruffydd ap Cynan ab Iago*, written in the lifetime of Gruffydd's

[1] Translated in *The Anglo-Saxon Chronicle*, ed. Garmonsway, xviii.
[2] For an admirable example of the contrast between the *Annales* and the *Brut*, sub 1022, see Jones, 'Historical Writing in Medieval Welsh', *Scottish Studies*, xii (1968), 26.
[3] *Ibid.*, 23.
[4] Lloyd, 'The Welsh Chronicles', *Proceedings of the British Academy*, xiv (1928), 376; Jones, trans. of Peniarth 20, xii.

son, Owain Gwynedd. This biography exaggerates the merits of its subject, as one would expect, but it is a good source and Sir John Lloyd's narrative of Gruffydd's reign would have been much more slender without it.[1]

Much more to be anticipated are the various annals of religious institutions in Wales and the marches. The most celebrated of these narratives is in the Book of Llandaff. This remarkable compilation was created to bolster the claims of the bishop of Llandaff in the twelfth century with six centuries of historical justification: but since criticism of the narrative is inseparable from examination of the charter memoranda which it contains and since it is part of the archives of the diocese, it is discussed instead in chapter 5.

The less spectacular narratives come from monastic scriptoria. Most monasteries maintained annals of some sort, whether brief and general, or localised, or at the farthest extreme, the 'vivid and colourful chronological encyclopaedia' of Matthew Paris, monk of St Albans. Very little survives from Wales itself although historical writing as background to the *Brut* was maintained at houses like Strata Florida and Whitland. Margam in Glamorgan is the only Welsh house for which real annals survive and they consume only thirty-seven pages of print in the Rolls Series edition. They begin in 1066 and lean heavily on William of Malmesbury until Stephen's reign. The local allusions become more frequent and the chronicle fuller up to 1232 when the unique manuscript ends abruptly.[2] The so-called 'register' of the Cistercian house of Conway, founded in the late twelfth century from Strata Florida, is even briefer, but incorporates the texts of some charters of the twelfth and thirteenth centuries before it peters out in 1284,[3] just after the abbey moved eight miles south to Maenan: if annals were maintained at the new site, they pre-

---

[1] Lloyd, *History*, ii, 379–468. The biography was edited by Arthur Jones as *The History of Gruffydd ap Cynan (1054–1137)* (Manchester 1910).

[2] *Annales Monastici*, i, ed. H. R. Luard (Rolls Series 36, London 1864), xiii–xv, 3–40.

[3] Edited by Sir Henry Ellis in *Camden Miscellany*, i (Camden Society, orig. series xxxix, 1847), 5–23.

sumably started a new book which has been lost. Thirdly, there is a tiny Cottonian manuscript, damaged in the fire of 1731, which contains annals of Llanthony from 1103 to 1203.[1] Lastly, there is a chronicle which seems to have attracted little attention, copied at the end of that abbreviation of Domesday which contains one of the *Annales Cambriae* texts. This further chronicle, spanning the years 1066 to 1286, seems to come from South Wales, probably from someone familiar with the Clares: there is interest in Bogo's birth, Richard's death and Gilbert's career, and in the burning and repair of Caerphilly Castle, as well as a range of local ecclesiastical news, about Margam and Neath and the bishoprics of Llandaff and St David's.[2]

As well as these chronicles actually written in Wales, there are several works from the English side of the border: the authors of these were in a position to be better informed about Welsh affairs than monks in East Anglia or in Sussex, though they did not always think to write down what a modern historian of Wales wants to know. The principal annals of this sort are from Tewkesbury (spanning 1066 to 1263), Worcester (1–1377), St Werbergh's, Chester (1–1297), Evesham (714–1418, and another 1377–1402) and St Peter's, Gloucester (compiled around 1400).[3]

Not only monasteries of the borderland show an interest in

[1] British Museum, Cotton MS Julius D x, fos. 31–53: the contents are listed in George Roberts, 'Llanthony Priory, Monmouthshire', *Arch. Camb.*, orig. series, i (1846), 202–3, and a part is printed in W. Dugdale, *Monasticon Anglicanum*, ed. J. Caley, H. Ellis and B. Bandinel (London 1817–30), vi (1), 128–34.

[2] Printed anonymously in *Arch. Camb.*, 3rd series, viii (1862), 272–83. The editorial to this volume (iv) suggests that it was compiled in Margam or Neath. It is, however, independent of the Margam Annals as we have them: Neath would be a more plausible guess, if it was written in a monastery.

[3] *Annales Monastici*, ed. Luard, i, 43–180; iv, 355–564; *Annales Cestrienses*, ed. R. C. Christie (Record Society for Lancashire and Cheshire xiv, 1887); *Chronicon Abbatiae de Evesham ad annum 1418*, ed. W. D. Macray (Rolls Series 29, London 1863); *Historia vitae et regni Ricardi II a monacho quodam de Evesham consignata*, ed. T. Hearne (Oxford 1729); *Historia et Cartularium Monasterii Sancti Petri Gloucestriae*, i, ed. W. H. Hart (Rolls Series 33, London 1863), 1–125 (see C. N. L. Brooke, 'St Peter of Gloucester and St Cadog of Llancarfan', *Celt and Saxon*, ed. N. K. Chadwick (Cambridge 1963), 260–76).

affairs touching Wales, but also others for special reasons. Battle Abbey in Sussex, for example, had a cell at Brecon and its late twelfth-century chronicle provides information about its eleventh-century patron Bernard of Neufmarché.[1] The lords of the march after the Norman Conquest commonly had extensive landed interests elsewhere as well: the Clares, for instance, had two *foci*, one in South Wales, the other in East Anglia, and their activities, which are part of Welsh history, are recorded in most of the major English chronicles. As a result, the general utility of English chronicles is very great. Dr Antonia Gransden's forthcoming book on chronicle-writing in England should supply a basic guide for students embarking on studies which require the discipline of properly understanding the form and purpose of these very diverse but indispensable compilations.

After the principal texts of the Welsh *Bruts* had been written, there was little chronicle-writing in Wales. The known monastic annals did not survive into the later fourteenth century and Professor Glanmor Williams was not surprised, considering the state of the Welsh monasteries.[2] But at least one other vernacular chronicle was compiled in Henry VI's reign: this raced breathlessly through the early history but expanded to give a valuable account of the Glyndŵr revolt from 1400 to 1415. Sir John Lloyd used this chronicle in his Ford Lectures of 1920 and, when he came to publish a revised version in 1931, he conveniently added a text and a translation of this section as an appendix. But the remainder of the chronicle (which occupies ten pages of the Peniarth transcript) is available only in five meagre lines of extracts in Gwenogvryn Evans's Historical Manuscripts Commission report.[3]

The early fifteenth century produced not only the Glyndŵr

[1] L. H. Nelson, *The Normans in South Wales, 1070–1171* (Austin 1966), 84–5.

[2] Glanmor Williams, *The Welsh Church from Conquest to Reformation* (Cardiff 1962), 178–81.

[3] J. E. Lloyd, *Owen Glendower* (Oxford 1931), 147–54; Historical Manuscripts Commission 48, *Report on Manuscripts in the Welsh Language*, i (2) (London 1899), 847.

annals, but also the celebrated chronicle of Adam of Usk.[1] This, too, is a record of contemporary events, by a lawyer, who came indeed from Usk in Monmouthshire, but who spent a not un-eventful life in England, Rome and France, before returning to Wales in about 1408 to share the hardships of Glyndŵr's support-ers. He was pardoned in 1411 and lived on until 1430: his brass still survives in the church at Usk, with an inscription that has caused a good deal of puzzlement finally resolved by Professor Morris-Jones fifty years ago.[2] The chronicle which Adam produced covers the period from 1377 to 1421, but the first seventeen years are scanty and the portion from 1404 to 1421 is disappointingly slender in content, especially about his ex-periences back in Wales: the years 1408 to 1411 are disposed of in one short paragraph. The real value of Adam's chronicle lies, then, in only ten years, and within these years the usurpation of the house of Lancaster and the lawyer's experiences on the con-tinent feature as large as the dramatic events in Wales. But even abroad there are two encounters with fellow Welshmen 'in whom I had placed my trust' but by whom 'I was clean stripped, at least on the second time, even to my breeches'; and in the earlier portion of the chronicle there is an eye-witness account of the trouble at Oxford University in 1388 and 1389, when southern English and Welsh students were pitted against the northerners.[3] Adam could have given a so much more vivid relation of this sort, but one must be grateful for what there is.

Two very readable writers have not yet been mentioned. Neither Walter Map nor Gerald of Wales was a chronicler, but their anecdotal works of literature have peculiar merits, and dangers, as sources. Walter Map, unlike Gerald, wrote little, but his *Courtiers' Trifles (De Nugis Curialium)* is justly famous.[4]

[1] *Chronicon Adae de Usk, AD 1377–1421*, ed. with trans. E. M. Thompson (2nd ed. London 1904).

[2] J. Morris-Jones, 'Adam of Usk's Epitaph', *Y Cymmrodor*, xxxi (1921), 112–34.

[3] *Chronicon*, ed. Thompson, 104 (283), 7 (147–8).

[4] Ed. M. R. James, *Anecdota Oxoniensia*, xiv (1914); trans. James, Cymmrodo-rion Record Series ix, 1923.

Walter's very name seems to have been an English joke about his Welsh origins: he came from the Hereford march, was about Henry II's court and lived on into the middle of John's reign. He was a sophisticated man of the world, a considerable wit. His *Trifles* are rather more than the deprecating title implies: there is serious satirical intent, not least against the Cistercian monks, amid the haphazard collection of gossip, memoirs and anecdotes. His importance for Welsh studies is his use of stories from the marches. Although Walter's adult life was spent first in Paris (from 1154 to 1160) and then in England, he clearly remained a Welshman.[1] The cosmopolitan Goliardic verses which are dubiously ascribed to Walter are less relevant and the poem, *Cambriae Epitome*, also ascribed to him, is simply a versification of some parts of Gerald's works, the *Description* and *Itinerary*.[2]

Gerald of Wales, Giraldus Cambrensis, was no chronicler, but a very prolific literary man during the years round 1200. In his large output there is a great deal of Welsh ore to be mined. Gerald was only partly Welsh: his father was a Norman, William de Barri, and his mother, Angharad, was only half-Welsh, the daughter of Gerald of Windsor and Nest, who was in turn the celebrated daughter of Rhys ap Tewdwr, condemned to be remembered as the Helen of Wales. Although born at Manorbier Castle in Pembrokeshire around 1146, Gerald was educated at St Peter's, Gloucester, and at Paris. Although appointed archdeacon of Brecon in 1174 by his uncle, the bishop of St David's, and although three times a potential bishop of St David's himself, he was largely an absentee and his vernacular was Anglo-Norman, his professional medium Latin. 'He saw himself as a cosmopolitan figure, feeling at home more in Paris and London than in Brecon';[3] and it is most proper that the most stimulating

[1] *D.N.B. sub* 'Map or Mapes'.

[2] *The Latin Poems commonly attributed to Walter Mapes*, ed. T. Wright (Camden Society, old series xvi, 1841), 131–46. The poem was popular: a fifteenth-century English version also exists (*ibid.*, 349–55).

[3] M. Richter, 'Giraldus Cambrensis: the Growth of the Welsh Nation', *N.L.W.J.*, xvi (1969–70), 313.

appreciation of his work as it affects the interpretation of twelfth-century Wales is by a German scholar.[1]

The best known works by Gerald are his early topographical tracts first on Ireland, then in the early 1190s on Wales. The *Itinerary through Wales* in which Gerald described the five-week tour which he took in the company of the Archbishop of Canterbury in 1188 to preach the third crusade, and the *Description of Wales* which he wrote about 1194 and revised later, have been familiar texts in Wales, through the Everyman translation. But valuable as it is to see something of Wales in the eyes of one twelfth-century man, and marvellously quotable though these short books are, the more substantial contribution which Gerald made to our historical understanding is his outpouring after 1200. After bishop Peter died in 1198, Gerald was elected to St David's, although he was not allowed to take his position and another was finally consecrated in 1203. In the years between 1198 and 1203, Gerald went to Rome to seek consecration and to revive the old question of the metropolitan jurisdiction of St David's over the other three Welsh dioceses. He failed, but the theological, legal and personal implications of this stormy debate were reflected in books such as *De Invectionibus*, the *Dialogus de jure et statu Menevensis ecclesie* and the *De Rebus a se Gestis*.[2] The use of these intense and not always internally consistent tracts is not straightforward, but they are essential for the ecclesiastical and intellectual history of Wales, and England, in the time of Richard and John. Dr Richter has expressed very well an attractive interpretation of Gerald around 1200, standing 'between two nations at a turning point in his life, and he did not know where he belonged. Giraldus never solved his deep emotional conflict. The only *nation* which he ever belonged to was the

---

[1] *Ibid.*, 193–252, 293–318; xvii (1971–72), 1–50.

[2] The Latin text of these three books is printed in an indifferent edition by J. S. Brewer in the Rolls Series 21, i (1861) and iii (1863). A better, but still uncritical, edition of *De Invectionibus* by W. S. Davies appeared as *Y Cymmrodor*, xxx (1930). A useful conflated *Autobiography of Giraldus Cambrensis* in English was published by Professor H. E. Butler in 1937.

class of scholars, the *natio* in the medieval academic sense.'[1]

The other writings of Gerald are also important. His *Gemma Ecclesiastica* was written, at Lincoln, for the instruction of clergy in Wales, particularly in his own archidiaconate of Brecon. The stories which enliven his liturgical and legal counsel (which is largely plagiarised) give a racy, if not necessarily balanced, view of the Welsh priesthood. The *Speculum Ecclesie*, which is unkind to monks, particularly Benedictines and Cistercians, again contains Welsh instances, which may or may not be credible. Unlike so many medieval writers, Gerald has the grace of readability and even in relatively unworthy books like the *Speculum*, his vivacity does not flag.[2]

Gerald also wrote a number of saints' lives. Hagiographical literature was a speciality of the Celtic world and edifying quasi-biographies of leading figures in the long-past 'age of saints' enjoyed a vogue in the twelfth and thirteenth centuries. Gerald's lives are merely part of a general literary, devotional and liturgical cult. This genre of writing is frustrating to use for historical purposes. The need for 'biographies' arises from the celebration of saints in the medieval liturgy. The medieval calendar of the year, day by day, showed in each area a mixture of great and inescapable saints like Peter and national or local saints. Before procedures for central approval of sanctification were established in the thirteenth century, local repute raised many a decent-living hermit or more sociable churchman to a place in the local calendar, with a mass said in his honour each year. In the liturgy the *lectio* would give some uplifting stories based on the saint's life: there was no interest in the chronological sequence of the saint's existence, for the important thing now was the unchanging annual feast-day. Moreover, the stories attached to long-dead saints increasingly came from a general corpus of such anecdotes but there was, where possible, a core of fact. The moral position

[1] Richter, *N.L.W.J.*, xvi (1969–70), 311.

[2] Eileen A. Williams, 'A Bibliography of Giraldus Cambrensis, c. 1147 to c. 1223', *N.L.W.J.*, xii (1961–62), 106–7; D. Knowles, *The Monastic Order in England* (2nd ed. Cambridge 1963), 667–74.

at its starkest is explained by a ninth-century Italian, Agnellus of Ravenna, who wrote an essentially hagiographical account of all the bishops of Ravenna up to his own time:

> Where I could not uncover a story or determine what kind of life they led, either from the most aged or from inscriptions or from any other source, to avoid a blank place in my list of holy pontiffs in proper order according to their ordination to the see one after another, I have, with the assistance of God through your prayers, made up a life for them. And I believe no deception is involved, for they were chaste and almsgiving preachers and procurers of men's souls for God.[1]

This use of a divine research assistant to document a halo is both understandable and laudable in the context of such authors: but historians today are trying to use these works of piety for alien purposes. This too is proper, but there are difficulties in extracting reliable data.

Wales, as part of the Celtic world, is well supplied with saints' lives. Eleven of these from one of the earliest manuscript collections, copied about 1200, have been edited with translation for the Board of Celtic Studies,[2] but the subsequent edition of *Rhigyfarch's Life of St David* by Chancellor James and the study of *Lifris's Life of St Cadoc* by Mr Emanuel show that for two of the lives at least there is a history of textual development which makes a text from only one stage in their development rather misleading.[3] The use which Professor Christopher Brooke has made of the Life of Cadoc is an instruction for beginners in this difficult field,[4] but comparable work on hagiographies which lack

[1] Quoted in C. W. Jones, *Saints' Lives and Chronicles*, 63.

[2] *Vitae Sanctorum Britanniae et Genealogiae*, ed. A. W. Wade-Evans (Board of Celtic Studies, History and Law Series ix, Cardiff 1944). See also an important study by S. M. Harris, 'The Kalendar of the *Vitae Sanctorum Wallensium*', *Journal of Historical Society of Church in Wales*, iii (1953), 3–53.

[3] *Rhigyfarch's Life of St David*, ed. J. W. James (Cardiff 1967); H. D. Emanuel, 'An Analysis of the Composition of the "Vita Cadoci" ', *N.L.W.J.*, vii (1951–52), 217–27.

[4] Brooke, *Celt and Saxon*, ed. Chadwick, 289–315.

critical editions is a necessary preliminary to more extended reappraisal.

Vernacular poetry as it flourished in Wales contains much historical information for those linguistically and critically qualified. Just as it is unthinkable to exclude Beowulf or The Wanderer or The Dream of the Rood from a survey of sources for Anglo-Saxon England, or Chaucer and Langland from a similar survey for later medieval England, so no introduction to Welsh sources is complete without a reminder that in the Old Welsh poetry, in the court poetry of the twelfth and thirteenth centuries and in the *cywyddau* of Chaucer's contemporaries Iolo Goch and Dafydd ap Gwilym and the works written under the patronage of the gentry of Wales in the fifteenth century there is an unusual wealth of historical allusion.[1] Lyrical poetry of itself is evidence, of course, of culture and taste, but the particular circumstances of Welsh bardic poetry give much of it a local habitation, a context which makes it a more flexible source.[2] The Latin poetry, too, like the lament of Rhigyfarch, David's biographer, written about 1094 in the face of the Norman invasion,[3] can supply an additional dimension of sensibility.

Closely linked with vernacular poetry in Welsh affections and manuscripts were genealogies. The passion of the race for geneal-ogy is reflected in the patronymic structure of personal names and the proverbial phrase 'as long as a Welsh pedigree'. Ability to recount the line of ancestors was of practical as well as emotional significance: for the royal houses, the pedigree was necessary evidence of its right to rule, for the ordinary people, it encapsulated the rights and responsibility of kindred and was fundamental to the establishment and survival of the *gafael*. The pedigree has

---

[1] A useful survey of recent work is by E. I. Rowlands, 'Iolo Goch', *Celtic Studies: Essays in Memory of Angus Matheson*, ed. J. Carney and D. Greene (London 1968), 124–46.

[2] For discussion and bibliography, see initially R. Geraint Gruffydd, 'Litera-ture', *Celtic Studies in Wales: a Survey*, ed. Elwyn Davies (Cardiff 1963), 103–39.

[3] *The Psalter and Martyrology of Ricemarch*, ed. H. J. Lawlor, i (Henry Brad-shaw Society xliv, London 1914), 121–3.

similar value for the modern historian, not only of native Welsh institutions but also of imported tenures and economic structure.[1]

Much depends, however, on the reliability of the surviving pedigrees. The 'ancient and authentic books' in which, Gerald of Wales tells us, the twelfth-century bards preserved the princely genealogies back to Adam have long since disappeared:[2] the only text from this early period (other than the entries in Nennius) which is at all comparable to the lost bardic books is the inscription on the pillar erected by a king of Powys early in the ninth century, the Pillar of Eliseg.[3] If it were not for the Life of Gruffydd ap Cynan, the short pedigrees in some saints' lives and in the twelfth-century compilation *Bonedd y Saint* (the 'lineage of the saints'), the tenth-century genealogies in the Harley MS 3859 (which also preserves the *Annales Cambriae* and an important text of Nennius), the fourteenth-century manuscripts of Llywelyn Offeiriad's pedigrees and some much later transcripts of lost thirteenth-century compilations, knowledge of pre-Conquest pedigrees would be very slender indeed: and only in these late transcripts do any but princely pedigrees figure.[4]

It is unfortunate that the early Welsh bards, unlike the Irish, did not incorporate their genealogical lore into their poems.[5] Only in the later Middle Ages, from Iolo Goch onwards, did genealogy become a feature of poetic expression, under the active encouragement of ambitious gentry.[6] A great number of manuscripts or transcripts of manuscripts containing ordinary late medieval pedigrees also survives, from clerical society as well as lay, but even more caution is required than with the early pedigrees, for 'family pride and the desire of genealogists to flatter often led to quite irresponsible invention'.[7]

[1] Cf. Francis Jones, 'An Approach to Welsh Genealogy', *Trans. Hon. Soc. Cymm.* (1948), 303–48.

[2] *Ibid.*, 319–20.

[3] *Early Welsh Genealogical Tracts*, ed. P. C. Bartrum (Cardiff 1966), 1–3.

[4] *Ibid.*, 5–122.    [5] Jones, *Trans. Hon. Soc. Cymm.* (1948), 334.

[6] *Ibid.*, 343.    [7] *Early Welsh Genealogical Tracts*, ed. Bartrum, viii.

Heraldry too became popular. It is significant that the oldest surviving European ordinary of arms (grouping together designs of a single sort, a professional manual of coat-armour) was preserved at Carmarthen throughout the later Middle Ages: it was indeed repaired in the fifteenth century with a membrane of the sheriffs' accounts.[1] This ordinary referred only to English blazons, but such a hand-book was as useful in Wales as in England to avoid unnecessary confusion. Welsh heraldry in general was distinctly undisciplined, compared to English, and, rather curiously, it is not nearly as useful an adjunct to genealogical study. Whereas in England, arms were inherited, with or without differences, and marriage alliances were often celebrated heraldically, one can find in Wales appalling laxity: there is a pleasing example of how in seven successive generations of one Welsh family five quite different blazons are recorded.[2]

The great flowering of both genealogy and heraldry, however, came in Yorkist and Tudor times. Guttun Owain and his associates, combining poetry with skilful genealogies, dominated the late fifteenth-century scene, together with the richly allusive poetry of bards like Lewis Glyn Cothi and Dafydd Nanmor, written mostly under the Yorkists. Subsequent genealogists and antiquaries continued to produce pedigrees, but the bardic tradition largely died with the school of Gruffydd Hiraethog which did not last into Stuart times.[3] Although, naturally enough, these later manuscripts repeat a great deal of the earlier, and errors of all sorts became established facts, 'there are few manuscripts which do not contribute something new and of interest . . .; perhaps an extra generation or two in the pedigree of a local family, an anecdote, or a quotation which has not survived elsewhere from some lost manuscript of importance'. But as Mr Bartrum has emphasised, the critical appraisal of this large and

[1] A. R. Wagner, *Aspilogia* i, *A Catalogue of English Medieval Rolls of Arms* (Harleian Society, vol. c, Oxford 1950), 58–9 and coloured plate V. Sir Anthony owns the roll.

[2] W. J. Hemp, 'Presidential Address,' *Arch. Camb.*, cv (1956), 4–5.

[3] Jones, *Trans. Hon. Soc. Cymm.* (1948), 352–78.

difficult corpus is only just beginning and it will be 'an arduous undertaking'.[1]

The genealogies have much to offer still, but there is a long row to hoe. A patriotic Welshman wrote for the Cymmrodorion Society in 1828 that by using the pedigrees 'the Welsh can tell who once occupied their ivy-mantled towers, their ancient manors, and such of their mansions as are desolate, and whose foundations are but faintly marked by detached and shapeless masses of stones and rubbish. To the unprejudiced antiquary and the travelled tourist such knowledge is always interesting, when good authority is annexed to the information; and on this point satisfactory evidence might be obtained were the scattered particles of genealogical knowledge, as subsisting in Wales, collected and arranged by men of talent and erudition, whose respectability of character and ability would inspire full confidence in their skill and fidelity.'[2] Whether all modern historians using genealogical material are sufficiently talented, erudite, respectable, skilful and faithful is less than certain, but these old-fashioned virtues enunciated before manuscript criticism was a developed art are appropriate not only for the nineteenth-century antiquaries but also for the student who would master the genealogical sources.

Finally in this review of narrative sources a brief mention must be made of books written or owned by medieval Welshmen. Most of these have, naturally, an ecclesiastical context and they contain evidence for the cultural and intellectual life of medieval Wales, although the content of the books does not necessarily concern Wales. As far as I know, no one has attempted to bring together in one list the books written by medieval Welshmen. But certainly they exist. A few titles may give some notion of the potential value. Thomas of Monmouth wrote the *Life and Miracles of St William of Norwich* around 1172.[3] Simon of

---

[1] P. C. Bartrum, 'Notes on the Welsh Genealogical Manuscripts', *Trans. Hon. Soc. Cymm.* (1968), 65.

[2] Ceninen Dy'gwyl Dewi, 'An Essay on Welsh Genealogies', *Trans. of the Cymmrodorion*, ii (1828), 143.

[3] Ed. A. Jessopp and M. R. James (Cambridge 1896).

Carmarthen's equally pious composition a century later, called *Par la priere de un men Compagnon* is possible evidence of Anglo-Norman in the Welsh cloister.[1] The Franciscan John of Wales, who died around 1255, wrote a whole series of learned compilations, many of which were printed in the first two centuries of movable type. Another John of Wales was a glossator of canon law at Bologna. Thomas of Wales, a Dominican (not the bishop of St David's), wrote widely about preaching and spent some time in the prison of the fourteenth-century Inquisition.[2] There are a number of other *Wallenses* to be found, and they are presumably Welsh, though usually expatriate. When only the vernacular form, some spelling of 'Waleys', is found, some caution is required; William Wallace, the Scottish hero of Cheshire stock, is a salutary example. His name is normally spelt Waleys in contemporary documents and he should not be considered Welsh.

Books written in Wales or with Welsh glosses also exist here and there in great libraries. For example, 'St Dunstan's Class-Book' at Bodley is the union of two Welsh manuscripts of the ninth or tenth century, brought together, with a Breton text, at Glastonbury; one of the texts of Ovid's *Art of Love* is glossed in Welsh;[3] while the celebrated Juvencus manuscript and the two Corpus Christi College, Cambridge, manuscripts, one originally from a Welsh exemplar, the other mostly written in ninth-century Wales, are essential links in the textual tradition of Martianus Capella, as well as evidence of Welsh scriptoria in the age of Hywel Dda.[4]

[1] Morgan Watkin, 'The Chronology of the Black Book of Carmarthen on the Basis of its Old French Phenomena', *N.L.W.J.*, xiv (1965–66), 215.

[2] Cf. *D.W.B.* and *D.N.B.* sub Wallensis and Johannes, and G. Hartwell Jones, 'Italian Influence on Celtic Culture', *Trans. Hon. Soc. Cymm.* (1905–6), 118–19. For a list of university-trained Welshmen, see Rhys W. Hays, 'Welsh Students at Oxford and Cambridge Universities in the Middle Ages', *Welsh History Review*, iv (1968–69), 355–61.

[3] Bodley, MS Auct. F. 4. 32. A facsimile was issued in 1961 by R. W. Hunt in the series *Umbrae Codicum Occidentalium*.

[4] T. A. M. Bishop, 'The Corpus Martianus Capella', *Trans. Cambridge Bibliographical Society*, iv (1964–68), 257–75.

At least fifty books from some twenty-two monastic or cathedral libraries of Wales have been identified. There may be many more but of the very substantial collection of Llanthony books, which mostly found their way to Lambeth Palace, only seven can be confidently ascribed to Welsh Llanthony: all the remaining volumes may not, however, be exclusively connected with Gloucestershire Llanthony. This sort of record is inevitably lopsided, created by chance survival: other than Llanthony, Dore (which may be regarded as Welsh for our purposes) is the only house whose books survive in any number. Any conclusions to be drawn from the titles and dates of the existing manuscripts would have to be tentative: sometimes they merely illustrate a known fact, like the relation of William the Conqueror kept at Brecon, which was a cell of Battle, itself named after the battle of Hastings.[1]

Liturgical books have a special interest. The most celebrated is the pontifical from Bangor Cathedral Library, written for one of the bishops called Anian, probably Anian II who occupied the see of Bangor from 1309 to 1328. This contains, as well as the usual formulae, a statement of the decrees of the otherwise unknown synod of Bangor held in July 1291.[2] The most interesting liturgically is the imperfect Sarum antiphonal, written in South Wales or western England, which contains the full office for St David's feast-day: much of the proper of this mass survives only in this recently discovered manuscript.[3]

The sum total of all these different kinds of literary source-material is not unimpressive. But the contrast with England, except perhaps in actual pedigrees, is very unfavourable. Despite the chronicles of the princes, the narratives leave unanswered

---

[1] *Medieval Libraries of Great Britain: a List of Surviving Books*, ed. N. R. Ker (Royal Historical Society, London 1964).

[2] J. C. Davies is firmly persuaded that the manuscript was made for Anian II (cf. his review of *Edward of Caernarvon* in *Journal of Historical Society of the Church in Wales*, i (1947), 183). T. Morris still prefers the old ascription to Anian I (1267-1305), 'The Liber Pontificalis Aniani of Bangor', *Trans. Anglesey Antiquarian Society and Field Club* (1962), 55-85, esp. 75.

[3] National Library of Wales, *Annual Report 1969-70*, 40-1.

many questions, and the decay of historical writing in the later Middle Ages is far more marked in Wales even than in England, which in turn is impoverished in the fifteenth century compared to France or Burgundy. Moreover, there is no inspired historical journalist in Wales as England had in Matthew Paris. There is no Welsh equivalent of the new genre of intimate biography inaugurated by Eadmer's *Life of Anselm*: the life of Gruffydd ap Cynan is hardly comparable. There is no magisterial contemporary history by a scholar high in church affairs such as Otto of Freising provided for part of the reign of his nephew Frederick Barbarossa. There is no intimate psychological revelation from any Welsh monk such as Guibert of Nogent wrote in the eleventh century. What price would not a historian pay for a Welsh Galbert of Bruges who, like a war correspondent, scribbled down on waxed tablets his eye-witness account of the siege of the castle of Bruges after the murder of Duke Charles the Good in 1127?—but no Welshman preserved for posterity the intimate impact of Edward I's soldiery. The evidence of silence is much less forcible in Wales even than in England. The remains of historical literature are lopsided: but this, for different reasons, is a common feature of the archives of Wales in general.

CHAPTER 2

# The Official Records of Wales and Their Preservation

The sources for later medieval English history are dominated by the public records. As the general editor of this series has rightly emphasised, from 1200 onwards the records produced and preserved by the English government give an indispensable and incomparable basis for most kinds of historical enquiry.[1] The enrolled copies of official letters, the complex of writing-department warrants, the difficult but rewarding financial records and the dismaying bulk of legal archives go on in largely unbroken sequence from the thirteenth century to the present day. There is nothing to compare with the English public records anywhere in Europe, not even the papal archives or the collections surviving in Florence. Certainly independent Wales has nothing at all to offer in comparison, and even for the period after the Edwardian Conquest only certain of the records generated in Wales by the various administrations there survive in regular series. Fortunately, there is much in the records created by the English government which has bearing on the history of Wales: but this is a different sort of source, although it shares the same repository with most of the Welsh records. This is because the records produced by the government in Wales were, for the most part, later amalgamated with the English public records, often, moreover, in a thorough way which disguises from the modern student the archival origin of the materials he uses in the Public Record Office. Since the origin of these records and their custody over the centuries is, or ought to be, a matter of concern to students, this chapter is devoted to a study of the surviving sections of the Welsh official records from their creation to their present incarceration in the

[1] G. R. Elton, *England, 1200–1640* (London 1969), *passim*.

Public Record Office, the National Library of Wales and various less official places.

The pre-Conquest princes of Wales certainly had clerks to issue documents, and in charge of these clerks was the 'priest of the household', who by the early thirteenth century controlled the issue of letters under the prince's seal.[1] In earlier centuries the Welsh rulers contemporary with the late Anglo-Saxon kings were presumably familiar with the diploma. Hywel Dda, for instance, was a witness to twelve surviving charters issued by Athelstan and Edred.[2] These charters may not all be genuine, but the conclusion is clear. Moreover, as discussed in chapter 5 below, the early charters in the Book of Llandaff show a strong Anglo-Saxon influence on their twelfth-century editor, coming through the cathedral priory at Worcester. But the *Book of Llandaff* shows also, better than any other collection of texts, the continuity of the Celtic charter, following its own diplomatic development probably from Mediterranean exemplars for half a millennium after the fall of Rome. The very different Anglo-Saxon diploma was not the only possible model, therefore, for the princes, and an extension of Dr Wendy Davies' work on the *Book of Llandaff* to embrace all pre-Conquest Welsh charters is needed.[3] There is at present no adequate context in which to place, for example, a *testimonium* issued in the twelfth century by Nicholas ap Gwrgant, bishop of Llandaff, where the bounds of property granted to Llantrisaint church by Gilbert de Clare are recited not in Latin, but in the vernacular Welsh.[4]

Unfortunately, copies of charters issued by Welsh princes are rare and original charters still rarer. As far as I know, the earliest originals to survive are twelve charters of Gwenwynwyn son of

[1] J. G. Edwards, 'The Royal Household and the Welsh Lawbooks', *Trans. Royal Historical Society*, 5th series, xiii (1963), 172.

[2] Tabulated in Lloyd, *History*, i, 353.

[3] See below, chapter 5, 143–6,

[4] P.R.O., Chancery Masters' Exhibits, C. 115/A. 1/K. 2/6683 section XV item xx. This document is omitted from J. Conway Davies's *Welsh Episcopal Acts*, ii, L. 121 to L. 192.

Owain Cyfeiliog of Powys, dated between 1185 and 1215.[1]
The text of Owain's own foundation grant to Strata Marcella
in 1170–71 survives also, but only in a fourteenth-century copy.[2]
This remarkable collection of Powys charters (all to Strata
Marcella) is without parallel. No such integrated cache survives
for the rest of the thirteenth century, but there are isolated original
charters from a member of the princely family of Arwystli
(1215), from Llywelyn ab Iorwerth (*c.* 1208), from Llywelyn ap
Gruffydd (1243) and from David ap Gruffydd (1260).[3] These
originals provide unique evidence of the physical structure of
documents issued by the princes, but only slightly less valuable
are a large number of documents which survive only in enrolments, cartularies or later inspected copies. It was the practice of
prudent landholders to pay for inspections of major title deeds, so
that in the case of Strata Marcella, for example, Edward II
in 1322 issued an *inspeximus* which recited in full the charters of
Henry III in 1232, of Gwenwynwyn in 1202, of John in 1200 and
of Owain Cyfeiliog in 1170 as well as a summary of the contents
of forty-five other charters (only eight of which survive in their
original form).[4] Moreover, evidence of the princely writing
departments survives in the register of *Littere Wallie*, known as

---

[1] E. D. Jones, N. G. Davies and R. F. Roberts, 'Five Strata Marcella Charters',
*N.L.W.J.*, v (1947–48), 50.

[2] Printed in W. Dugdale, *Monasticon Anglicanum*, ed. J. Caley, H. Ellis and
B. Bandinel (London 1817–30), v, 637.

[3] These five charters are all printed, with facsimiles, in *N.L.W.J.*, v (1947–48),
53, 52; iii (1943–44), 158–62, 29–32, respectively.

[4] *Calendar of Charter Rolls, 1300–1326*, 438–41; J. C. Davies, 'The Records of
the Abbey of Ystrad Marchell', *Montgomeryshire Collections*, li (1949–50),
8–15. Strata Florida obtained the apotheosis of an *inspeximus* in March 1508,
when Henry VII inspected a patent of 1425, which in turn inspected a charter
of 1380, in turn inspecting one of 1369, in turn inspecting one of 1336, in turn
inspecting one of 1320, in turn inspecting one of 1285 (which itself inspected a
native charter of 1184 and two more royal charters, one of Henry II, the other
of John) plus four native charters of 1198–99 and 1202, and giving the text of
another (Cardiff Central Library, D. D. Cardiganshire, no number; *Calendar
of Patent Rolls, 1494–1509*, 567; *1422–1429*, 294–8; *Arch. Camb.*, original series,
iii (1848), 195).

Liber A, documents from or concerning Wales from 1217 to 1292 copied by English Exchequer clerks, probably before 1295;[1] and other thirteenth-century Welsh documents survive among the fearful miscellany called 'Ancient Correspondence' in the Public Record Office.[2]

It is high time that proper diplomatic examination was made of these remains of the Welsh documents. Twenty years ago Dr Conway Davies urged such study of the princes' charters.[3] Nearly thirty years ago he drew attention to the apparent notarial influence on the charter of David ap Gruffydd in 1260, which was dated by anno domini and the Roman kalends, not by feast-days and regnal years.[4] Yet as late as 1237 there were no notaries public at all in the whole of England—the legatine council meeting in London made a special point of this—and the first notarial instruments known in England date from 1259, only the year before David's grant.[5] Was Master Cadwgan Gervase a notary precociously in Wales? Questions like this may have a simple enough answer—a clerk can use notarial styles without being a notary public—but wherever one looks in the official letters and grants of the princes, basic questions leap up and subside unsatisfied.

Although such records could be consolidated into a small *regesta principum Wallie*, the contrast with the evidence for the English Chancery is overwhelming. The contrast even with Scotland is striking. Already by the mid-twelfth century the Scottish Chancellor conducted his affairs in a way very similar to his English counterpart. There survive at least twenty-five,

---

[1] *Littere Wallie*, ed. J. G. Edwards (Board of Celtic Studies, History and Law Series, v, Cardiff 1940). Liber A remained unbound in quaternions until after 1400 (E. L. G. Stones, 'The Appeal to History in Anglo-Scottish Relations between 1291 and 1401', *Archives*, ix (1969–70), 80).

[2] J. G. Edwards, *Calendar of Ancient Correspondence concerning Wales* (Board of Celtic Studies, History and Law Series ii, Cardiff 1935).

[3] Davies, *Montgomeryshire Collections*, li (1949–50), 6–7.

[4] Davies, *N.L.W.J.*, iii (1943–44), 32.

[5] P. Chaplais, 'Master John de Branketre and the Office of Notary in Chancery, 1355–1375,' *Journal of the Society of Archivists*, iv (1970–71), 169.

and probably twenty-nine, original charters issued by Malcolm IV, who reigned only for twelve and a half years.[1] The surviving grants of this short-lived king alone are more numerous than all the surviving original charters of all the native princes of Wales. Moreover, Edward I does not seem to have brought records back from Wales in the way he did from Scotland. This in turn made the Welsh archives more vulnerable than the Scottish. As Professor Stones had remarked, 'It is not too much to say that whatever documents Edward I removed from Edinburgh had a better chance of survival among the English records than those which remained in Scotland.'[2] It is a great pity that Edward did not find more, or wish to bring back more, Welsh documents. Many of those which he did bring back seem to have been copied into Liber A in 1292–95. Although the provenance of the originals from which these copies were made has not been analysed, most came presumably from Wales, although some may possibly be English copies of documents issued by Henry III and Edward I. The likelihood is, however, that the two receptacles kept in the Exchequer inside the main coffer C, one marked with a drawing of a Welsh archer, the other with a drawing of a Welsh spearman, contained documents brought back from Wales:[3] and there is a reasonable presumption that most, if not all, of these were transcribed in Liber A.

There was also in the Treasury of Receipt at Westminster, in Edward II's reign, a coffer containing 'various quires and rolls in the Welsh language, very foreign to the English tongue' and in Edward II's library deposited in the Treasury there was a small book 'de Ydiomate Anglicis ignorato' whose *incipit* was in Welsh.[4] This book, and perhaps some of the contents of the coffer,

---

[1] *The Acts of Malcolm IV King of Scots, 1153–1165*, ed. G. W. S. Barrow (Edinburgh 1960), 28–30, 57.

[2] *Anglo-Scottish Relations, 1174–1328*, ed. E. L. G. Stones (London 1965), xxxi.

[3] *Littere Wallie*, ed. Edwards, xxviii–xxix.

[4] *The Antient Kalendars and Inventories of the Treasury of His Majesty's Exchequer*, ed. F. Palgrave (London 1836), i, 106, 116. The cryptic *incipit* is 'Edmygaw douit duyrmydd diuas'. For interpretations of it by Aneurin Owen and

was in all probability a literary text, but the rolls may possibly have been administrative in origin. The compilers of the inventories were, however, contemptuously proud of their inability to read Welsh, and none of the items seems to have survived: so there is little point in speculation, in particular about the possibility of business records in the vernacular. All that can be guessed with confidence is that both these records in the Treasury of Receipt and the other princely records in the Exchequer and Wardrobe copied into Liber A were chance spoils of war, not really comparable with the records of Scotland concerning 'the subjection of the people or of the land of Scotland to the King of England' or 'touching the freedom of Scotland', which were to be returned to Scotland under the Treaty of Northampton in 1328.[1] The corollary seems inescapable: that no substantial, systematic Welsh archive was thought worthy of preservation and removal to Westminster. This does not prove that there was no Welsh archive—it is inconceivable that the thirteenth-century princes had no accumulation of records—but it strengthens the presumption that there was no administrative organisation creating, preserving and in particular enrolling records on the model and scale of England.

The loss is incalculable for the writing of Welsh history in the thirteenth century. By contrast to the very substantial legal records of England, there is virtually nothing to demonstrate the actual practice of Welsh law. English historians who lament the lacunae in English legal records of the thirteenth century might perhaps be comforted by the pathetic pleasure with which Welsh historians greet the discovery of two whole judgments in the time of Llywelyn ab Iorwerth,[2] and the large dependence placed on the Assize Roll of 1277 to 1284 which is part of the records of

another unnamed (and unsound) scholar, see *ibid.*, i, lxxxii, lxxxiii, cxlii, cxliii. Professor Melville Richards tells me that no modern Welsh philologist has addressed himself to the line.

[1] E. L. G. Stones, 'The Treaty of Northampton, 1328', *History*, xxxviii (1953), 59–60.

[2] See Davies, *Montgomeryshire Collections*, li (1949–50), 15–17.

England.[1] It is ironic that the 'marvellous slowness'[2] with which Welsh law vanished after the Norman and Edwardian Conquests should be documented only by the records of lords marcher and by the Welsh lawbooks. These lawbooks are justly famous and certainly incorporate legislation of the princes, but they are not themselves records of that legislation as the Anglo-Saxon laws are.

The Anglo-Saxon laws contain the legislation issued by successive Anglo-Saxon and Anglo-Danish kings. They are essentially official ordinances (although they are often restating older laws) and rightly take their place among English royal records. The Welsh lawbooks, by contrast, are basically private compilations. They belong more naturally to the type of legal literature of which Henry Bracton's *Concerning the Laws and Customs of England* is the most familiar example: they are 'lawyers' textbooks' not 'mandatory pronouncements'.[3] They are associated with the name of Hywel Dda, but no manuscript survives from the two centuries after Hywel's death around 950; the major achievements in editing both the Welsh and the Latin texts in recent years are gradually opening the way to an assessment of the importance of Hywel's own contribution, to a better understanding of the inter-relationships of the groups of manuscript tradition, and the amount of earlier material common to several or all of the manuscripts.[4] The lawyers responsible for these texts as they evolved are shadowy men, far more shadowy than Henry Bracton: but it is clear that they had a practical purpose in mind. They organised their material by topics into what Sir Goronwy Edwards has neatly dubbed 'tractates':[5] these topics are both

---

[1] *The Welsh Assize Roll, 1277–1284*, ed. J. C. Davies (Board of Celtic Studies, History and Law Series, vii, Cardiff 1940).

[2] J. G. Edwards, 'The Historical Study of the Welsh Lawbooks', *Trans. Royal Historical Society*, 5th series, xii (1962), 142.    [3] *Ibid.*, 147.

[4] Cf. H. D. Emanuel, 'Studies in the Welsh Laws', *Celtic Studies in Wales: a Survey*, ed. Elwyn Davies (Cardiff 1963), 73–100. To the editions listed there can now be added Dr Emanuel's own invaluable *The Latin Texts of the Welsh Laws* (Board of Celtic Studies, History and Law Series, xxii, Cardiff 1967).

[5] Edwards, *Trans. Royal Historical Society*, 5th series, xii (1962), 143–4.

procedural and substantive. But the various texts are rarely of the first importance for their own day. Those from before 1300 are particularly valuable for pre-Norman legal institutions, those of the later Middle Ages for the thirteenth century, while it is the existing private court records of the marches and South Wales which are especially valuable for the continuing use of Welsh law after the Edwardian Conquest.[1]

Official court records of the Principality before or after the Conquest play little part in supplementing this material: the prince's court can be glimpsed only through occasional chronicle references, allusions in letters, a few extracts and the like.[2] This is unfortunate, for the laws raise the most fundamental questions about Welsh society.[3] The large literature which is building up around the strong framework of critically edited texts, of scholarly colloquia and a Welsh Laws sub-committee of the Board of Celtic Studies, bears witness to the dominant role which the laws play in understanding early Wales. But these secondary speculations would be much better informed if the laws also existed as datable dooms like those of Ethelred the Unready or Cnut, or as parliamentary legislation like that of Edward I; and they would be still better informed if there was a substantial case-law available from official court-records such as exist in England in increasing numbers from the thirteenth century onwards.

Although the existence of such records can be surmised for the last century of the independent princes, little is knowable about

---

[1] Cf. T. Jones Pierce, 'Social and Historical Aspects of the Welsh Laws', *Welsh History Review*, special number, 1963, *The Welsh Laws*, 48–9.

[2] Cf. T. Jones Pierce, 'The Laws of Wales—the Last Phase', *Trans. Hon. Soc. Cymm.* (1963), 30–2.

[3] For example, the recent unfinished debate about the origin of the *gwely* (T. Jones Pierce, 'Landlords in Wales: A. The Nobility and Gentry,' *The Agrarian History of England and Wales*, iv, ed. J. Thirsk (Cambridge 1967), 357–81; Dafydd Jenkins, 'A Lawyer looks at Welsh Land Law', *Trans. Hon. Soc. Cymm.* (1967), 241–7): or about the estate of *priodolder* (Pierce, 'The Law of Wales—the Last Phase', *Trans. Hon. Soc. Cymm.* (1963), 7–26; Jenkins, *op. cit.*, 220–40).

Welsh record-keeping before Edward I's Conquest. With the Statute of Rhuddlan in 1284, the land we now know as Wales was divided for the next two and a half centuries into three distinct sections. One of these, the marcher lordships in the south and east, was largely independent and its records are discussed in chapter 4. The two other sections were on the one hand Flintshire, which was for administrative and legal purposes amalgamated with the liberty of Chester and on the other hand the five counties which were to form the principality. These five counties were in turn divided into the two existing shires of Cardigan and Carmarthen which formed West Wales, or South Wales, and the three newly created shires of Anglesey, Caernarvon and Merioneth which formed North Wales.[1]

No fully formed administrative system was legislated in 1284, but the five shires were clearly outside the English shire system. The Welsh shires looked not to Westminster but to Caernarvon, Cardigan and Carmarthen. Their finance was under a treasurer or chamberlain or receiver: all these terms are used, but 'chamberlain' was to survive. The treasury of North Wales with its accounting branch, the Exchequer, settled at Caernarvon. The local official accounted to it and it accounted to Westminster. As a check on its activities, there was a controller, that is to say, a 'counter-roller', an official who kept a separate account-roll, which was also sent to the Exchequer at Westminster. To add to the confusion of the terminology, the controller is also known as the chancellor in the 1280s, and the duties were presently taken over by the third leading official, the Justice of North Wales appointed under the terms of the statute.[2]

Initially the 'chancery' work, mainly connected with legal writs, was done, in all probability, by a sub-department of the Caernarvon treasury, but under Prince Edward's administration

[1] The most lucid explanation of the divisions is by J. G. Edwards, *The Principality of Wales, 1267–1967: a Study in Constitutional History* (Caernarvon 1969), 9–16.

[2] See W. H. Waters, *The Edwardian Settlement of North Wales in its Administrative and Legal Aspects (1284–1343)* (Cardiff 1935), *passim*.

from 1301 to 1307 a greater range of duties fell to the chancellor: it is clear that some system of enrolment of letters issued by the prince developed, as it had in England a century earlier, that sealed warrants were used, that the privy seal and great seal of the Principality engendered their own archives.

Below these central offices in Caernarvon were the sheriffs in the newly formed counties, and below them a variety of local officials; alongside these were the officials of the boroughs and the coroners who were responsible, like the sheriffs, to Caernarvon.

An analogous situation obtained in West or South Wales, with administrative centres at Cardigan and Carmarthen.

The administrative records generated by this system survive very unequally. The enrolments of grants are completely lost. It is true that four volumes and one fragment survive from registers kept by the Black Prince: but the whole registers refer respectively to his affairs in general in England, Wales, Cornwall and Chester (1346 to 1348), to Devon and Cornwall, to Chester and Flint and to England (all three from 1351 to 1365): nothing survives for South Wales and only twelve mutilated membranes survive for North Wales, only twelve sides of these membranes bear writing and they contain only thirty-four documents for 1354 to 1356.[1] These registers are, moreover, the Prince's: he is giving instructions to his officials. The register, even if it survived in full, would not replace the lost administrative records of the Caernarvon writing department. The recognizance rolls of the Chester Chancery are merely supplemented by the Chester register. These chances of survival again emphasise how much better documented is the county of Flint than the rest of Wales. The officers of North Wales certainly did keep their own copies, although they had apparently been remiss about this early in Henry VII's reign. At the Beaumaris sessions held in May 1494 it was provided that the chamberlain of North Wales, his deputy, sheriffs, escheators and other officials 'that make out any Processe

[1] *Register of Edward the Black Prince* (4 vols., London 1930–33). The fragment for North Wales is calendared in iii, 489–96.

for the Prince or taketh any Inquisicion before them, write and put all such processe and all other things belonginge to their said Office in a booke and at the yeres end to make the Substaunce of the same booke to be entred in parchement and put into the said Exchequere or Treasorie of Carnervan aforesaid *as of old time it hath bene accustomed*, there to remayne of Record'.[1] Unfortunately none of these books has survived into modern times, unless *The Record of Caernarvon* is indeed one of them, as Sir Henry Ellis thought. This compilation of extents, statutes, *quo warranto* proceedings, petitions, regulations, writs and the like was certainly made for the convenience of the fifteenth-century administrators of North Wales, and its value is immense:[2] but its value is so great only because all the local series of records from which the extracts were taken have perished. A comparable volume in an English context would be of interest primarily for the purpose which lay behind the selection of items, not as the sole surviving evidence for the information each entry contained.

On the other hand, the financial records are, by Welsh standards, well preserved. The original rolls of the chamberlains' accounts themselves survive in large numbers in the Public Record Office. Moreover, since the chamberlains were required to make periodic accounts at the English Exchequer of Receipt, these accounts were enrolled on the pipe roll and its duplicate, the chancellor's roll.[3] The series of pipe and chancellor's rolls is preserved virtually unbroken, so that the text of many of the missing chamberlain's rolls can be recovered if one is strong enough and tall enough to hurl the pipe roll over the five-foot high 'horse'

---

[1] *Registrum vulgariter nuncupatum 'The Record of Caernarvon'*, ed. H. Ellis (Record Commission, London 1838), 295–6.

[2] *Ibid., passim.* The Record Commission edition (in record type) was made from the copy in the British Museum, Harley MS 696. What appears to be the original kept in the Caernarvon Exchequer has now been rediscovered: it is among the Baron Hill collection in the library of the University College of North Wales at Bangor.

[3] The basic finding-aids to these records are in *Lists and Indexes* v (London 1894, revised ed. New York 1963) and for the early Tudors, xxxiv (London 1910). Foreign Accounts are in xi (London 1900).

in the Record Office and patient enough to walk round and round it to read the successive membranes. Thus although all the thirteenth-century chamberlain's rolls have perished, the ones for North Wales are completely enrolled from 1284 to 1301 and for West Wales from 1298 to 1301; while the broken original series for North Wales from 1303 to the end of Edward II's reign can be made perfect by four enrolled accounts.[1] Although three ordinances of the English Exchequer in the 1320s reformed the accounting procedures, all of these 'foreign' accounts, different from the normal shire accounts of the English sheriffs, were not removed from the bulky pipe roll to form separate rolls until 1368 (although the separate auditing provided for forty years before had been effective).[2] After 1368 therefore the enrolment system alters.

A thorough administrative history of the Principality is one of the many basic gaps in the secondary literature, but it seems plain that chamberlains' accounts had ceased to be enrolled after the Black Prince took control of his principality in 1343 and only a handful of fifteenth-century accounts, in different circumstances, came to Westminster for audit and enrolment—for South Wales, the receivers' accounts for the whole of the princeless reign of Henry V, and for North Wales, the chamberlains' accounts for 1426 to 1430 and 1435 to 1436 (when Henry VI was still a minor).[3] As a result of the infrequency of enrolment, the gaps in the series of original accounts cannot be made good. Taking into consideration stray rolls in the British Museum, the Duchy of Cornwall office and the Duchy of Lancaster records, the gaps in the accounts for North Wales from 1303 to 1543 (the position of chamberlain continued after 1536) total 113 years.

[1] P.R.O., Exchequer, Pipe Rolls, E. 372/131, 136, 138, 146 (North Wales); 146, 176, 154, 170 (West or South Wales): Special Collections, Ministers' Accounts, S.C. 6/1211/1, 2A, 2B, 3, 6, 7; 1212/1–12; 1213/3; 1214/4. Cf. the use made of these and similar accounts in R. A. Brown, H. M. Colvin and A. J. Taylor, *The History of the King's Works* (London 1963), particularly ii, Appendix, 1027–8.

[2] *Guide to the Contents of the Public Record Office*, i (London 1963), 73–4.

[3] P.R.O., Exchequer, Foreign Accounts, E. 364/64, 73, 37, 64.

Only about half of the chamberlains' accounts for North Wales then survive in any form: the longest gap is during the later years of Edward III, from 1353 to 1377. The second longest is in Edward IV's reign from 1468 to 1483, the next longest from 1438 to 1448. The remaining gaps are quite small, three of seven years, one of five, and the rest four or less. Possibly some of these gaps, like the analogous gaps in the South Wales series, can be filled from rolls 'which strayed into other official archives or into private ownership long ago', but the only original chamberlains' accounts not listed in the obvious place in the *List and Index of Ministers' Accounts*, parts 1 and 2, are:

*North Wales*

| | |
|---|---|
| 1352–53 | Duchy of Lancaster records, P.R.O., D.L.29/636/10338 |
| 1393–94 | B.M., Additional Roll 29595 |
| ?c. 1434–35 | One membrane attached as cover to private accounts of 1434–35. N.L.W., Badminton 1563. |
| 1437–38 | B.M., Additional Roll 29597 |
| 1468–69 | P.R.O., D.L.29/636/10339 |
| 1469–70 | P.R.O., D.L.29/636/10340 |
| 1481–82 | Duchy of Cornwall Office |
| 1483–84 | P.R.O., D.L.29/636/10341 |
| 1519–20 | Duchy of Cornwall Office |

*South Wales*

| | |
|---|---|
| 1431–33 | B.M., Additional Roll 29596 |
| 1519–20 | Duchy of Cornwall Office[1] |

The distinction which I have made between enrolment and 'original' is a slightly specious one. Certainly more than one copy of each roll would be made in Wales (including the counter-rolls): the roll which has chanced to survive the centuries does

[1] British Museum, Additional Rolls 26595 and 26596 are printed as a supplement to *Arch. Camb.*, 6th series, xii (1912), Original Documents, 34–44, 1–25. Photographic copies of the Duchy of Cornwall records were presented to the National Library by Prince Charles in celebration of his inauguration (*National Library of Wales Annual Report, 1968–69*, 14–15, 22).

not necessarily have more weight as evidence than the copy on the pipe roll. Mr Waters used the pipe roll copies extensively for his administrative study of North Wales[1] and Miss Myvanwy Rhys printed five accounts from the pipe rolls in her edition of *Ministers' Accounts for West Wales, 1277 to 1306*,[2] but the texts published in the *Bulletin of the Board of Celtic Studies* have been from 'original' rolls only,[3] and it seems that scholars need to be reminded again of the wealth lying in the pipe rolls. Moreover, a proper comparison of the texts where they survive both in 'original' and in enrolments should be undertaken, for the content is not always the same. For example, the chamberlain's 'original' account for North Wales covering the year 1315 to 1316 does not include details of decayed rents, or stock and furnishings of the castles, but the enrolment on the pipe roll does, adding an enormous amount of detailed information which would otherwise be lost: the enrolled account fills two rotulets completely, or something close on twenty feet of parchment.[4]

In conjunction with these enrolments, the information on the memoranda rolls, both of the King's Remembrancer and the Lord Treasurer's Remembrancer, is essential for a comprehensive view of the financial and archival position: it is on the memoranda roll, for example, that the loss of the original chamberlains' accounts up to 1294 is uniquely recorded and explained. It is to be hoped that the work on these records done by Mrs Fryde on behalf of the Board of Celtic Studies will be published: Mrs Fryde's survey covers all memoranda rolls from 1282 to 1343.

Subsidiary accounts, the files of local ministers accounting to the chamberlains, were rarely enrolled at Westminster. Original rolls survive intermittently and are scattered in the Public Record Office among Ministers' Accounts, Duchy of Lancaster records, and the Accounts Various, Sheriffs' Accounts and Miscel-

---

[1] See above, 57 n.2.

[2] Cymmrodorion Record Series, xiii (London 1936).

[3] *B.B.C.S.*, ii (1923–25), 49–86 [West Wales, 1301–2]; ix (1937–39), 51–63 [North Wales, 1291–92]; i (1921–23), 256–75 [North Wales, 1304–5].

[4] P.R.O., E. 372/163; S.C. 6/1121/7.

lanea of the King's Remembrancer.[1] There are also two splendid sets of audit rolls, one for the officials of Cardiganshire in 1445–46, the other for those of Carmarthenshire in 1454–55, which have strayed into the archives of the Duke of Beaufort.[2]

The composition of these mixed files is complex and they are rather scattered. Most of the information about the accounts for South Wales will soon be available in Dr Ralph Griffiths' annotated list of office-holders to be published by the University of Wales Press, but the compilation of a similar, elaborate biographical list for North Wales will take some time, and, as an interim measure, a consolidated check-list of the North Welsh accounts and subsidiary documents would be a boon. The situation in which each student of later medieval Wales has to hack his own path through the undergrowth is doubtless educational in a way, but it wastes everyone's time and has not been in the interests of scholarship.

There is also one stray account, or copy of an account, of the issues of the Exchequers of Wales for 1426 to 1429. This document shows the income from the issue of documents over these years, at the rate of 2s for a protection and a *supersedeas* and 6d for everything else. The business seems to have increased, with internal fluctuations: fifty-five 6d writs and eight protections in 1426–27, totalling 27s 6d, in 1427–28, eighty-one 6d writs (sixty-two of them *recordares*) and five protections, totalling 50s 6d, in 1428–29, sixty-nine writs (only thirty-six or thirty-seven *recordares*, but a large increase in transcripts of fines from six to fourteen), eleven or twelve protections and one *supersedeas*.[3]

The records produced by the justices' sessions were ill-protected from loss over the centuries and actual plea rolls in the Public

---

[1] P.R.O., S.C. 6, various; D.L. 29, various; E. 101/600/1–33, 507/29; E. 199/57/1, 2, 10–28; E. 163/24/1, 4/4/47. Two accounts of the escheators for North Wales are enrolled on the pipe roll (E. 372/169, 184). For those in print, see *Handlist of Scottish and Welsh Record Publications* (British Records Association, London 1954), 31.

[2] N.L.W., Badminton MSS 1561, 1560a.

[3] P.R.O., Exchequer of Receipt, Accounts Various, E. 101/514/20. There is a discrepancy in the addition of the 1428–29 section.

Record Office for the period before 1543 exist only for Anglesey and Caernarvon. But fragments, copies and extracts exist in widely scattered places. Inside the Public Record Office, two battered membranes of pleas of Carmarthen containing cases of 1317–18, 1320, 1327 and 1332 will be found among Chancery Miscellanea.[1]

There is also an exceedingly important volume of transcripts, made in the early sixteenth century from the pleas and inquisitions preserved among the principality records.[2] The records from which these copies were selected then survived for the whole period of the Principality, although there is no way of telling whether the Tudor copyists were selecting from a very large archive or preserving most of the pathetic remains of an archive. It is, however, clear from the number of fourteenth-century documents transcribed that Glyndŵr did not destroy the archives, or certainly not with the success of the revolting peasants in London's Inns of Court in 1381. Dr Beverley Smith's edition of Welsh legal proceedings will put this, and other chance survivors, into a proper context. Until this volume appears in the Board's History and Law series, students are dependent on their own assessment of such materials. And these materials are very scattered, even inside the Record Office and even one class of record: eight additional folios, for example, which seem rightly to belong to this volume of transcripts, are bound in with Marian valuations of English lands in another volume preserved by the Court of Augmentations.[3]

Collections of deeds will often contain extracts from the sessions rolls, when these were concerned with property. Many of the major deed collections discussed under private muniments contain such documents, others are to be found in the exhibits in the Court of Wards, as mentioned in the next chapter, others are

[1] P.R.O., Chancery, Miscellanea, C. 47/10/32/15. The 1327 case is mutilated.

[2] P.R.O., Exchequer, Augmentation Office, Miscellaneous Books, E. 315/166.

[3] P.R.O., E. 315/167, fos. 1–8.

simply strays in, for example, Shrewsbury Public Library,[1] and others survive only in antiquaries' transcripts.[2]

Because the Flintshire records were left with the relatively well-organised Chester records, which suffered less confusion after the Act of 1543 than the Caernarvon records, they survived better than those from the Principality. Moreover, they received very favoured treatment by way of listing and even calendaring in the nineteenth-century Public Record Office. The Flintshire Historical Society, too, has been very vigorous since its inception sixty years ago, and in its publications a number of plea rolls, as well as ministers' accounts, have been conveniently calendared or translated. There is not the problem of dispersal or reliance on later copies. I know of only one plea roll of Flint which is out of custody, the roll for 1316–17 deposited at the University College of North Wales in 1958 by Lord Langford of Bodrhyddan: but the mere fact that this roll appeared unexpectedly encourages archive-spotters to maintain their vigilance.

The subsidiary materials, which make the English archives so extraordinarily fruitful, are mostly lost for Wales. The odd documents, mostly produced and preserved by the English Chancery, which were formed into the vast P.R.O. class of Chancery Miscellanea, have a section specifically created by the nineteenth-century archivists to accommodate documents relating to Wales. These are basically English documents, although there are many letters from Welsh law-officers in answer to English writs of *certiorari*: the point is, however, that this section is much larger itself than the entire archive of official Welsh legal records for the Principality and Flint combined.

The only exception to the general lack of subsidiary legal documents is, predictably, Flint; though even for Flint the materials are very thin, and the thinness is emphasised because they share classes in the public records with the impressive Chester

---

[1] E.g., Shrewsbury Public Library, MSS 190, 192 (Caernarvon Sessions, 1481, 1545). MS 191 is an exemplification of an inquisition *post mortem* taken at Harlech by the escheator in April 1446 after the death of John Vivian of Harlech.

[2] See chapter 6 below.

records. But there are a few useful items to be found. A bundle of small membranes, for example, containing the names of those indicted before the sheriff during the third quarter of the fourteenth century survives as Chester 20/8 and a very fine file of records from the tourns and inquisitions organised by the sheriff, again in the later fourteenth century, is Chester 19/8. Chester 24/237 is a large box containing original files of Flintshire judicial writs in Edward III's reign, a file of petitions and writs *precipimus* from Edward III to Edward IV and some damaged remains of Yorkist court records.

There also survive a few English assize rolls, records of specific commissions of oyer and terminer which relate to the Principality and the marches. The most important of these, the records of the commission which heard cases in the marches from 1277 to 1284, has been calendared by Dr Conway Davies:[1] but it is not a record of the Welsh administration. It is an English record although it was perhaps used by the justices of the later Principality as a collection of precedents: but the implications of its storage in the old Wallia Miscellanea bags in the English Treasury of Receipt are not self-evident. The Wallia class seem to have contained English documents relating to Wales as much as documents brought from Wales.

As a result of the way in which records were stored in Wales, which is discussed below, our sources for the administration of medieval Wales are very patchy. If an Englishman petitioned parliament about the conduct of royal justice in England, as the abbot of Vale Royal petitioned in 1442 about the sessions in Carmarthenshire and Cardiganshire, a student could immediately search voluminous records of the English courts around that time. But when the student reads how the abbot of Vale Royal complained that he had been indicted in the Principality for alleged felonies, that he had been outlawed for failure to attend in these distant parts before he had received even one summons, that he dared not go to Carmarthen even with a safe conduct for fear of assault and particularly not at the time of the annual Great

[1] Board of Celtic Studies, History and Law Series vii (Cardiff 1940).

Sessions, the student has very little hope of finding any ancillary evidence from legal records. Yet the abbot had some very specific and interesting proposals for reforming aspects of the procedure around the writ *capias* in Wales: it is very doubtful whether it is now possible to discover the success of his proposals or the justice of his complaints.[1]

The administrative reorganisation of Wales subsequent to the statute of 1284 had created a series of small imitations of some parts of English practice and these arrangements remained basically unchanged until the Henrician statutes. The shiring of Wales and the appointment of justices of the peace under the two Acts of 1536 was certainly a fundamental change in the administration of law and order, but the creation of courts of Great Sessions in 1543 was the final watershed. This is the reason for the terminal date of this book. It is also the reason for the lamentable history of the preservation of the medieval records of Wales and the basis for the present division of the existing plea rolls of Wales between London and Aberystwyth. The records generated by the Justices of the Peace, the Quarter Sessions archives, do not concern this survey, although two indictment rolls for Caernarvonshire in fact survive for 1541 and 1542.[2] The history of the other legal records of Wales, however, is relevant, for it helps to explain the present situation.

The Act of 1543 establishing the circuits of the Great Sessions made no provision for the transfer of earlier records to the new legal authorities: it merely provided that existing records of the earlier sessions should be kept by the new prothonotaries in each county, who now attended on the justices for the four circuits of three counties apiece. The legal records, such as they existed in Henry VIII's reign, therefore, became the responsibility of the new law officers. This arrangement lasted for nearly three hundred years.

After Edmund Burke interested himself in the Welsh judicature

[1] *Rotuli Parliamentorum* (London 1783), v, 43.
[2] *Calendar of the Caernarvonshire Quarter Sessions Records*, i, *1541–1558*, ed. W. Ogwen Williams (Caernarvon 1956), 2–29.

there was a series of investigations and reports given to parliament from 1798 to 1820, but only after the general enquiry into the entire English and Welsh judicial system ordered by Lord Lyndhurst in 1828 was the system itself changed. Despite solid Welsh opposition—only one Welsh M.P. voted in favour of the Judicature Act—the Great Sessions were abolished as from 1830.[1] The Act provided that legal records throughout England, Wales and the palatinates, should, 'unless otherwise provided by Law, be kept by the same Persons and in the same Places as before the passing of this Act . . . , provided always that in case of the Death of any such Person before any other Provision shall have been made for keeping such Records, Muniments, and Writings, the Custody thereof shall be with the Clerks of the Peace of the several Counties to which Counties the same shall respectively belong'.[2] But since after 1830 the prothonotaries had no longer any financial interest in maintaining the records, the keeping of the legal records throughout England and Wales rapidly became scandalous.

The legal records of Flint had, however, a rather different history. Until the Act of 1543, and in some respects even later, Flintshire records were part of the Chester records. The series of so-called 'recognizance rolls' of Chester contain copies of documents issued by the administration for both Chester and Flint. The title commonly used in the fifteenth century is 'counties palatine of Chester and Flint' and the justices of Chester held the sessions in Flint. The combined records were kept in Chester Castle even after the 1543 Act which provided for a separate prothonotary for Flint, Denbigh and Montgomery. This was because of the influence of the existing prothonotary of Chester and Flint, John Birkenhead, who lived until 1555, and three members of his family who thereafter obtained a grant for their lives in survivorship: and the office bound Chester and Flint together as far as record-keeping went until the Act of 1830.[3]

---

[1] M. H. James, 'Montgomeryshire and the Abolition of the Court of Great Sessions, 1817–1830,' *Montgomeryshire Collections*, lx (1967–68), 85–103.

[2] 11 George IV and 1 William IV, c. 70 s. 27.

[3] *First Report of the Royal Commission on Public Records appointed to inquire into*

The clerk of the peace in Flintshire, which had enjoyed virtual judicial independence since 1543, kept Great Sessions records only from 1748 onwards. The major series in Chester Castle was disrupted by a fire there in 1817, by over-zealous antiquaries and finally, as elsewhere, by the dissolution of the old legal order under the statute of 1830.[1]

The care and attention which the Welsh records, both legal and administrative, received was minimal and the losses were probably heavy and sustained. The process of loss is very well illustrated by a letter from Humphrey Jones to Sir John Wynn of Gwydir in 1626. Jones had gone to the Exchequer at Caernarvon to look for a 'deed' which Sir John wanted; he had found all the inquisitions in a bag and he took the bagful home to search at his leisure. He may or may not have returned them.[2] There are two rival, or complementary, theories about the removal of the Caernarvon Exchequer records to London: between the reigns of Elizabeth and George III the Auditors of the Exchequer for Wales seem to have brought to London as exhibits and precedents both Welsh accounts and plea rolls, while the local Caernarvon tradition in 1840 was that a mass removal of early records took place in 1767 when the Exchequer tower was rebuilt and converted into Caernarvon Town Hall.[3] Both explanations may very well be true: they would repay investigation. However the Welsh records got there, certainly most of the splendid series of Chamberlains' accounts, both for North and South Wales, had reached London by the early nineteenth century.

This was uncommonly fortunate, for around 1810 or 1820 the masses of early records which still remained at Caernarvon, in a

*and report on the State of the Public Records and Local Records of a Public Nature of England and Wales*, i (2) (London 1912), 156 (Sir Henry Maxwell-Lyte's note on Flintshire records).

---

[1] *Ibid.*, 152b, from the memorandum on the Welsh records by Sir Vincent Evans, Henry Owen and Llewelyn Williams.

[2] *Calendar of Wynn (of Gwydir) Papers, 1516–1690* (Aberystwyth 1926), no. 1390.

[3] *First Report of Royal Commission on Public Records*, i (2), 150; *D.K.R.*, i (1840), 112.

cellar of the record building, were sold by the hundredweight on the magistrates' orders, thrown on middens and 'wheeled into the Menai as rotten and worthless'. The market in those records which were not destroyed was cornered by a local entrepreneur, David Williams of Turkey Shore, who sold the parchment principally to tailors, presumably to stiffen clothes. By 1840 only two Jacobean plea rolls were not being worn by the gentlemen of Caernarvonshire.[1]

In this year 1840 Mr W. H. Black reported to the Master of the Rolls (as Keeper of the Public Records) on what he had found in his recent survey of the legal records of Wales and Chester. He carefully and damningly described the conditions under which Welsh records struggled to survive. The least insalubrious was Cardiff Shire Hall, where the room was light and airy and the records, from Henry VIII's reign on, were in good condition, in locked presses many of which Black had to have broken open.[2] The most unattractive repository was in Presteign. There Mr Black was obliged to force the town-crier's wife to remove her furniture and her carpet from her parlour in the new Shire Hall, before the door to the record vault could even be opened. Because of the remarkable dampness of the stone, and the lack of ventilation, the great heap of old parchments on the floor of the vault had putrefied so that the parlour had become uninhabitable. In trying to diminish the stench of mouldering, rat-infested parchment some years previously, ventilation holes had been cut and a stove provided in a neighbouring passage to warm the atmosphere: but the workmen engaged on these improvements scattered a large quantity of limestone chips all over the records, adding to their distress. Black was convinced that only his action in having this Augean stable cleansed (at his own expense) prevented actual fermentation taking place.[3]

All this was very regrettable, though it should be remembered that when in 1661 William Prynne became keeper of the English records in the Tower of London he found 'many rare antient Precious Pearls and Golden Records' lying 'through the Negli-

[1] *D.K.R.*, i (1840), 90–1.     [2] *Ibid.*, 99.     [3] *Ibid.*, 97–8.

gence, Nescience, or Sloathfullnesse of their Former Keepers . . .
in one confused Chaos under corroding, putrefying Cobwebs,
Dust, Filth'.[1] But this does not excuse Presteign.

Between the extremes of Presteign and Cardiff came Chester
Castle where, despite confusion and past damage from
'damp, disorder, dirt and perhaps vermin', the early records did
survive in number, and there was liberal accommodation. They
were not well arranged and a number of early rolls had been
collected together in a box labelled 'Illegible Illingworth'.[2] Fire
was a constant threat at Brecknock and Ruthin, damp at Caernarvon and Dolgellau; while the adequate buildings at Pool and
Haverfordwest were both about to be demolished. Mr Black
recommended therefore that all the records of North Wales
should be housed with 'Illegible Illingworth' in Chester Castle,
although he did add thoughtfully that the record rooms 'are
only 50 yards distant from the magazine of gunpowder'.[3]

Black detected also 'a strong public feeling' against the removal
of the records from North Wales. But the creation of the Public
Record Office in Chancery Lane, not just as an ideal (as it was in
1840, only eighteen months after the enabling Act) but as a
capacious Gothic pile, made possible another sort of consolidation for the records of Wales. The foundations of the Public
Record Office were not in fact laid until 1851, but during the
1840s in preparation for the repository a massive work of consolidation of records was undertaken.

In 1845 the first steps with the Welsh archives were taken.
Welsh records already in the Chapter House and in other major
repositories would be transferred automatically to Chancery
Lane when the time came, but the legal records had to come
from Welshpool (the chancery records of Montgomery, Denbigh
and Flint), the Great Sessions equity records for Glamorgan,
Brecknock and Radnor from Clements Inn (where they had
been removed from the Shire Hall at Brecon) and the Chester

---

[1] W. Prynne, *Brevia Parliamentaria Rediviva* [part iii] (London 1662), Epistle
Dedicatory.
[2] *D.K.R.*, i (1840), 80.    [3] *Ibid.*, 115–16.

circuit records from 15 Bedford Square and 62 Lincoln's Inn Fields.[1] These legal records, now transferred to the Rolls House or to Chancery, were all post-medieval, however, and the bulk of the records remained to be collected from fourteen Welsh repositories. Despite the efforts made by some areas—Caernarvon as late as 1853 spent £1,000 in constructing a new repository[2]—Lord Romilly, the new Master of the Rolls, with his Public Record Office partly habitable, issued a warrant in July 1854 for the transfer of all the records to London, and Charles Roberts of the Record Office set off immediately on an epic collecting tour in Welsh repositories.

Starting from Chester on 24 July 1854, Roberts moved to Ruthin and on to Caernarvon on 26 July. There he asked the clerk to rearrange the Anglesey and Caernarvon records, while he returned to Chester Castle, which was to be the staging depot for North Wales. On 6 September Roberts returned to Caernarvon, where sorting was partially done. He arranged for suitable wooden containers to be made and went on to Dolgellau, where he packed the records in two large boxes and eleven bags. He was obliged to hire an elderly stage coach to take this load the forty-five miles to the nearest railhead, at Caernarvon. The Dolgellau and Caernarvon records were then sent by train to Chester, and Roberts moved on to Welshpool. The Welshpool records, despite the clearance of 1845, filled three boxes and forty bags, broke the springs of the open van taking them to Oswestry and almost missed the only train to Chester.

From 20 to 23 September Roberts stayed at Chester, then went to collect the Ruthin records. Like most Welsh repositories, Ruthin was an uncomfortable distance from the railway system: to get his loot to Mold Station Roberts had to start loading at 5 a.m., emptying two rooms in the Town Hall and transporting seventeen filthy sacks brought in hampers and barrels from the vaults of Wrexham Church in 1827.[3] It was on this day, 28 Sep-

---

[1] *D.K.R.*, xx (1859), Appendix 10, 193–4.

[2] B. R. Parry, 'The Caernarvonshire Record Office', *Archives*, vii (1965–66), 35.   [3] *D.K.R.*, i (1840), 88.

tember, that Roberts was shown the two boxes in the loft of Ruthin Town Hall, which were to prove to contain the spectacular set of seigneurial court rolls for Ruthin lordship.

Once Ruthin records arrived at Chester, North Wales was emptied of its archives and five of the biggest luggage vans which the North Western Railway could supply were sent to London filled to the brim with Welsh records. The records arrived in Chancery Lane on 13 October and weighed in at thirteen tons.

November 1854 was spent by Roberts on similar expeditions in South Wales, to Cardiff, Carmarthen and Haverfordwest, transferring the archives to London in three of the Great Western Railway's most capacious horse-boxes.[1]

In 1855 Roberts completed his task, collecting four more tons from Brecknock, Cardigan and Presteign[2] and in 1857 gained a well-earned promotion to be Secretary of the Public Record Office.[3]

Once all the surviving records produced by the administration in Wales, medieval and modern, were at last brought together, the Public Record Office proceeded to disperse them among many classes. Sir Henry Maxwell-Lyte was, in many ways, a great Deputy Keeper but some of the procedures under his regime would not be countenanced today. In particular, the idea of tearing records of a certain sort from their context and creating a 'special collection' of court rolls, or account rolls, or rentals and surveys is no longer fashionable. The integrity of the original archival unit was less respected then than now. Although de Wailly had coined the phrase *respect des fonds* as early as 1841, when he took stock of the Archives Nationales in Paris, and although archivists like Maxwell-Lyte were deeply learned in administrative history, yet aberrations like Special Collections were still possible. The creation of artificial classes of documents like this is behaviour quite different from the current debate among

[1] *D.K.R.*, xvi (1855), Appendix 2, Roberts' report, 35–41.

[2] *D.K.R.*, xvii (1856), 38–40.

[3] *First Report of Royal Commission on Public Records*, i (2), 154.

archivists whether there is justification for splitting up a family
archive as Mr Emmison of Essex did with the Petre deposit or
Mr Collis of Somerset with the Mildmay.[1] No sane archivist
nowadays would tear court rolls or accounts from their Chancery
or Exchequer classes, although he might usefully compile a
consolidated finding aid.

Maxwell-Lyte, however, supervised the creation of the celebrated, or infamous, S.C. classes, the 'special collections'. Welsh
records did not suffer uniquely, but they did suffer: the Chamberlains' rolls were taken and put in S.C.6, Ministers' Accounts, the
court rolls, whether official or private, went into S.C. 2, the
rentals and surveys into S.C. 11 and S.C. 12. In further 'rationalisation' Maxwell-Lyte annexed the plea rolls of the Great Sessions
of Wales to the English plea roll series in the *Lists and Indexes*.
Other Welsh records, mainly more modern documents subsidiary
to the plea rolls, were only roughly sorted until the twentieth
century.[2] The only records from Wales which received any really
thorough treatment were the Flint–Chester series: the 'recognizance' rolls of the Chester Chancery, the deeds, inquisitions
and writs of dower enrolled on the Chester Plea Rolls between
the reigns of Henry III and Edward III, the final concords for
Edward I's reign and early Tudor warrants, signed Bills and privy
seals were all calendared in a series of Deputy Keeper's Reports.[3]

The position of the Welsh records was not helped by the
apparent animus which Maxwell-Lyte bore towards Wales. The
evidence which he gave to the Royal Commission in 1912 is at

[1] F. G. Emmison, ' "Repatriation" of "Foreign" Estate and Family Archives',
*Archives*, ii (1953–56), 467–76; R. B. Pugh, 'Quod dominus conjunxit Carto-
phylax non separet', *ibid.*, iii (1957–58), 39–42; symposium, 'Some Views on
"Sanctity"', *ibid.*, 159–71.

[2] *First Report of Royal Commission on Public Records*, i (2), 154–5. For the first
brief survey of all the Welsh records, see *D.K.R.*, xxiv (1863), Appendix 11,
54–61.

[3] *D.K.R.*, xxxvi (1875), xxxvii (1876), xxxix (1878), recognizance rolls;
xxvi (1865), xxvii (1866), xxviii (1867), plea rolls; xxviii (1867), fines; xxvi
(1865), warrants. There was also a helpful list of officials published in xxxi
(1870) and an index to plaintiffs and defendants in equity cases from Henry
VIII to Mary, xxv (1864).

times contemptuous, particularly towards the National Library. In particular, he seems to have been anxious to destroy the more modern records of the Great Sessions. The nine Commissioners, however, included three prominent Welshmen, all associated with the new National Library, Sir Vincent Evans, a governor, Henry Owen, the treasurer, and W. Llewelyn Williams, *ex officio* a governor as a member of parliament for Carmarthen Boroughs. All three, moreover, were also prominent in the Honourable Society of Cymmrodorion. The Commission noted acidly that from 1908 onwards 'recommendations and criticisms submitted [by Welsh scholars to the Record Office] seem to have caused some irritation in official quarters and to have evoked a promise to call the attention of the "Destruction Committee" to these Welsh records'.[1] The result was that the modern records of the Great Sessions were removed to the National Library of Wales; 'They were documents', said Maxwell-Lyte, 'which, if we had not had very great regard to Welsh feeling, we should have sent to be pulped.'[2]

The medieval and Tudor records had never been in danger of pulping (since only documents created after 1660 could legally be destroyed, under the amending statute of 1898),[3] but they had suffered considerable delay in sorting and then were victims of an inflexible system of classification which affected an uncommonly high proportion of the records surviving for the period before 1543.

Again in 1962 the legal records were the victims of a final solution to the Welsh problem. This was doubtless an honest attempt to satisfy Welsh aspirations and to make a more logical reapportionment. The basis of this last attempt at rationalisation was that all records of the Great Sessions as created by the Henrician legislation should go to Aberystwyth to join their more modern counterparts which had gone there to escape destruction over half a century before. The difficulty is that the actual procedure

[1] *First Report of Royal Commission on Public Records*, i (2), 155.
[2] *Ibid.*, i (3), *Minutes of Evidence*, 12–13, question 324.
[3] *Ibid.*, i (1), *Report*, 16.

of sessions in ancient counties such as Flint and Caernarvon was continuous: the statute of 1536 enunciated the principle of holding Great Sessions, but the organisation of these courts in the new shires was not effected until after an order of June 1540, and statutory sanction for the administrative arrangements of circuits was not given until the Act of 1543.[1] It seems, however, that 1541 was the critical year in the new counties, and in 1962 the legal records from the regnal year 1541–42 onwards were transferred to Aberystwyth.

The effects of this division are not entirely happy. As a result of the gesture to Wales, the fine set of plea rolls for Flintshire (Chester 30), which survive intermittently from 12 Edward I onwards, is no longer a set. The first forty-two rolls remain in London, the rest are in Aberystwyth: Chester 30/42, in London, has the pleas and gaol deliveries of 11 January and 3 May 1541; Chester 30/43, in Aberystwyth, contains the remaining sessions for 1541 and 1542. The series technically changes when the justice of Chester added to his circuit the counties of Denbigh and Montgomery under the statute of 1543, but that is a technicality: any student of a topic which is illuminated by the legal records of Flint will not find his materials affected by the new jurisdiction; but he will find them two hundred miles apart. As it happens, the problem is solved for most counties other than Flint, because there are no plea rolls for Brecknock, Cardigan, Carmarthen, Denbigh, Glamorgan, Merioneth, Montgomery, Pembroke and Radnor before 1541, so all pleas from these counties are to be found in the National Library.[2] Caernarvon, however, has one late fourteenth-century roll and two others for 24 and 25 Henry VIII, so rolls 1, 2 and 3 of Wales 20 are in London, while Wales 20/4 onwards (still keeping their Record Office call numbers) are all in Aberystwyth. Similarly all the Anglesey plea

[1] See P. R. Roberts, 'The Union with England and the Identity of Anglican Wales,' *Trans. Royal Historical Society*, 5th series, xxii (1972), forthcoming.

[2] The call numbers which these rolls had in the Public Record Office are, somewhat confusingly, retained in Aberystwyth.

rolls except one, which covers the first eight years of Henry VIII's reign, have gone to Wales.

The records of the lordship of Ruthin constituting the class Wales 15, were not transferred to Aberystwyth 'being unrelated to the Court of Great Sessions'. This is undeniable, but it is also true that the National Library has a large collection of Ruthin records which are exactly complementary to Wales 15. Since these records came to Chancery Lane simply as a salvage operation arising in the first instance from Charles Roberts' interest in the boxes of court rolls, there is nothing uncommonly sacred about their presence among the English records. The more significant early records of Ruthin, the court rolls themselves from 1294 to 1654, were classed in the nineteenth century with Special Collections, S.C. 2, and it is clear that there can be no trifling with the synthetic sanctity of that archive group. Yet one Welsh deed in the equally artificial class of Ancient Deeds series F (Wales 29/36) and a bundle of thirty-nine deeds from the FF series (Wales 30/51) were transferred to Wales in 1962, although they are not obviously sessions records any more than the Ruthin records: and, furthermore, although both classes Wales 29 and 30 are mainly composed of Cheshire documents, at least three medieval Flintshire deeds, one Cardigan deed of 1546 and a Denbighshire bond of 1590 remain in London.

Neither logic nor consideration for the user triumphed in 1962. Even in the legal records themselves there are anomalies. 1541 was the great dividing line, used ruthlessly in bisecting Flint, Anglesey and Caernarvon plea rolls. But a gaol file for Merioneth survives for 1513–14 (Wales 4/296/1): it is the only Welsh gaol file surviving from the period before 1541. Where is the Merioneth gaol file? It is at Aberystwyth.

Less escapable anomalies exist in the treatment of the classes of miscellanea. Wales 28/235 contains a bundle of miscellaneous Flintshire documents spanning five centuries up to 1830. Presumably the medieval material is supplementary in some way to the plea rolls still in London, but Wales 28/235 is now at Aberystwyth along with two bundles of Denbighshire 'prisoners' papers'

(Wales 28/13, 14), both covering the years 1540 to 1830.

The circumstances of the transfer do seem to be in keeping with the general messiness of Welsh archival practices over the centuries. Things have not gone smoothly for the records of Wales, and the modern student is the sufferer: particularly the modern student of early Tudor Wales who does not happen to live at Aberystwyth. For if he were in Aberystwyth he would find that the National Library thoughtfully obtained photographic copies of all the earlier plea rolls, which remained in London. But a student in the Public Record Office—and that is where most students of Tudor Wales ought to be based—will find that there was no reciprocal arrangement in London.

# CHAPTER 3

# The Records of the English Government

The official records produced by the activities of the English government are essential sources for medieval Wales. They contain evidence of all manner of English actions which affected Wales, Welshmen, the marches and the lords of the march: the affairs of Wales and England are reflected in a wide variety of record. Moreover, the English government, particularly after the Edwardian Conquest, had occasion to keep office copies of many documents produced by the administrators of Wales. This might be done in the Exchequer in the course of normal business, particularly auditing, or in the Chancery or the law courts in response to questions, writs *certiorari*, sent from Westminster. As the previous chapter made plain, these English copies are not infrequently the only surviving texts. As well as making copies, the English departments, in particular the Exchequer and the law courts, acquired in their normal routine many Welsh documents, often documents from private estates. The Court of Augmentations, created to meet the dissolution of the monasteries, was the most spectacular of the courts which acquired Welsh records, but other law courts, particularly equity and prerogative courts, heard many cases touching Wales and retained not only the record of the suit but also curious items which were originally exhibits.

In another book in this series, Professor Elton has given an admirable introduction to the English official records.[1] What he says there does not need to be repeated here, but some indication of the series in which information relevant to Wales can be found is appropriate. The archives of Chancery, both the enrolments of letters sent out (the Close, Patent, Charter, Fine, Liberate, Welsh, Gascon, Norman and Scots rolls) and the much less complete,

[1] Elton, *England, 1200–1640*, chap. 2.

but still enormous, files of warrants, are essential to the student of Welsh no less than the student of English history. The most obvious are the Welsh rolls, of course, a special series of rolls created for the specific needs of the Edwardian Conquest. These seven rolls, which were published in calendar form in 1912,[1] contain basically copies of documents issued under the great seal of England from 1277 to 1294, but there are also copies of some other documents, including letters from Llywelyn. Some items appear on other Chancery enrolments and some were copied into Liber A. The most spectacular single entry is the celebrated report on the laws and customs of Wales made in 1281 by the three English commissioners, but the entire series of enrolments is fundamental to the history of the Conquest. The Welsh rolls also contain copies of a few private deeds: a schedule, for example, enrolled documents concerning the sons of Gruffydd ap Gwenwynwyn, or an *inspeximus* of the charters of Strata Florida dating back to the twelfth century.[2] But the rolls contain basically the political and military record of the English government's conquest of Wales.

Throughout the other enrolments of Chancery letters, there are royal grants, instructions to officials, appointments of all sorts, pardons, authorisation for payments, all the multifarious business of the writing department. Inevitably, a proportion of these letters touches on the marches, on Wales and on Welshmen and marchers, at home or abroad. Because Welshmen abroad are an aspect of Welsh history, the Scots, Norman and Gascon rolls, which may have seemed improbable sources in the list, are useful: they record, among other things, a good deal about soldiers in English service. It is quite impossible to give examples of the information available in these hundreds of beautifully-preserved rolls: they contain the story of English government from 1200 onwards, the day to day running of the kingdom, from humdrum routine to high crisis. But they are not beyond criticism, nor are all the series of equal value at all periods. Some of the lesser

[1] *Calendar of Various Chancery Rolls, 1277–1326* (London 1912), 157–362.
[2] *Ibid.*, 328–32, 298–301.

series do not exist continuously: the Norman rolls were not maintained between the loss of Normandy by John in 1205-6, and Henry V's renewed campaigns after Agincourt, and they end again in 1422. The Gascon rolls are slender memorials of two hundred years of English rule, covering the years 1254 to 1469. The Liberate rolls, ordering payments, were discontinued in 1436 after a long decline. The Close rolls also declined rapidly after the fourteenth century, and an increasing number of letters was issued by the privy seal or signet office clerks (whose records are relatively ill-preserved), and after 1534, although the Close rolls continued, they contained only private deeds enrolled there for safe evidential keeping by private individuals. And even when series are unbroken, like the Patent rolls, there is always the element of human inefficiency to reduce their comprehensive rightness. Finally, the officials of the palatinates and liberties, including Lancaster, Chester, Wales and the marches, are inevitably much less frequently the recipients of royal letters than the ministers in ordinary royal England.

So the searcher ought not to be surprised if the Chancery records fail him in any specific quest. But he should keep his sense of proportion. Because of the clerks who made the Chancery enrolments, and those modern clerks who have calendared and indexed most of the medieval rolls, a unique means of entry into the affairs of government is available.[1] Its excellence is far more striking than its shortcomings. England should take pride, moreover, not only in her incomparable records but also in her Record Office where the finding aids are fuller and more accessible and the staff more helpful and better informed than in any other comparable institution in the whole of Europe.

Chancery also maintained immense files of replies to inquisitions, mostly about the lands and heirs of recently deceased tenants-in-chief. These inquisitions *post mortem*, for all their unreliability, make possible the history of landownership and

[1] For the details of calendars and indexes, see the appropriate classes in the *Guide to the Contents of the Public Record Office*, i (London 1963) and *British National Archives* (H.M.S.O. Sectional List 24, current edition).

family relationships as no other single series of documents can do. Such inquisitions in the Principality of Wales were heard by the Prince's officers, of course, and do not appear in the Chancery files (they were nearly all lost long ago, probably in Caernarvon): some of the marcher lordships were debatable land. North Welsh lordships which lay outside the Principality, but which had formed part of Llywelyn's Principality, were technically held in chief of the Prince (unlike the Norman lordships), but royal escheators usually took inquisitions into the bargain.[1] Lordships of the southern march were regularly subject to such royal inquisitions. Such records refer only to those who held land directly of the crown: although such tenants were by no means always magnates, the majority were men of substance, and all the great barons were tenants in chief for at least part of their lands. From this source a great deal can be learned about the marcher lords. A corollary to the system was that royal officials, who held the property until the heir proved his age and title, maintained accounts which were regularly kept and usually enrolled at the English Exchequer. These are often frustrating accounts if the period is short, but some marcher lands stayed in royal hands for years after the inquisition *post mortem* was taken.

The miscellanea which are regarded as Chancery records (C. 47), since they were housed, like Chancery records, in the Tower of London before the Record Office was created, contain a considerable bulk of documents relating to Wales. These should initially be sought out in the List and Index Society's photographic copy of the manuscript description of bundle 10, in which documents obviously bearing on Wales, Ireland and the Channel Islands were assembled in the nineteenth century, but materials for Wales and more particularly the march lurk in many of the other 145 bundles. Many of the miscellanea are merely copies of

---

[1] J. G. Edwards, *The Principality of Wales, 1267–1967, a Study in Constitutional History* (Caernarvon 1969), Appendix B, 31–4. One example of double jeopardy is Ruthin in 1353: on the death of Roger Grey, both the Prince's officers and the royal escheators took the lordship into their hands (*ibid.*, 32; *Calendar of Inquisitions Post Mortem*, x (1921) no. 10 ).

documents better preserved among the enrolments, warrants, inquisitions, Exchequer records and legal records (and the Record Office staff over the years has pencilled on the references to these other records), but many more are unique to this class: a few preserve extracts from lost records of the Principality and many are necessary sources for the lords and lordships of the march.

Chancery was also a court of law, but the legal records are collected together for discussion later in this chapter.

The records of the English Exchequer, unlike those of the Welsh Exchequer, are 'many and majestic'[1] and contain much basic source material for the Principality and the marches. Even the oldest of all English Exchequer records, Domesday Book, is a basic source for early Wales. Flintshire, the cantreds of Rhos and Rhufoniog in what became Denbighshire and even a small part of Gwynedd itself are included in the Cheshire folios. This section of Domesday is less helpful than most of the English descriptions, partly because there is uncommon vagueness about the very abbreviated entries, partly because of the still unresolved problem of identifying the names, and this becomes worse as the survey looks westward beyond Wat's Dyke. As a result Professor Tait could make a penetrating appraisal of Domesday Flint, but nothing comparable is possible for Domesday Denbighshire.[2] The description of the other neighbouring counties, Shropshire, Hereford and Gloucester, all include parts of what is now Wales. The Gloucestershire account of the lands beyond the Wye which William fitz Osbern and his son held up to 1075, is, like the North Wales section, less full and systematic than the main corpus; in Ewias and Archenfield, the Welsh parts of Herefordshire, the statistics are again less complete and the descriptions of part of modern Monmouth and Radnor are highly

[1] Elton, *England, 1200–1640*, 47.

[2] *Liber Censualis vocatus Domesday Book*, i (London 1783), 269; *The Domesday Geography of North England*, ed. H. C. Darby and I. S. Maxwell (Cambridge 1962), 383–90; J. Tait, 'Flintshire in Domesday Book', *Flintshire Historical Society Publications*, xi (1925), 1–37.

selective, though very valuable as an indication of Norman penetration. The unstable borderland of Shropshire, still recovering from extensive Welsh ravages in the preceding decades, did not produce many entries, but the information available about the march in general in the mid-eleventh century is better contrasted favourably with the silence from Welsh Wales than with the astonishing, though intractable, comprehensiveness about English land-holding in 1086.[1]

Although Domesday Book held so little for Wales, two of the four manuscripts of the official abbreviation of Domesday, made in the twelfth century, were owned by Welsh religious houses and, moreover, the later one (probably from Strata Florida) seems to be a line by line copy of the earlier (mid-thirteenth century) book owned by Margam.[2] Furthermore one of the Latin texts of the *Annales Cambriae* is written on the later manuscript. All this is presumably coincidence, but it may serve to emphasise the importance of Domesday texts for Welsh studies.

Nor is this all. Domesday Book remains as a basic, everyday reference book in the English Exchequer. But it rapidly became if not obsolete at least lacking in up-to-date information: this did not prompt the officials to create a new Domesday, for the weight of tradition was heavy and the hidation in particular, but also annual value and tenancy of honours given in 1086, retained some usefulness a century later. One exceptional man, however, Master Thomas Brown, who came to Henry II's Exchequer from the court of Sicily after Roger II's death, had a copy made of the entries for Herefordshire (where he had property) and added in marginal notes the names of many of the later tenants. All of these tenants, with the exception of Bernard of Neufmarché (the lord of Brecknock), lived some time in the reign of Henry II. Moreover, Brown (or his scribes) identified some manors unnamed in Domesday. As a list of Angevin tenants, it is valuable, though

---

[1] *The Domesday Geography of Midland England*, ed. H. C. Darby and I. B. Terrett (Cambridge 1954), 1–159.

[2] British Museum, Arundel MS 153 (Margam); P.R.O., E. 164/1 (Strata Florida).

incomplete; as a topographical guide it improves on 1086; as a compilation it is unique.[1] The marches of Wales are well served by Domesday documents; as they are by Exchequer documents in general.

In examining the fate of the accounts of the officials in the Principality, attention was drawn to the enrolments of many Welsh accounts on the great roll of the Pipe, its duplicate, the Chancellor's roll, and, later, on the various foreign rolls. It was also emphasised that some original Welsh rolls survive in various Exchequer classes, particularly those generated by the King's Remembrancer.[2] But there are also many other financial documents of all kinds which have Welsh relevance among these classes and elsewhere. The Memoranda rolls, of both the Lord Treasurer's Remembrancer and the King's Remembrancer, are the most striking example. Mrs Fryde has analysed the rolls from 1282 to 1327 for their Welsh content and exploited them up to 1343. She has collated all the Welsh accounts preserved on the Memoranda rolls with the particulars in Special Collections and Accounts Various and with the enrolments on the Pipe rolls. She has collected together the invaluable information about otherwise unknown subsidies and ecclesiastical accounts, the accounts of the customs collectors at Haverfordwest, new information about the expenses of the Edwardian castles and supplementary information about lands in the king's hands and prisoners taken after the rebellion of Madoc ap Llywelyn.[3] The importance of this neglected source is enormous: the Memoranda rolls give so much incidental background to the accounts which have so dominated Welsh interests

[1] *Herefordshire Domesday circa 1160–1170*, ed. with full facsimile and transcript by V. H. Galbraith and J. Tait (Pipe Roll Society, new series xxv for 1947–48, London 1950), *passim*. The manuscript is in Oxford, Balliol College MS 350.

[2] See above.

[3] Mrs Fryde's analysis of the Memoranda rolls is lodged with the Board of Celtic Studies. Pending publication, a copy of the typescript is available at the Public Record Office: this has an introduction discussing Welsh affairs as represented on the rolls and an index. In preparation are articles on the changes in the administration of Wales under Edward I and Edward II and on councils and consent in post-Conquest Wales.

hitherto. Mrs Fryde has produced an essential guide to sixty years of these rolls. There is plenty of material arising from her guide to occupy several energies, and there is still uncharted the whole period after 1343. Although probably while the Black Prince lived there is relatively little about Wales on Memoranda rolls, the fifteenth-century rolls deserve investigation.

The Memoranda rolls are the most significant under-used Exchequer record series, but the more familiar should not be overlooked. The general class realistically entitled 'Accounts, Various' from the Exchequer of Receipt is usefully listed item by item in a *List and Index* volume (xxxv, 1912) and its typescript additions, but it has still surprises to offer the searcher. The variety is so great that one can only counsel the student to read right through, to remember that muster-rolls of English army commanders often give information about Welsh soldiers and to look hard at something described as 'fragments of accounts relating to Wales' (one of these 'fragments' is part of the lost assessment of Merioneth, giving the livestock of each Welshman in detail).[1]

Furthermore, since English (and Italian) money financed the Welsh wars of the thirteenth century, since the Principality and marches were not immune from taxation after the Conquest, since men and lands from what is now Wales engaged the interest of the Exchequer bureaucracy in innumerable ways both before and after the Conquest, the whole archive of the medieval Exchequer has potential relevance.

The taxation records are poorly preserved. Even in England no county has extant assessments in the period 1290 to 1334 when all sixteen grants of lay taxation were accompanied by personal assessments. After vill quotas replaced individual taxpayers as the basis for subsidies in 1334, only general conclusions about relative prosperity can be drawn from the surviving assessments, while the poll taxes of Richard II's minority which ignited the peasants' revolt are very tricky to interpret. But many of these

[1] P.R.O., Exchequer of Receipt, Accounts Various, E. 101/506/15 mm. 1–2. Cf. C. Thomas, 'Thirteenth-Century Farm Economies in North Wales', *Agricultural History Review*, xvi (1968), 1–14.

English difficulties do not trouble the Welsh historian: he has no poll-tax records, and very few assessments at all save for 1293. Except for three Caernarvonshire commotes in the later fourteenth century and a subsidy account of the under-chancellor for North Wales in 1394, there is a blank until Henry VIII's reign. The usefulness of these few existing lists of taxpayers is limited: all property-owners were not included, for there was a minimum qualification except in 1301 and there are no Welsh assessments for 1301.[1] Some parts of Caernarvonshire and Merioneth are fortunate in having a complete assessment of livestock held by each assessed taxpayer: this is of uncommon value. Even the simple name and sum assessed gives useful genealogical information and gives some indication of the distribution of wealth within a given area.

Even more valuable for the social and economic history of the march is the Exchequer collection of extents and accounts, both original and enrolled, which relate to estates taken into the king's hand for a time, either through the death of a tenant-in-chief or through forfeiture in time of trouble. The troubles of Edward II's reign were particularly productive of such documents. Much of the class of Ancient Extents in the King's Remembrancer's office (E. 142) is taken up by detailed surveys of the lands forfeited from the 'contrariants' (the supporters of Thomas of Lancaster), the Despensers and, in turn, Roger Mortimer: these are of the greatest relevance to Welsh history. Many of the accounts of local officials in these and other marcher properties, most notably those of the Clare family, were formerly in the King's Remembrancer's archives but were withdrawn to create the class of 'special collections', Ministers' Accounts (S.C. 6), in the nineteenth century.

Also in the Special Collections are to be found most of the surviving court rolls from public and private jurisdictions in Wales (S.C. 2); sixty-two volumes containing over a thousand items of Ancient Correspondence (S.C. 1); upwards of seventeen thousand Ancient Petitions (S.C. 8); and well over a thousand Rentals and Surveys (S.C. 11, rolls, and S.C. 12, portfolios).

[1] M. W. Beresford, *Lay Subsidies and Poll Taxes* (Bridge Place 1963).

These four classes all contain Welsh materials. The court rolls are readily assessed through the topographical *List and Index* vi (1896), the Rentals and Surveys similarly in xxv (1908). The complex class of petitions is based on a genuine archival group of parliamentary petitions, but, as a report of 1924 confessed, 'it has suffered more than most other classes from the mangling reconstruction of successive generations of archivists, and from extensive but incomplete additions from other classes'.[1] Some of this mangling has been mitigated by the issue of an alphabetical list of petitioners: this is virtually the only means of access to the collection.

A guide to these petitions with relevance to Wales is long over-due in the Board of Celtic Studies' History and Law Series. Until an integrated list appears, there is little alternative to working through the alphabetical index. Even those integrated groups of petitions to the Prince of Wales and his council which were later added to S.C. 8 from the Exchequer archives are not at all a handy collection of Welsh material.[2] Almost all the petitions come to the Prince in his other capacities, principally as Duke of Cornwall: out of the seventy-seven petitions of this sort made in the Yorkist period only six have reference to Wales.[3] Scattered through the other 344 files are Welsh petitions, however, cover-ing a wide variety of topics, directed to the English king, or to parliament or to the chancellor.

Finally the Ancient Correspondence: thanks to the labours of Sir Goronwy Edwards, Miss Friend and Miss Dale, the letters of Welsh interest, spanning the period from John to Henry VII, are available in an exemplary printed calendar.[4]

The central courts of justice which had settled in Westminster by the thirteenth century did not have direct jurisdiction over

---

[1] *Lists and Indexes*, i (revised ed. New York 1966), 2.

[2] P.R.O., S.C. 8/333/E. 996–E. 1101B, E 1102–E. 1118; 344/E. 1262–E. 1316; 345/E. 1338–E. 1359.

[3] See typescript of S.C. 8 Addenda, P.R.O., Round Room, 12/122.

[4] J. G. Edwards, *Calendar of Ancient Correspondence Concerning Wales* (Board of Celtic Studies, History and Law Series, ii, Cardiff 1935).

Wales or the marcher lordships: the Principality had its own judicial system, whose paltry remains were discussed in chapter 2, while the marcher lords had their own sessions, as discussed in chapter 4. Yet the central English courts took cognisance of cases which concerned Wales and Welshmen, either because they were asked by litigants or because part of the action touched an English county: it is particularly unfortunate that any search in the common law rolls for anything specific should be so protracted. The formal plea rolls of King's Bench, which survive from 1272 onwards are, however, much more manageable than those of Common Pleas, which run from 1235: not only are there some medieval guides to the contents of the King's Bench rolls (inadequate enough, it is true, but better than nothing) but the rolls themselves are much smaller. The rolls of Common Pleas march on in majestic series, one roll to a term, four terms to a year, each roll the length of a man, containing up to six hundred membranes piled on top of each other, sewn at the top with stout rope and begrimed with ages of understandable neglect: they require two assistants to carry them to the table in the Record Office, and once on the table they have to be swivelled round each time a membrane is turned, for the membranes are written from the same top downwards on each side: this involves a turning diameter of some twelve feet unless one closes the roll each time. Mercifully, all legal records are not like that: yet on these great rolls there is the greatest single untapped source for English medieval history, and cases touching Wales are surely there. Cases arising from the marcher counties can easily be identified, since the county is always named in the margin. Normally, however, the Common Pleas' records have to be neglected except when a term, year and rotulet reference is given from some other medieval document.[1]

It is more practicable to look through the King's Bench rolls for a series of years, even without help from a contemporary repertory. It was here that the celebrated case against John Kynas-

[1] See M. Hastings, *The Court of Common Pleas in Fifteenth Century England* (Ithaca 1947).

ton of Stocks was recorded in 1400: the presentment described how Owain Glyndŵr and his associates assembled in Glyndyfrdwy in September and went on to the first attacks of the great rebellion.[1] Even more interesting, however, are the separate files of indictments preserved by King's Bench, the Ancient Indictments. These are the files of indictments taken before commissions of the peace or justices of oyer and terminer, the normal way of beginning criminal cases in the later Middle Ages. Either the crown lawyers drew up the indictment and sought a verdict on this from a grand jury or the jury made a presentment itself. The documents arising from this procedure, often noting the plea offered by the accused and occasionally noting the verdict, were sent to King's Bench although the cases were not necessarily called into the central court. Although the earlier fourteenth-century files are arranged under counties, the term indictment files are continuous from 1385 onwards.[2] The reorganisation of the class by Mr C. A. F. Meekings, who knows more about medieval legal records than anyone else, has reinforced the archival integrity of the indictments, but for topographical purposes the indictments after 1385 are still uncharted. There is no alternative to working steadily through the hundreds of files, unless the searcher is working inside a very narrow time-scale. With these indictments, as with other legal records, it should be remembered that the marcher counties are not the only areas which may contain materials for Welsh history: Dr Griffiths has recently demonstrated the value of five Oxfordshire indictments for illustrating the reaction of Welsh students to Glyndŵr's rebellion.[3]

The most approachable of all legal records are those from the equity jurisdiction of Chancery, since the equity court used the canon-law procedures of written bills and answers, rejoinders

---

[1] J. E. Lloyd, *Owen Glendower* (Oxford 1931), 30-2.

[2] See R. Virgoe, 'Some Ancient Indictments in the King's Bench referring to Kent, 1450-1452', *Kent Records*, xviii, *Documents Illustrative of Medieval Kentish Society*, ed. F. R. H. Du Boulay (Ashford 1964), 214-15.

[3] R. Griffiths, 'Some Partisans of Owain Glyndŵr at Oxford', *B.B.C.S.*, xx (1962-64), 282-92.

and replications. Instead of using a 'register of writs' to inaugurate actions, as the common law courts did, cases in Chancery's equity court were started by a petition to the Chancellor, the 'bill', and thereafter the defendant's answer and written interrogation of witnesses set the case further on its course. The bundle of parchment resulting from all this in any one case is the 'proceedings', and Early Chancery Proceedings, beginning in Richard II's reign, and very numerous for the fifteenth century, are very approachable and chatty vernacular documents compared to the formal Latin of the common-law plea rolls. There is available, moreover, a separate index of names and places to the catalogue of cases given in tabulated form in *Lists and Indexes*: although it may offend some sensibilities, the Harleian Society indexer's convention of listing Welshmen under *ap* has advantages.[1] There is also a convenient printed inventory of most of the cases concerning Wales, grouped under counties in chronological order: this, however, has no index.[2]

The problems of using these records are twofold. First, they are normally datable only by the name of the Chancellor to whom the bill is addressed and by any other internal evidence. Secondly, it is very rare to find a full set of documents: sometimes there is only a bill (especially before 1440), rarely are there interrogatories, very seldom is there any note of the decision.[3] The proceedings therefore are apt to give one imprecisely dated allegations which, like many Ancient Indictments, are not necessarily true. Although

[1] *Lists and Indexes*, xii (1901), up to Edward IV; xvi (1903), 1467–85; xx (1906), 1485–1500; xxix (1908), 1500–15; xxxviii (1912), 1515–29; xlviii (1922), 1529–38; l (1927), 1533–38; li (1929), 1538–44. *An Index of Persons Named in Early Chancery Proceedings, Richard II (1385) to Edward IV (1467)*, ed. C. A. Walmisley (Harleian Society lxxviii, London 1927; lxxix, London 1928).

[2] E. A. Lewis, *An Inventory of Early Chancery Proceedings Concerning Wales* (Board of Celtic Studies, History and Law Series iii, Cardiff 1937). It is fairly exhaustive for the Welsh counties, less so for the marches.

[3] M. E. Avery, 'The History of the Equitable Jurisdiction of Chancery Before 1460', *Bulletin of Institute of Historical Research*, xlii (1969), 129–44. Enrolment of Chancery decisions began only in 1534 and then only at the request of the parties: systematic daily entries in books began in 1544.

in law a man is presumed innocent until proved guilty, far too many historians seem to approach indictments and bills with a presumption of guilt. This is a venial sin, perhaps, for it spoils a good story to stress that it is unsupported vilification, but much harm can be done by a failure to realise that not everything that appears in Chancery bills is true. There is nowadays something of a reaction to the claims made for the total authenticity and the 'unimpugnable veracity' of medieval records. As Professor Cheney demonstrated in his stimulating inaugural at Cambridge, records can be just as fallible, biased and misleading as chronicles, and he might very well have vouched to warranty the equity records of Chancery.[1]

The positive contribution which the Early Chancery Proceedings can make to Welsh social, ecclesiastical and legal history can perhaps be illustrated by this bill levied by the Prior of Abergavenny in the time when Cardinal Kemp was Chancellor (1450–54). The prior complained that Mwrog ap David ap Thomas had sent his brother Ieuan to the Roman curia to sue against the prior

as for the fyndynge of a preste dayly to synge wythin the chapell of Kydwarton' within the parissh of Burgavenne, in which cause oon' Maister Robert ap Thomas by grete soteltee bytwene hym & the forseid Ieuan was made juge, and, as God knowith, ayenste right, gaf juggement ayenste youre seyde besecher, soo that an excummengement [excommunication] ys come doun ayenste hym and, graceous lorde, it stondith so that if your forseid besecher shulde serve a *premuniri fac(ias)* ayenste the forseid Muroc, Ieuan & Robert, hit wold not avayle hym by cause they dwell in Walys; where uppon', if it please youre graceous lordesshupp to considre the premisses and thereuppon' to graunte severell wryttes under grete peynys direct to the forseid Muroc, Ieuan & Robert to appere before the kynge in his Chauncere uppon' a certeyn' day to be examynyd uppon' the mater beforseid and to doo & resseve as conscience askith & requyrith for the love of God & in wey of cheritee.[2]

[1] C. R. Cheney, *The Records of Medieval England* (Cambridge 1956).
[2] P.R.O., Early Chancery Proceedings, C. 1/22/194. No date is hazarded in Lewis's *Inventory*.

The prerogative courts followed procedures similar to those of Chancery, and their records pose the same problems of imprecise dating, lack of decisions, unsupported allegations. But, despite these limitations, the records of the courts of Star Chamber and Requests are a necessary and useful source for Tudor Wales as for Tudor England. The rather disorganised bundles of Star Chamber Proceedings are listed from 1485 to 1558 in *List and Index* xiii (1901), which is in turn indexed in the new duplicated Supplementary Series iv (1966),[1] while the Board of Celtic Studies inaugurated its History and Law Series in 1929 with a catalogue of those proceedings up to the court's dissolution in 1641 which concern Wales, arranged reign by reign, county by county.[2] The books of orders and decrees have perished, but some later transcripts made from them, covering the years 1487 to 1543, do survive.[3]

The situation in the Court of Requests is rather better, for the proceedings (of which thirteen bundles belong to the reigns of Henry VII and Henry VIII), available through *List and Index* xxi (1906), are supplemented by order and decree books.[4]

The records of the council in the marches of Wales would, of course, be of cardinal importance for the history of the late fifteenth and the sixteenth century. But as long ago as 1574 it was reported to the English government 'that the Records of that Court are not so orderlie kept but by deliverie of the same to the Councellours at the Barr, Attorneys and Clerkes out of the Court and office the same are many tymes imbeselled, rased, or falsified'.[5] The earliest surviving register of the court, compiled

---

[1] A selection is printed in the Selden Society Publications, xvi (1902), 1477–1509, and xxv (1911), 1509–44. See Elton, *England 1200–1640*, 57–64.

[2] I. ab O. Edwards, *A Catalogue of Star Chamber Proceedings relating to Wales* (Board of Celtic Studies, History and Law Series, i, Cardiff 1929).

[3] The earlier ones are printed in *Select Cases in the Council of Henry VII*, ed. C. G. Bayne and W. H. Dunham jr. (Selden Society lxxv, 1958).

[4] Cf. *Select Cases in the Court of Requests, 1497–1569*, ed. I. S. Leadam (Selden Society xii, 1898). See Elton, *England 1200–1640*, 57–64.

[5] David Lewis, 'The Court of the President and Council of Wales and the Marches from 1478 to 1575', *Y Cymmrodor*, xii (1897), 9–10, quoting British Museum, Lansdowne MS 155, fos. 235–6.

between 1569 and 1591, was for centuries out of custody and found a refuge in the Bodleian Library only around 1800. This register contains a few documents of earlier date, but of the two earliest, one, of 1535, is preserved also at Hereford and the other, of 1538, concerns only game.[1] The activities of the Council before Elizabeth's reign can be resurrected only through miscellaneous survivals in the State Papers, in the Chancery records, in the great collections of Tudor official papers preserved in the Cotton, Harley and Lansdowne collections in the British Museum and from various archives of marcher families.[2]

The 'exhibits' which survive in considerable quantity from the law courts contain a fascinating medley of historical documents. The two principal classes containing Welsh material are from the Masters in Chancery and from the Court of Wards. The Chancery Masters, who were defined in 1413 and reformed in 1852, had come to have the particular responsibility of reporting to the court of Chancery on matters of fact: 'In Chancery there is a certain impatience about disputes of fact; these have to be resolved as incidents to the real operation of equity.'[3] It is, and was, the task of the masters to master these facts. As a result of these responsibilities, exhibits accumulated in the offices of the masters. Since some Chancery proceedings have been very protracted (there is one case about a trust which started in the twelfth century, was properly investigated last in 1274 and is still attracting applications today), the exhibits descended from one master to his successor.[4] Today these collections make up thirteen classes (C. 103 to C. 115), mostly arranged under the last eleven masters in Chancery who were the final heritors. They are reasonably well catalogued in a manuscript list which has been duplicated by the List and Index Society and have a pleasing diversity, varying

[1] R. Flenley, *A Calendar of the Register of the Queen's Majesty's Council in the Dominion and Principality of Wales and the Marches of the Same [1535], 1569–1591* (Cymmrodorion Record Series viii, London 1916), I, 47–8.

[2] Penry Williams, *The Council in the Marches of Wales under Elizabeth* (Cardiff 1958), 362–6.

[3] R. E. Ball, 'The Chancery Master,' *Law Quarterly Review*, lxxvii (1961), 348.

[4] *Ibid.*, 347.

from the entire archive of the Million Bank of the eighteenth century to a box of coral and glass beads belonging to a bankrupt named Ross.[1] But they contain also 'the Duchess of Norfolk's deeds'.

Now after the dissolution of Llanthony Secunda in Gloucestershire, the lands were granted to Arthur Porter: Porter's great-granddaughter married John Scudamore of Holme Lacy in Herefordshire and in 1771 Scudamore's great-great-great-granddaughter Frances married Charles Howard, later Duke of Norfolk. Some of the muniments of Llanthony descended to Duchess Frances, who was declared a lunatic shortly after her marriage: as a result of her insanity, her estate came into Chancery after her husband's death in 1815 and the Llanthony muniments went to one of the masters. These muniments are the finest set of cartularies and registers surviving from any house with Welsh connections. In fact there is a good deal about Wales, for Llanthony Secunda was founded in 1136 as a daughter of the original Llanthony in Monmouthshire: the two houses separated in 1205 and remained independent until 1481 when Llanthony Prima became a cell of its own daughter house. As a result, the cartularies and registers of Llanthony Secunda contain material of the first importance for early march history, for the relationship between the two houses, especially at the two critical periods of reorganisation, for the Gloucestershire house's endowment in Wales (Caldecot and Llantrisaint), and for miscellaneous information such as an inventory of the small treasure of Welsh Llanthony stored in Gloucestershire in 1380.[2] The eight cartularies and five letter-books of the Gloucestershire priory contain too a remarkable number of otherwise unknown documents issued by Welsh bishops, mainly of Llandaff, from the twelfth century

---

[1] P.R.O., Chancery Masters' Exhibits, C. 114/9–23; C. 104/151. As well as the classes C. 103 to C. 115, there is a separate collection of court rolls, C. 116, which are not included in the List and Index of Court Rolls. They contain, however, no Welsh records before the reign of Elizabeth (C. 116/77–96, 191–5). There are several medieval rolls for Easthope in Shropshire (C. 116/213).

[2] P.R.O., C. 115/A. 7/K. 2/6684 fo. 49r.

onwards.[1] The late-thirteenth-century cartulary of St Peter's Abbey in Gloucester (which also came to the Chancery from Holme Lacy in 1817) has been in print for more than a century and its relevance to marcher history is well known.[2] The extraordinary richness of the Llanthony collection awaits systematic exploitation.

The Llanthony cartularies and registers are the only exciting Welsh sources among the Masters' Exhibits, but there are other odds and ends, such as a grant of property within the lordship of Usk made to Welshmen in January 1428, lying beside proceedings in a consular court in Italy in 1686–87, and splendidly detailed Welsh farm accounts of 1657–59 among the detritus of John Lloyd, a seventeenth-century financier;[3] or deeds from the Shropshire fee of Golston which survive from the early thirteenth century onwards in a collection with extraordinarily fine records of Cheswardine in the seventeenth and eighteenth centuries.[4]

The exhibits in the Court of Wards are much more staid. They consist almost entirely of deeds, roughly listed in the sixth Report of the Deputy Keeper.[5] There is a number of neglected Welsh deeds in this collection, the more interesting because some of them are in the form of estreats from the sessions of the medieval Principality. These estreats give not only the usual topographical, genealogical and legal information common to deeds, but also the date and place of otherwise unrecorded sessions and the name of the presiding justice.[6] Furthermore, the Wards' exhibits include a substantial part of the Welsh and Cheshire archive of the Bulkeley family,[7] which is a major supplement to the much larger

[1] R. I. Jack, 'An Archival Case-History: the Cartularies and Registers of Llanthony Priory in Gloucestershire', *Journal of Society of Archivists*, iv (1970–73), forthcoming.

[2] *Historia et Cartularium Monasterii Sancti Petri Gloucestriae*, ed. W. H. Hart (Rolls Series 33, 1863–67), i, 127–392; ii; iii.          [3] P.R.O., C. 108/146.

[4] P.R.O., C. 108/314 (two large boxes: the Golston deeds are in one of the two small deed-boxes in Box 1).

[5] *D.K.R.*, vi (1845), Appendix 2, 1–87.          [6] P.R.O., Wards 2/4/17/1–9.

[7] P.R.O., Wards 2/14/53A/1 to 16/53K/9. There are several fine private seals in this collection and a splendid specimen of the seal of the borough of Beaumaris attached to a deed of 1568 (16/53I/28).

Baron Hill deposit in the University College of North Wales at Bangor. The only other substantial single groups seem to be the Flint and Cheshire records of a More family, and twenty deeds of the bishop and chapter of St Asaph, but there are Welsh deeds in eight more of the forty-eight boxes.[1]

As well as these records of courts and of the two great administrative departments, Chancery and Exchequer, there are the collections of State Papers which begin in 1509. These records of correspondence increasingly add a new dimension of personality and informality to the public records. They suffer from a lack of system, in contrast to the Chancery rolls, but they balance this with giving insight into motive and negotiation. They do not contain the whole truth, although they seduce their users into over-reliance: but they are the principal source for the background to the Welsh Acts of 1536 and 1543, and in all manner of ways give incidental information. Their variety is such that it is impossible to epitomise.

Finally, the royal council and parliament have left remains which contain relevant material. The council records survive only intermittently: before 1540 minutes of proceedings are available in proper registered form only for 1392–93 and 1421–35, 'but the normal method of recording decisions was in the form of endorsements on draft documents or petitions', which have suffered much loss over the years but still survive in quite large number among the Treasury of Receipt archives, the Chancery files of warrants, the special class of Ancient Petitions and, outside the Record Office, among the great collections assembled by Sir Robert Cotton, now in the British Museum.[2] The Parliamentary records include such petitions endorsed by the council and, on the

---

[1] There is no way at present of ascertaining the division into boxes of bundles 147 onwards: bundles 146R to 146T are in box 42. The relevant parts of the collection are in bundles 164E and 164G. The St Asaph collection is 4/19/1–20. References for other Welsh materials up to Henry VIII's death are Wards 2/2/10/4; 4/17/1–9; 7/23A/41; 9/29B/2; 18/78/1, 2; 34/131/1, 2; ?/147/2, 3, 5; ?/164G/10, 14.

[2] A. L. Brown, 'The King's Councillors in Fifteenth-Century England', *Trans. Royal Historical Society*, 5th series, xix (1969), 95–6.

so-called 'Rolls of Parliament', record many other petitions which survive in no other form. It is in these petitions that most of the direct Welsh allusions can be found, for until after the statute of 1536 there was no Welsh representation in the English parliament: the twenty-four North Welshmen and the same number of South Welshmen who were to attend the York parliament of 1322 and the twenty-three (whose names are known) who were returned by North Wales for the Westminster parliament of 1326–27 are isolated exceptions.[1] But again, the activities of knights, burgesses and lords from the marcher counties of England often have relevance to Welsh affairs, while petitioners from Welsh Wales appear sporadically on the rolls recording business transacted in parliament.

In this inadequate survey, I have deliberately given more space to the less familiar. Welsh history has suffered such grievous losses that a more adventurous approach is needed. But this should not obscure the fact that it is in the basic English records of Chancery, Exchequer and the law courts, together with the 'special collections', that most material for Welsh history will be found. Wales is very lucky to have been associated with the best-documented country in Europe. To use this enormous archive properly, a student of Welsh history requires, however, a sound grasp of the administrative history of medieval England,[2] familiarity with the Record Office finding-aids, and a flair for detecting the relevant amid a mass of irrelevance.

[1] W. R. Williams, *The Parliamentary History of the Principality of Wales* (Brecknock 1895), iv–v. The parliament of 1542 was the first Tudor parliament attended by Welsh representatives (cf. P. S. Edwards, 'Parliamentary Representation of Wales and Monmouthshire, 1542–58', Cambridge Ph.D. thesis, 1970).

[2] This is best approached through S. B. Chrimes, *An Introduction to the Administrative History of Mediaeval England* (2nd ed. Oxford 1959), and V. H. Galbraith, *An Introduction to the Use of the Public Records* (London 1934), and *Studies in the Public Records* (London 1948).

CHAPTER 4

# *Archives of Individuals and Corporations*

The largest single category of record surviving from medieval Wales comprises the various accounts, court rolls, rentals, surveys, deeds and so forth created by the day-to-day administration, the consolidation and acquisition of estates, lay and ecclesiastical, in what is now Wales. Unlike the situation obtaining in most other categories of Welsh sources, the sheer bulk is quite daunting. But, despite the quantity, there are very few long, consecutive runs of such estate documents: this makes the thousands of account rolls less meaningful than they would be if individual properties had continuous series, year after year for a prolonged period. Court rolls are usually better preserved, for they contain the evidence of every copyholder's title and precedents for future cases: sooner or later, they are often dispersed or neglected, but they stood a better chance than account rolls of surviving into relatively modern times. Rentals were renewed infrequently, and surveys were taken usually for special purposes, so these are not common among the surviving records. Deeds, which are necessary to every lord and corporation to prove title to the various elements of the estate in an age of excessive litigation over landed property, are still very numerous, either in their original form, or in copies enrolled at the landholder's expense on the dorse of the Close rolls in the royal Chancery, or in the compilations known as cartularies. Deeds go back in time long before the earliest court rolls or accounts (which are rarely found before the late thirteenth century), so they have a unique value for estates of the eleventh and twelfth centuries, not only for establishment of title, but for topographical, agricultural, genealogical and tenurial information. This value is to some extent retained by later deeds, but they tend increasingly to be stereotyped texts with names, places and dates changing. For peasant genealogies, they are increasingly displaced by the court rolls, but when there are no court rolls, of course, the deeds are indispensable. Unlike the various administrative records, moreover, deeds survive from peasant families: the peasant no less than the lord was anxious to retain his proofs of title and accumulated extracts from court rolls and various deeds registering purchase and exchange as was appropriate to his own legal standing and that of the property which he acquired or inherited.

In the nature of things, these remains of medieval private archives are now scattered hither and yon. Although many English collections are still to be found in a repository within the county where the property is situated, most of the greater families owned land in several counties and the records may or may not have been kept together over the centuries. Sometimes the dis-integration of an estate meant that the records of each geographical segment passed to the new owner of that segment; sometimes this did not happen, except for the current, essential records; sometimes political, martial or family disaster brought all or part of the estate into royal hands or into the hands of a palatinate prince, so that some of the records went into royal or palatinate hands from which they may or may not ever have emerged. All manner of permutations are possible, and can be exemplified, in the descent of estate collections. As a result, one can never be sure that some accounts or court rolls or deeds relevant to one's interests do not survive until a very comprehensive survey of finding-aids to all the repositories in the British Isles has been completed: and even then, despite the surveys made over the last century by the Historical Manuscripts Commission, there is always the possibility that somewhere in a country house or a solicitor's office or a factor's rooms or a parish chest[1] there still lurk such rolls and evidences.

Of course, university vacations, sabbaticals, research fellow-ships, life itself, are too short to pursue materials which one has no

---

[1] An example from a parish chest is the constable's account for Castle Isabel, 1340–41, found, with other accounts, among the Worfield parish records in Shropshire (Shropshire Record Office, 1374/1/Account rolls).

reason to think in existence through all the most unlikely places in the country. Of course, too, it is a mistake to avoid the obvious in a snobbish preoccupation with the remote. In the Public Record Office, the British Museum, the National Library of Wales, Cardiff Central Library and the University College of North Wales Library at Bangor, there is more documentation of Welsh estates than an army of researchers could exhaust in a generation. But estate documents are fully usable only in a proper context, and the great, but rather arbitrary, collections in these five major repositories are often insufficient to supply this context. The total bulk is large, but no single repository is exhaustive in its holdings for any one estate, much less any one family, much less still any one area: and since research is likely to be centred on a geographical or family unit, it is necessary for each individual student to be aware of the other two hundred repositories in England and Wales.

To establish the whereabouts of apparently relevant documents, some familiarity with basic finding aids is a prerequisite. Most students will be aware of the new edition of the *Guide to the Contents of the Public Record Office* published in 1963 with a third volume largely irrelevant to medievalists appearing in 1968. This admirable guide gives comprehensive information about the detailed lists or calendars of the classes which it describes briefly. As discussed in chapter 3, the most important of the classes relevant to a Welsh medievalist and containing estate documents are very well listed in the printed *List and Index* series: the special collections of accounts, court rolls and rentals-and-surveys are all in this series and are readily available in major libraries. It should be noted, however, that the copies kept in the Record Office itself have been corrected and amplified over the years: these corrections have been incorporated in the recent Kraus reprint of the *List and Index* series, which is accordingly more accurate than the original edition. The collection of 'ancient deeds' in the Record Office (some sixty thousand before 1603) is partly calendared in six massive printed volumes produced between 1890 and 1915, but many more are calendared only in manuscript lists in the Round Room. Cartularies in the Record Office are listed by Godfrey Davis in his *Cartularies of Great Britain*.

In general, therefore, it is possible to know in advance whether appropriate private estate documents are housed in the Public Record Office and to know, moreover, the precise call-number for each document.

In 1900 and 1912 the British Museum published an index of religious houses and other corporations, and a separate *index locorum* as keys to the documents known as 'charters and rolls'. The distinction between 'charters and rolls' and 'manuscripts' is sometimes blurred, but most of the estate documents other than cartularies are properly among charters and rolls. The indexes printed in 1900 and 1912 refer to the charters and rolls referred to by their original provenance as Harley, Cotton, Royal, Sloane, Egerton, Campbell, Lansdowne, Topham and Wolley as well as the Additional Charters and Rolls.[1] But in the last seventy years a great many additional Additional Charters have been acquired by the Museum: those acquired up to 1945 are now noted in the successive volumes of the *Catalogue of Additions to the Manuscripts* and a manuscript calendar or latterly a list is maintained in the Manuscript Room itself: beyond that, the annual notices in the *British Museum Quarterly*, the 'migrations of manuscripts' feature in the *Bulletin of the Institute of Historical Research* and enquiry at the Manuscript Room are the best finding aids available. Cartularies are, of course, listed by Godfrey Davis, and other estate documents classed as 'manuscripts' can perhaps be found through the scandalously inadequate printed catalogues of the Harleian manuscripts and the Cottonian manuscripts, and the more satisfactory printed catalogues of the Royal, Sloane and Additional manuscripts. Recourse to the Manuscript Room's subject indexes, particularly the topographical index, can often be of supple-

[1] The expressions 'Additional Charter' and 'Additional Roll' seem to confuse newcomers to the Museum collections. The two form one collection with integrated numbers: Additional Charter 62767, for example, is followed by Additional Roll 62768. The Harley Charters on the other hand are a quite distinct series from the Harley Rolls.

mentary assistance, but cannot remove the need for private enterprise.

The National Library of Wales has received an impressive number of estate archives since its foundation in 1907. This has been a mixed blessing. On the credit side must firmly be put the advantages of centralisation, the facilities offered to readers and to manuscripts, the expertise of the staff, the availability of a journal to publicise holdings. But the debit side is weighty too. Aberystwyth is peculiarly inaccessible except by private car, since the lines of communication in Wales run east to west, not north to south; the library is essentially an artificial creation, founded in despite of the existing major library in Cardiff, the centre of population; the pressure which the National Library has increasingly put on owners of lay and ecclesiastical archives to deposit in Aberystwyth has effectively deprived the local record offices of a spread of deposits comparable to those in English county offices; and the burden of listing estate collections is diverting specialist manpower from the literary manuscripts which are, arguably, the principal concern of the library. In fact, especially since the recent further accession of the Great Sessions records, the National Library has become in a limited way a Welsh equivalent of the Public Record Office and the British Museum rolled into one, while at the same time attracting private archives which in England would normally go to local offices: a closer parallel would be Scotland, except that, unlike Wales, there are no county record offices in Scotland, where centralisation in Register House, Edinburgh, is still more complete. Although the present situation in Aberystwyth does not infringe article II of the library's royal charter, it might well be thought a major extension and change of emphasis: the object of the library, the charter of 1907 stipulated

> shall be the collection preservation and maintenance of manuscripts printed books periodical publications newspapers pictures engravings and prints musical publications and works of all kinds whatsoever especially manuscripts printed books and other works which have been or shall be composed in Welsh or any other Celtic language

or which relate or shall relate to the antiquities language literature philology history religion arts crafts and industries of the Welsh and other Celtic peoples as well as all literary works whether connected or not with Welsh subjects composed written or printed in whatsoever language on whatsoever subject and wheresoever published [to further university education in Wales][1]

The great majority of the bound lists in the manuscript section of the library in 1971 contain not antiquities, language, literature, philology, religion, arts, crafts and industries, but history, and the special sort of history which is based on estate collections. The very number of these collections has produced (with commendable speed) virtually the same number of lists, handsomely bound and arranged in alphabetical order. But there are a great many and the majority are very slim: they are titled, moreover, for the most part by the country house in which they last reposed. Since there is no general guide, such as one would find in most English county record offices (which are exactly comparable), the searcher must either make his own list of useful collections from the brief accession notes in the annual reports of the library or the longer notices of major deposits in the library's journal, or else, the only entirely foolproof way (since the printed notes are not up to date), he must resign himself to the tedious but rewarding task of working steadily through shelf after shelf of the bound inventories.

The most important medieval estate collections are probably Chirk Castle, Badminton (from the Duke of Beaufort on loan only),[2] Wynnstay (which came in two exciting deposits), Margam (which is largely available in print),[3] and Bute (which breaches the topographical system of reference and which is

---

[1] National Library of Wales, *Charter of Incorporation and Report on the Progress of the Library* (Oswestry 1909), 9.

[2] The Duke of Beaufort's deposit is available for consultation only if the searcher has written permission from the Duke's estate agents, Messrs. Humbert and Flint, at Badminton in Gloucestershire.

[3] *A Descriptive Catalogue of the Penrice and Margam Abbey Manuscripts*, ed. W. de G. Birch (6 vols., London 1893–1905).

still only roughly listed). But there are significant medieval records also in deposits such as Ruthin, Peniarth (estate), Rûg (for Denbighshire), Sotheby (for Anglesey), Puleston and St Pierre. The collections of the Pembrokeshire antiquary George Owen, in the Bronwydd collection, contain essential transcripts and some medieval documents, and the riches of the foundation collection from Hengwrt via Peniarth are still not fully exploited. But scholars will find much of value here and there in the other collections.

It is quite impossible to give any brief indication of the contents of these collections. But highlights catch the eye: the receivers' accounts for Chirk for most of the fourteenth century, the court rolls of Porthcaseg in Monmouthshire in broken series from 1262 to 1527, a superb rental of the town of Newport in Pembrokeshire made in 1434, accounts of the bailiff of Dinas Powys in Glamorgan from 1373 to 1456 or a bundle of twenty-one accounts of various officials in the lordship of Senghennydd mainly from Henry VI's reign.[1]

The only repository in Wales which remotely resembles an English local record office is, ironically, Cardiff Central Library. This library has great collections for its own area of Glamorgan: but it is much more than that. By its acquisition of the more significant section of Sir Thomas Phillipps' Welsh manuscripts in 1896, some seven hundred of them, Cardiff created itself a *de facto* National Library in the capital of Wales. The creation of the library at Aberystwyth came only after understandably bitter wrangling in the early years of this century: but Sir John Williams and Robert Vaughan of Hengwrt won the day and the potentiality of Cardiff Central Library has not been realised. The comparison between the grandiosity of the Aberystwyth Library and the rather decayed Victorian charm and inadequate accommodation at Cardiff is only too striking, but Cardiff's collections deserve to be much better known outside Wales. The only way to find out

[1] N.L.W., Chirk Castle MSS, D. 1–D. 44; Badminton MSS, 1639–1662; Bronwydd MSS (first deposit), 301; Bute MSS, box 93, parcel A, nos. 105–116, and box 91, parcel A, nos. 1–5, 5a, 6–20.

what is contained in the reference section of the Central Library is by going to Cardiff. The only useful preliminaries for literary manuscripts is to read the Historical Manuscripts Commission report on manuscripts in the Welsh language[1] and for estate documents to study the twenty-eight pages of the *Handlist of Early Documents (before 1500) in the MS Department of the Reference Library* (Cardiff 1926) or the handbook published in 1931 describing the 'exhibition illustrating the history and topography of Wales'.

At the Central Library itself there are two types of access to the collections. The manuscripts, which are grouped together by size rather than topic or provenance, can be reached only through an accessions list, one line to each manuscript across a double page of a ledger: this catalogue is as constrictive in its way as the Easter tables were for the early medieval annalists and, again like the annalists, the Cardiff librarians have broken free of these limitations, in their case when dealing with the tens of thousands of 'deposited documents'. The division between manuscripts and documents is analogous to the British Museum's distinction between manuscripts and charters and rolls: at Cardiff, however, unlike London, the calendars of the documents are arranged chronologically in loose-leaf folders under counties, and are referred to in the form 'D.D. Flint 5'.

. Although there are substantially more medieval documents at Cardiff than appear on the 1926 list, the number is not very large. Some, however, like an unprinted early charter from Montgomeryshire and two twelfth-century Neath charters,[2] are important, and there are useful uncatalogued sets of receivers' accounts for the lordship of Builth and Elfael during much of Henry VIII's reign. Here too can be found the record of the

[1] Historical Manuscripts Commission 48, *Report on Manuscripts in the Welsh Language*, ii (1) (London 1902), 91–345. This describes eighty-one of the Cardiff manuscripts and twenty-six of the Hafod manuscripts at that time merely loaned to Cardiff.

[2] Cardiff Central Library, D.D. Montgomeryshire, unnumbered; A. G. Foster, 'Two Deeds relating to Neath Abbey', *South Wales and Monmouthshire Record Society Publication*, ii, ed. W. Rees and H. J. Randall (1950), 201–6.

Chepstow sessions of 1415 which Mr T. B. Pugh printed in 1963.[1]

As a result of this city repository, Glamorgan County Record Office, ten minutes' walk away, is starved of major estate collections: of those which it has, only the Fonmon Castle and the recently-acquired Dynevor collections contain any important early materials. In any case, the greatest of all Glamorgan archives, the Margam Abbey estate collection, on which G. T. Clark worked so tirelessly in the nineteenth century, was not deposited anywhere in South Wales, but in Aberystwyth. The North Wales record offices are no better off than those in the south. The two major estate archives of North Wales which evaded the National Library are not in Caernarvon or Hawarden, but at Bangor, in the University College Library. The Baron Hill manuscripts were deposited in 1937 by Sir Richard Williams Bulkeley, the head of that family of Bulkeley which has played a dominant role in Anglesey politics since William Bulkeley from Cheshire married into the leading native family of North-West Wales around 1440 and became a burgess of Beaumaris.[2] This splendid archive contains many medieval deeds of Caernarvon and Anglesey, including a great many for the boroughs of Beaumaris and Conway in the fifteenth century, estreats and final concords from the sessions of North Wales, and what seems to be the Welsh Exchequer copy of the 'Record of Caernarvon'. The other outstanding estate collection at Bangor is from Lord Mostyn covering Flintshire, Denbighshire and Caernarvonshire; the results of Mr A. D. Carr's work on the Mostyn archives are awaited with interest.

The two repositories in London and the three in Wales certainly contain the larger part of surviving estate archives for Wales and the march. But they do not contain everything, and for any study of a lordship, an area or a family it is prudent to look beyond.

---

[1] *The Marcher Lordships of South Wales, 1415–1536: Select Documents*, ed. T. B. Pugh (Board of Celtic Studies, History and Law Series, xx, Cardiff 1963), 49–75.

[2] D. Cyril Jones, 'The Bulkeleys of Beaumaris, 1440–1547', *Trans. Anglesey Antiquarian Society and Field Club* (1961), 1–5.

The best vantage-point is the National Register of Archives maintained by the Historical Manuscripts Commission at its offices in Quality Court, just a little above the Public Record Office in Chancery Lane. This splendid institution is a central finding aid to manuscripts in England and Wales. It is more, for it is a finding-aid to finding-aids. Repositories and other owners or custodians of archives send more or less summary lists of collections to the Commission, which files them and, in a fairly general way, indexes them. Over fourteen thousand such lists are now available at Quality Court, with an unpretentious index by county, by general topic and by personal name. Too much detail should not be expected of these indexes, but when used with understanding and imagination they lead the searcher to useful materials often located in highly unlikely places. The Registrar and her assistants, moreover, publish each year a *List of Accessions to Repositories* throughout the British Isles, including Eire. Although this list is only as good as the information supplied by the various repositories, and although there is no alternative to reading right through the book (which is now over one hundred pages long), time spent on the series of lists is rarely unrewarded. Without the National Register, I should, for example, have been quite unaware, and likely to remain unaware, that Nottinghamshire Record Office acquired in 1968 a remarkable bundle of thirty accounts of the estate in various parts of England and Wales belonging to Thomas the great Earl of Lancaster: and furthermore, which enhances the value of the collection, all accounts seem to be for the same year 1316–17, so that they supply fairly full information about Lancaster's landed revenues and supplement the holdings of the Public Record Office for the lordship of Denbigh and elsewhere. Without the National Register, students in London would not have access to the admirable list of Stafford manuscripts prepared in the Staffordshire Record Office: this is one of the greatest collections of march accounts in existence, although only recently available to scholars.[1] Without the

[1] The Stafford archive includes, *inter alia*, declared accounts of the receiver responsible for Brecon and Hay in 1447–48, 1454–55 and 1488–89, and various

National Register, one would be unlikely to realise that the archives of a Lewis family, which include deeds from the medieval lordship of Senghennydd in Glamorgan, are deposited in the Wiltshire Record Office, since these Lewises held land both in South Wales and in Wiltshire. Without the National Register it would be hard to follow the migrations of manuscripts reported on in years gone past by the Historical Manuscripts Commission. Few things are more frustrating than to discover that documents briefly listed by the Commission's inspectors are not now obviously accessible.[1] If anyone can help, it is the staff of the National Register. 'The historian, essentially, wants more documents than he can really use.'[2] In his quest for this excess of evidence, one of the historian's principal allies is the Royal Commission on Historical Manuscripts and its principal handmaiden, the Registrar.

One further depressing thought. Some collections have escaped from Britain altogether. Most of these are of sufficient importance or notoriety to be known at the National Register, but it is not its business to maintain this information unless the documents were once listed by the H.M.C. Only one significant Welsh collection, however, falls into this category. The Ellesmere archive was in 1917 bought more or less in its entirety by Henry E. Huntington, the American millionaire, and is now in the library which he endowed in San Marino, California. This notable collection contains, as well as Tudor state papers, estate documents for the medieval lordship of Bromfield and Yale. The quantity of early Welsh records is not large—some deeds, six account rolls and eight court rolls before 1543, and five of these account rolls and two of the court rolls (both for Wrexham town) are post 1500.[3]

accounts for Hay in 1380–81 (Stafford County Record Office), D. 641/1/2/19, 22, 246, 245).

---

[1] The present location, as far as it was known in 1967, of all collections reported on over the last century by the H.M.C. is given as Appendix 3 to *The Twenty-Fifth Report of the Royal Commission on Historical Manuscripts, 1963–1967* (London 1967), 99–142.

[2] Henry James, *The Aspern Papers*. Cf. F. Ranger, 'The Historical Manuscripts Commission and Northern History', *Northern History*, v (1970), 192.

[3] J. Preston, 'Collections of English Historical Manuscripts in the Huntington

After tracking down relevant materials, the researcher unfamiliar with such documents requires to do some preliminary work of another kind. Knowledge of medieval accounting practice, of the law dispensed in manorial courts and of medieval conveyancing is necessary. A book of this sort cannot give instruction on the technicalities of the law. The law in the court rolls of the marcher lordships is more complex than the customary law of English manors, for as well as the custom of the march there is Welsh custom to be reckoned with. More than one sort of law was recognised in these courts. The recent researches of Dr R. R. Davies are at long last giving a sound foundation for future users of the court rolls: an aspiring student must read Dr Davies' articles and the older works cited there.[1] This book can, however, give some guidance about medieval accounts and about the use of court rolls.

Court rolls were, like all proper records, compiled for the administrative needs of the community which created them. As Mrs Thirsk commented in her review of an edition of the Tottenham court rolls, 'one does not usually expect to obtain a picture of the farming economy from reading the court rolls of its manors'.[2] Yet too many students do expect too much from a series of manorial court records. The rolls record briefly such matters as the fining of those who failed to answer the summons to attend, the entry of heirs on to their copyhold inheritance and the payment of succession duty, the presentation of local offences such as stealing or poaching or having an affray, the sentencing of the guilty and the compounding of disagreements between individuals. In the marcher lordships where the royal writ did not run, more serious offences were also heard in the seigneurial courts. The Ruthin rolls, for instance, in 1400–1 contain charges

Library', *Archives*, vi (1963–64), 96–7. Another account roll of the lordship of Bromfield and Yale, for 1475–76, has recently been found in the Trevor-Roper deposit in Flintshire County Record Office.

[1] R. R. Davies, 'The Survival of the Blood-Feud in Medieval Wales', *History*, liv (1969), 338–57; 'The Law of the March', *Welsh History Review*, v (1970), 1–30.

[2] *Agricultural History Review*, xii (1964), 62.

against the large gang under Owain Glyndŵr which attacked the town and robbed its inhabitants at the very opening of the revolt: and the few accused who were actually in custody were hanged.[1] The courts of the lords marcher were in many ways a combination of English manorial courts and royal common-law courts, so they give fuller information than the rolls of Tottenham in rural Middlesex. But one must still not expect too much: for only such matters as came within the jurisdiction of the court are recorded, and many of these are recorded in a very formal manner. They may display crime, but only detected crime. Many cases drag on, as in the central court at Westminster, with excuses (essoins) and delays and the giving of pledges: and there are many unfinished stories as a result, even in the rare cases where the series of rolls is unbroken. Even the Ruthin collection, famous as one of the most complete sets in existence for any locality in Britain, is not as complete as it seems. There are four separate jurisdictions within the lordship—Ruthin town and each of the three commotes (Dogfeiling, Llannerch and Colion). Although there are indeed few years from late in Edward I's reign until the Commonwealth for which there are no rolls, the sets for each individual jurisdiction are significantly less complete, and one missing membrane ruins a statistic. Indeed, to seek for statistical information at all from court rolls is unwise. Yet in the court rolls one comes closest to the possibility of tabulating information about medieval people, their numbers, their trades, their lands, their crimes, and the intimate relationship between Welshmen and Englishmen living cheek by jowl.[2] Over a long

[1] R. I. Jack, 'Owain Glyn Dŵr and the Lordship of Ruthin', *Welsh History Review*, ii (1964–65), 309–12.

[2] A very useful set of court rolls for this purpose is the Clun collection. There are thirty-one rolls extant for the period 1328–99, eighteen for 1400–99 and five for 1500–61 in the Shropshire Record Office, Powis Collection: cf. G. E. A. Raspin, 'Transcript and Descriptive List of the Medieval Court Rolls of the Marcher Lordship of Clun deposited in the Salop Record Office by the Earl of Powis', Diploma in Archive Administration thesis, London 1963. Copies of this thesis are available in the University of London Library, in University College, London, and at Shropshire Record Office. There does not

period the rolls can yield a vivid impression of the family complexes, the consolidation or wasting of inheritances, the natural resources used or abused in the area, the incidence of theft and violence and so forth. Although the court rolls of South Wales and the march have their own unique features, a careful reading of the work of scholars such as Professor Ault or Professor Levett, preceded by Nathaniel Hone's famous and still indispensable Antiquary's Book, is desirable before settling down to master the handwriting and contractions of the original manuscripts.[1]

The composition of manorial accounts was governed by the lord's need to give his officers an honourable discharge after they had fulfilled their responsibilities. The form of the account is charge balanced by discharge. The accountant—whether he is a humble hayward, or a bailiff responsible for a whole manor, or a receiver responsible for the revenues of an entire lordship or honour, or a steward answering for household expenditure—has a clearly delimited area of responsibility. He admits responsibility for the revenues and costs of this area. If all that he is charged with exceeds his allowances (his discharge), what remains is his *debet*, the money for which he is answerable but has not discharged on his account. If his discharge is greater than his charge, then he has a 'surplus', a *superplusagium*, which is not at all the same as the modern notion of a surplus. On the contrary, the accountant who shows a 'surplus' has spent more than he received.

The charge and discharge are set out normally in the form shown at the top of page 117.

In the common 'Westminster form' of account (which is the only one that I have found used by Welsh accountants), the arrears are the *debet* from the previous year's account, the surplus heading the discharge similarly the surplus from the previous

appear to be a copy at Aberystwyth. The only other long run of court rolls, for Cawrse and Overgorddwr, is at Longleat.

---

[1] *Court Rolls of the Abbey of Ramsey and of the Honor of Clare*, ed. W. O. Ault (New Haven 1928), Introduction; A. E. Levett, *Studies in Manorial History*, ed. H. M. Cam, M. Coate and L. S. Sutherland (Oxford 1938); N. J. Hone, *The Manor and Manorial Records* (London 1906).

---

arrears [if any]
receipts
foreign receipts
   TOTAL  CHARGE

surplus [if any]
expenses
foreign expenses
liveries of money
   TOTAL  DISCHARGE

DEBET or SURPLUS

---

account: arrears and surplus cannot, of course, appear on the same account, and if by some miracle, the previous year's discharge exactly balanced the charge, neither would appear (or arrears would be shown as nil).[1]

The receipts are made up, in the case of a manorial account, of rents, leases, issues of demesne lands or land temporarily in the lord's hand (in the nonage of an heir for instance), perquisites of the manorial courts, sales of wood, profits of parkland and agistments and so forth. Foreign receipts are simply extraordinary revenue coming from sources not in the minister's area of responsibility. The sum given for rents is not, however, the sum really received: it is merely the sum chargeable to the accountant. On the discharge there will usually be an item 'decays of rent': these 'decays' include the rent of land which is currently untenanted (and so in the lord's hand), any charitable remittances of rent which the lord may have granted and any decreases in rent since the last rental was compiled (which may have been decades earlier). To calculate the amount of income from rent on this manor which the lord actually received, those decays on the discharge must be deducted from the rents on the charge. The genuine expenses on the discharge were very varied and are

[1] See D. Oschinsky, 'Notes on the Editing and Interpretation of Estate Accounts', *Archives*, ix (1969–70), 84–9, 142–52; *Walter of Henley and Other Treatises on Estate Management and Accounting* (Oxford 1971), 213–34, and S. M. Jack, 'An Historical Defence of Single Entry Book-keeping', *Abacus*, ii (1966), 145–58.

often of great interest: fees of local officials who are named, assigned annual fees paid to indentured servants, clients or patrons of the lord, costs of repairs to houses or fences or byres or folds, costs of enclosure, rents paid to other landowners for property within the accountant's jurisdiction, tithes, alms and miscellaneous items.[1]

If the account comes from a property where demesne farming is still pursued, or where there is a horse-stud, or the lord has sheep grazing on the hills, there will also be a stock account, usually on the dorse of the parchment roll. This accounts, again in a charge and discharge form, for the crops and animals on the property: the amount of various grains reaped, consumed, sold or handed over to a household servant (who would account separately), the amount of seed corn bought, the number of cattle or pigs or horses or sheep at the beginning of the accounting year (usually Michaelmas, 29 September), their natural increase and the number sold, or dead of murrain, or consumed during the year.

This method of account, to discharge the minister, is not at all the same thing as a profit-and-loss account. But lords, even monastic lords, were not at all indifferent to the question of whether they were running their estates profitably or not. It is true up to a point that 'the abbey was not intended to be a profit-making enterprise',[2] but it could not afford to incur persistent losses. Monastic vigilance is reflected in the records of monastic temporalities. When the proctors, themselves monks, who attended to the Irish endowments of Llanthony priory in Gloucestershire rendered account in 1381, they were specifically praised for having been 'wise and prudent, behaving in the interests of good governance and husbandry, living for the convenience and well-being of their chief house of Llanthony'.[3] The thirteenth-

---

[1] For discussion and a number of manorial accounts in English, see *The Grey of Ruthin Valor: the Valor of the English Lands of Edmund Grey, Earl of Kent, drawn up from the ministers' accounts of 1467–68*, ed. R. I. Jack (Sydney 1965: Bedfordshire Historical Record Society Publications xlvi, 1967).

[2] H. P. R. Finberg, *Tavistock Abbey: A Study in the Social and Economic History of Devon* (Cambridge Studies in Medieval Literature and Thought, new series ii, Cambridge 1951), 219.

[3] P.R.O., Chancery Masters' Exhibits, C. 115/A. 2/K. 1/6681 fo. 287d.

century treatise on how to be a successful steward, the *Senes-chaucie*, was insistent that

> accounts ought to be audited at each manor. On each manor by itself one may thereby hear the account and know profit and loss as well as the performance and improvement made by the steward, bailiff, reeve, and the others. Whenever they have made a profit or caused loss during the year this will be seen through the audit in a day or two; and it will be easy to recognize good sense and improvements or folly, if such has been committed.[1]

It is not without significance that the accounts both of Edmund Grey of Ruthin and Richard Beauchamp of Warwick, lord of Glamorgan, both extracted a *valor* at the end of some accounts of their officials.[2]

Ministers' accounts supply not only a basic source for the economic structure and viability of an estate, but also a wide variety of incidental information about retainers, servants, associates, tenants, mills, visits, charities and so on. But it should be obvious that an isolated account is much less useful than a series of accounts: and a bailiff's account alone is much less useful than a collection of interlocking accounts of officials above and below him. Best of all is a consecutive run of such collections for a number of years. Since accounts were neither evidence nor precedent in the way that court rolls were, they were vulnerable to loss within a few years of their audit. But as a result the historian is equally vulnerable to misinterpretation. A fairly dramatic example is afforded by the account of the receiver-general of Richard Beauchamp, Earl of Warwick. Two accounts survive, one for 1420–21 (at Longleat), the other for 1422–23 (at Warwick Castle). The years during Beauchamp's absence on the French campaigns of Henry V had seen an enormous excess of discharge over charge building up. In 1420–21 the 'surplus' was over £2,600, in September 1422 still over £1,600. Had the

[1] Oschinsky, *Walter of Henley*, 289. This is the new, standard text of *Senes-chaucie* and the other tracts, replacing Miss Lamond's, published in 1890.

[2] *The Grey of Ruthin Valor*, ed. Jack, 9; N.L.W., Bute MSS, box 63, packet A, bundle D (six accounts of the reeve of Llyswyrny).

account for 1420–21 been the only survivor, it would have been easy to assume massive cumulative extravagance, probably on building. But the 1422–23 account covers the year when Warwick returned, registered alarm and engaged a real financial expert from the royal Exchequer to investigate the receiver's accounts for the previous six years. This expert, John Thorlthorp, found that the receiver-general had been overstating his discharge by the colossal, cumulated sum of £3,000. When this correction was incorporated in the 1422–23 account it converted a 'surplus' of £1,672 into a *debet* of almost £1,400. The receiver petitioned the lord, no doubt because this *debet* would ruin him, whether his crime had been embezzlement or incompetence, and Warwick 'forgave' him £1,187, so that the final *debet* was only £185.[1] The moral of this story is that accounts of other estates may be as misleading as the 1420–21 account of Warwick's receiver. Where only an isolated account survives, let the historian beware.

Estate management produced, from time to time, surveys and rentals. North Wales is uncommonly lucky in having the celebrated survey of the lordship of Denbigh, which Sir Paul Vinogradoff and Mr Morgan edited in 1914, with the help of their Oxford seminar.[2] This huge survey of 1334 has attracted many scholars anxious to solve the problems of Welsh settlement and landholding, but it has not been squeezed dry: in fact it is still extraordinarily juicy. Not only can North Wales boast of the Denbigh survey, but the same county has published editions of two other major extents, Bromfield and Yale in 1315 and Chirkland in 1391–93,[3] and there is more Bromfield material in Peniarth MS 404. The 'Record of Caernarvon', an unpublished extent of the bishop of Bangor's lands in Acta 3,[4] three major rentals of the

[1] C. D. Ross, *The Estates and Finances of Richard Beauchamp, Earl of Warwick* (Dugdale Society Occasional Papers, xii, Oxford 1956), 14–18.

[2] *Survey of the Honour of Denbigh 1334*, ed. P. Vinogradoff and F. Morgan (British Academy, Records of the Social and Economic History of England and Wales, i, London 1914).

[3] *The First Extent of Bromfield and Yale, A.D. 1315*, ed. T. P. Ellis (Cymmrodorion Record Series, xi, London 1924); *The Extent of Chirkland (1391–1393)*, ed. G. P. Jones (London 1933).
     [4] See below, 136–7.

lordship of Ruthin[1] and other documents, mainly in the Public Record Office, give surprisingly rich source material also for North Wales. In South Wales the Clare estate and the various forfeitures of Edward II's reign produced a crop of extents, often associated with inquisitions *post mortem*, and the Black Book of St David's is a comparable compilation. A bibliography of these extents ought to be issued with any bibliography of accounts and lists of officials.

The other major category of estate archives contains deeds. A substantial collection of deeds can be used for a variety of purposes: it can document family history, the consolidation of an estate, great or small, local topography, land usage, field systems, forms of tenure. Deeds may survive as the original pieces of parchment, and the five major repositories have thousands upon thousands of medieval and Tudor deeds. Those for Glamorgan have been largely printed by the loving efforts of G. T. Clark and the energies of Walter de Gray Birch in the nineteenth century,[2] but other areas are less fortunate. The text of deeds may also survive in cartularies, bound registers of documents which the owners felt to have some practical value for reference, precedent or evidence. Over 1,300 cartularies survive in any form, original or transcript, complete or mutilated, from England, Wales and Scotland, but only 158 of these are secular.[3] At least seven of these are of interest to Welsh historians, the Bohun, Mortimer (three in all), Stafford, Sutton[4] and Fort of Llanstephan: probably others,

[1] Melville Richards, 'Records of Denbighshire Lordships, I, The Lordship of Dyffryn-Clwyd in 1465', *Trans. Denbighshire Historical Society*, xv (1966), 15–54; R. I. Jack, 'Records of Denbighshire Lordships, II, The Lordship of Dyffryn Clwyd in 1324', *ibid.*, xvii (1968), 7–53; P.R.O., Special Collections, Rentals and Surveys, S.C. 12/24/1.

[2] G. T. Clark, *Cartae et Alia Munimenta quae ad Dominium de Glamorgan pertinent* (4 vols. Dowlais and Cardiff 1885–93; 2nd, posthumous, ed. 6 vols., Cardiff 1910); *A Descriptive Catalogue of the Penrice and Margam Abbey Manuscripts*, ed. W. de G. Birch (London 1893–1905).

[3] G. R. C. Davis, *Medieval Cartularies of Great Britain: a Short Catalogue* (London 1958).

[4] This cartulary, containing the evidences for Deuddwr in Montgomeryshire, mainly in the reign of Henry VIII, but compiled after 1563, was untraced by Dr Davis: it is in Cardiff Central Library, MS 5.2.

like the Herefordshire Pedwardine cartulary, would also be of value, but the total is not large. If from the religious corporations one takes away the Red Book of St Asaph, the Statute Book of St David's and the Book of Llandaff,[1] all listed by Dr Godfrey Davis, one is left with an eighteenth-century copy of the lost Brecon register, the handful of documents in the Conway book, a seventeenth-century transcript of Carmarthen Priory's cartulary, scattered snippets from the lost Dore register, which once was at Holme Lacy along with the great Llanthony collection, the complexities of the fourteen cartularies and registers of Llanthony Secunda themselves, Tudor and Stuart extracts from the untraced cartulary of Neath and a few charters of Tintern copied in the sixteenth century. Add to these the great Shropshire cartularies, Haughmond, Lilleshall, Shrewsbury, Wenlock and Wombridge, the Gloucestershire books of the cathedral itself, Tewkesbury Abbey and Newent Priory, and the Herefordshire registers of its cathedral, St Guthlac's priory in Hereford, Leominster and Wormsley, and one has listed in two sentences most of the known cartularies of relevance to Wales.

The predominance of corporations is not surprising. Until the dissolution of the monasteries, religious institutions had much greater stability than secular landholders. Not only monastic corporations, but also boroughs maintained their archives. But many of the boroughs of modern Wales received their medieval charters from lords of the march, and after the Henrician Acts and the granting of new charters these seigneurial charters, which had been the most treasured of municipal documents, lost their value and were not always preserved by the reformed boroughs, although they may be found there or in the archives of the medieval lords. Other boroughs, like Swansea or Cardiff, have kept a firm hold on their charters,[2] and an analysis of the Welsh towns in the works of Ballard, Tait and Weinbaum is a

[1] See below, 143–6.
[2] *Cardiff Records*, ed. J. H. Matthews (6 vols., Cardiff 1898–1911); *Charters Granted to Swansea*, ed. G. G. Francis (London 1867); cf. *The Charters of the Borough of Newport in Gwynllwg*, ed. W. Rees (Newport 1951).

simple enough task:[1] a more general survey would be a useful
adjunct to E. A. Lewis's famous extended essay on *The Mediaeval
Boroughs of Snowdonia.* Other borough records, such as court
rolls and accounts of local officials, can be found sporadically:
the Caernarvon court rolls for 1361 to 1402 were found in the
spare room of an Anglesey solicitor,[2] the account of the reeve
of Caerphilly town for 1428–29 is among the Bute manuscripts,
the rental of the Pembrokeshire Newport for 1434 survives in
George Owen's Bronwydd papers,[3] much information about the
towns is in the Public Record Office ministers' accounts, but for
most towns, even Cardiff, the usual wide net has to be cast.
The contrast with English municipal archives is as great as most
of similar comparisons throughout this book.[4] Indeed it is in
Hereford city records that there can be found the basic information about the customs of various Welsh towns, for at various
times towns as far apart as Caernarvon, Haverfordwest and Cardiff
obtained their customs by writing to Hereford.[5] The physical
hazards of the searcher for estate and corporation records are
less than those of the ecclesiastical historian, but until the essential
bibliographies of estate archives are compiled and published, an
initiative test is there to be overcome.

The whole history of the keeping of private records, whether
family or monastic or municipal, is peculiarly involved. Records
of dissolved monasteries often reached private hands after they
had been received into the Court of Augmentations: the searcher
must be familiar not only with the Augmentations records in the

[1] *British Borough Charters, 1042–1216,* ed. A. Ballard (Cambridge 1913);
*British Borough Charters, 1217–1307,* ed. A. Ballard and J. Tait (Cambridge
1923); *British Borough Charters, 1307–1660,* ed. M. Weinbaum (Cambridge
1943).
[2] *Caernarvon Court Rolls, 1361–1402,* ed. G. P. Jones and Hugh Owen
(Caernarvonshire Historical Society, Record Series, i, Caernarvon 1951).
[3] N.L.W., Bronwydd MSS (first deposit), 301.
[4] Cf. Elton, *England, 1200–1640,* 119–28.
[5] R. Johnson, *The Ancient Customs of the City of Hereford* (London 1882),
24–45. Rhuddlan's request for information in 1348 is, however, in *The Record
of Caernarvon,* ed. Ellis, 130.

Public Record Office, but also with the families who, in the six-teenth century, received grants of land formerly owned by the monastery in which he may be interested. Muniments might or might not be preserved by the new owners, but it is prudent to find out. But this in turn involves a student of medieval monaster-ies in the genealogy of landed families from the Tudor period to the present day, just as the arrangement of estate archives at the National Library of Wales calls for an encyclopaedic knowledge of Welsh families and their country seats. Even titles are not a sufficient guide; because of family settlements and the vagaries of peerage law over the centuries the lands and muniments may not necessarily follow the title. All this makes for intellectual exhilaration, and there are great rewards for passing the initiative test.

# CHAPTER 5

## *Ecclesiastical Records*

Just as the main series of Chancery records produced by the secular administration of medieval Wales has been lost, so the ecclesiastical records are gravely deficient. A remarkable amount of information can still be amassed about the activities and personnel of the Church in Wales. Dr Conway Davies has published two volumes of documents produced by the pre-Conquest Church, and Professor Glanmor Williams has written a massive, and exemplary, history of the Church 'from Conquest to Reformation'.[1] But the sources published by Dr Davies are not, in the main, ecclesiastical archives maintained by the Church over the centuries: they are compiled from all manner of records mainly created by the recipients of the grants. And Professor Williams would be the first to agree that in writing his book he was largely deprived of basic records which every historian of the English Church in this period would regard as his birthright.

The fundamental ecclesiastical record is the episcopal register.[2] The register was the official copy of business transacted by the bishop as ruler of his diocese. In some ways registers resemble the Chancery rolls of the royal administration, but differ in one vital respect: they often contain copies of letters received as well as letters despatched. To this extent, therefore, they are a fuller record than the Chancery rolls: on the other hand, they are much more selective. It is clear that copies were kept only of letters felt to be of importance. For the most part, what was of

[1] *Episcopal Acts and Cognate Documents relating to Welsh Dioceses, 1066–1272*, ed. J. C. Davies (Historical Society of Church in Wales, i, 1946, ii, 1949); Glanmor Williams, *The Welsh Church from Conquest to Reformation* (Cardiff 1962).

[2] The most convenient introduction to episcopal registers is E. F. Jacob, *The Medieval Registers of Canterbury and York: Some Points of Comparison* (St Anthony's Hall Publication, iv, London 1953).

importance to the episcopal administration is also of importance to the historian, but what had no evidential value to the bishop is not necessarily unimportant today. The registers are, however, an invaluable source, particularly for details of ordinations and movements of clergy in the diocese, and for the characteristic business correspondence of a leading ecclesiastical statesman. For the historian's convenience, the register ranks with the Chancery rolls or private cartularies in bringing together a whole corpus of related information. Without the register, the Close roll, the Patent roll or the cartulary, the historian would have to search high and low amidst scattered collections of all sorts, public and private, to create a similar corpus. This is why the reign of King John has a unique importance for English medievalists. To gauge the convenience of the government enrolments, one cannot do better than to read through the three volumes of the *Acta Regum Anglo-Normannorum* and note the variety of sources and repositories from which the materials are drawn. To assess the importance of the episcopal register, one ought to look at the labours of Professor Kathleen Major in recreating from many sources some of the contents of the lost register of Stephen Langton, Archbishop of Canterbury from 1207 to 1228.[1]

Registers survive for most English dioceses in large numbers from the early thirteenth century onwards: the revolution in ecclesiastical record-keeping is almost simultaneous with that in government. No diocese has an unbroken series, because of fire, decay, theft or borrowing, but Canterbury is almost complete from 1279 (it lacks only 1327–49 and 1636–60) and York from 1225. The contrast with Wales is depressing. All the available surviving ecclesiastical records of Wales have been deposited in the National Library by the Representative Body of the Church in Wales: St David's has one complete early register, covering the

[1] *Acta Stephani Langton, Cantuariensis Archiepiscopi, A.D. 1207–1228*, ed. K. Major (Canterbury and York Society l, Oxford 1950). Cf. *The Acta of the Bishops of Chichester, 1075–1207* (Canterbury and York Society lvi, Torquay 1964), which H. Mayr-Harting compiled from eighteen repositories.

years 1397 to 1410 and then, after a gap of seventy-two years, parts of registers spanning the years from 1482 intermittently to 1518.[1] Only for Guy Mone, bishop during the ten years ending in 1407, and for Hugh Pavy (1485 to 1496) are there complete registers for their entire episcopacies. The register of Chichele (bishop from 1408 to 1414, when he was translated to Canterbury) stops short in 1410; the acts of the short-lived Franciscan Richard Martin, who died only nine and a half months after his translation to St David's in July 1482, are recorded only up to December of that year; and Edward Vaughan's episcopacy from 1509 to 1522 is recorded only for its middle years, 1512 to 1518. After 1518 the registers do not resume until Mary's reign, with Henry Morgan in 1554.[2] The registers of Benedict Nicholls and Thomas Rodburn (1417 to 1442) and other parts of the registers of Chichele and Hiot the vicar-general, were still in existence in the eighteenth century, for Edward Yardley used them in his *Menevia Sacra*, but, despite valiant efforts to find them through his heirs, his sale catalogue and the Society for Promoting Christian Knowledge (which Yardley endowed), they remain lost.[3]

Three stray fragments of St David's records have, however, been found, two in Oxford, the other at Hereford. The earliest fragment is a small collection of near-contemporary transcripts from the register of Thomas Bek, who held the see through the Edwardian Conquest period until his death in 1293. These extracts are in a composite volume in the Bodleian and, despite Dr Conway Davies' hope expressed in 1946 that they would be published 'at an early date', the student has still to go to Oxford to discover their contents.[4] The other two fragments are, how-

[1] Published in Cymmrodorion Record Series vi, London 1917. The originals are bound in one volume, N.L.W., SD/BR/1.

[2] N.L.W., SD/BR/2. Cf. Glanmor Williams, 'The Second Volume of St David's Registers, 1554–64', *B.B.C.S.*, xiv (1950–52), 45–54.

[3] J. le Neve, *Fasti Ecclesiae Anglicanae, 1300–1541*, xi, *Welsh Dioceses* (London 1965), foreword by Bridget Jones.

[4] Bodley, MS Auct. F. 5.25, fos. 151–5; *A Summary Catalogue of Western Manuscripts in the Bodleian Library at Oxford*, ii (2) (Oxford 1937), 816–7, no. 4056; *Episcopal Acts*, ed. Davies, i, 8.

I                                          129

ever, in print. One is a fly-leaf of a fourteenth-century manuscript in Hereford Cathedral, containing seven of the acts of the archbishop of Canterbury's vicar-general during the vacancy in 1389.[1] The other is a group of four leaves from Stephen Patrington's register, covering the summer and autumn of 1415, which caught the eye of Neil Ker in New College MS 360 and was printed by Dr Emanuel in 1950.[2]

The diocese of Bangor has preserved fragments of early fifteenth-century registers, six folios of parchment containing presentations to benefices between 1408 and 1417.[3] There are also copies of the presentations from 1408 to 1410, probably made in the sixteenth century.[4] No more registers or copies of registers survive before 1512. It is possible that no registers were maintained for much of this period, for the absentee English bishops from 1417 onwards are said to have allowed the cathedral to fall into some decay, and the improvement in Bangor's situation is attributed to Henry Deane, bishop from 1496 to 1500.[5] Certainly the register series resumes from 1512 to 1525 and, after a further gap, from 1542 onwards.[6]

The registers of St Asaph survive only from 1536.[7] The worst preserved series is that of Llandaff. The first register of Llandaff dates from 1819, although there are drafts for a register going back two years previously, and the subscription books (an aspect of post-medieval register material) start in 1660.[8]

[1] H. D. Emanuel, 'Early St David's Records', *N.L.W.J.*, viii (1953–54), 258, 261.

[2] H. D. Emanuel, 'A Fragment of the Register of Stephen Patryngton, Bishop of St David's', *Journal of Historical Society of Church in Wales*, ii (1950), 31–45.

[3] N.L.W., B/BR/1, fos. 1–6; A. I. Pryce, 'The Register of Benedict, Bishop of Bangor, 1408–1417', *Arch. Camb.*, 7th series, ii (1922), 80–107.

[4] N.L.W., B/Misc./272. The National Library list suggests a fifteenth-century date, but a sixteenth-century date would be more convincing on palaeographic grounds.

[5] A. I. Price, *The Diocese of Bangor in the Sixteenth Century, being a Digest of the Registers of the Bishops, A.D. 1512–1646* (Bangor 1923), x.

[6] *Ibid.*, passim. The originals are now N.L.W. B/BR/1 and 2.

[7] N.L.W., SA/BR/1.

[8] Cardiff Central Library, MS 3.468. A photographic copy of this 1819–21

There are then only a few fragments of Welsh registers at all before 1397, only a short section of the early fifteenth century survives in any form for Bangor, St Asaph begins in Henry VIII's reign and Llandaff is a total blank before the seventeenth century. A certain amount of supplementary material for St Asaph and the relatively well documented St David's exists in later transcripts. These are in the main capitular rather than diocesan. Episcopal statutes, regulating cathedral life, and other documents were collected in the time of Edward Vaughan, bishop of St David's from 1509 to 1522. This 'Statute-Book of St David's' was an official compilation, probably made directly from the original manuscripts, which included one twelfth-century bull and some score of thirteenth-century documents. The series of statutes is of the greatest importance and, although the original compilation is lost, the text in the Tudor copy among the Harleian manuscripts in the British Museum (6280), and the later transcripts in the National Library of Wales (which has five) and St. John's College, Cambridge, is reasonably sound. The documents which date from before 1272 have been calendared by Dr Conway Davies in his *Episcopal Acts*, but an edition of the whole is long overdue.[1]

Overdue, too, though a more delicate task, is a published edition of the St Asaph counterpart, the celebrated Llyfr Coch Asaph.[2] The original red-bound manuscript was lost, or at least mislaid, long ago, probably in the seventeenth century: it was a sort of register, not a formal episcopal one, but a more miscellaneous compilation. Although it contained presentations it also contained statutes of the bishop's household, bulls, grants and other documents of a very varied nature. It even listed at one point the contents of seven boxes of documents, labelled A to I, inspected in 1311 at Meliden, an episcopal manor. It was probably

register is in N.L.W., LL/BR/1. The drafts for 1817–19 are N.L.W., LL/BR/14. The subscription book starting in 1660 is LL/SB/1. Some capitular records begin in 1573 (LLCh/1).

---

[1] Cf. *Episcopal Acts*, ed. Davies, i, 25 n. 139.

[2] The master's thesis by O. E. Jones, examining the Red Book, has not been published. It was completed at Aberystwyth in 1968.

compiled in the time of Llywelyn of Bromfield (1293 to 1314) and contained about seventy documents before 1272. The scope of the contents is known from an epitome made from the original in 1602,[1] when already about a quarter of the original number of folios was missing, some thirty-seven out of 151. Even these 114 folios which survived until 1602 have not been fully transcribed. A sixteenth-century copy kept by St Asaph Cathedral, and now in the National Library, contains only seventeen folios (all from the first twenty-three), although it seems to give a fairly full text for this limited portion. The other three transcripts which survive are inter-related. The oldest and best is in the hand of the greatest of Welsh antiquaries, Robert Vaughan of Hengwrt (who is discussed below in chapter 6). The so-called 'Nefydd' transcript is copied from Vaughan and the St Asaph 'no. 2' from the 'Nefydd', although both have other documents added from familiar sources originally copied by Vaughan into another book. When these two separate transcript-traditions are amalgamated, some forty-three folios of the original Red Book are available. This is better than nothing, and comparison of the surviving items with the epitome of what survived in 1602 seems to indicate that most of the apparently important documents were transcribed.[2]

The records of St Asaph are supplemented, not only by the remains of the Red Book, but also by an early Elizabethan collection of ordinations, collations and a few other documents: these cover the period from 1501 to 1571, but there are only three ordinations noted from the period of Henry VIII, and none before 1524, and only twenty-four presentations or collations before 1544.[3]

The registers of dioceses adjacent to Wales often survive and contain relevant information. The diocese of Hereford bordered

---

[1] Printed in *Arch. Camb.*, 3rd series, xiv (1868), 151–66.

[2] D. L. Evans, 'Llyfr Coch Asaph', *N.L.W.J.*, iv (1945–46), 177–83; *Episcopal Acts*, ed. Davies, i, 26–7.

[3] G. Milwyn Griffiths, 'A St Asaph "Register" of Episcopal Acts, 1506–1571', *Journal of Historical Society of Church in Wales*, vi (1956), 25–49.

on St David's, Llandaff and St Asaph. In striking contrast to its Welsh neighbours, Hereford's registers survive in unbroken series from 1275 to 1492 (resuming twelve years later): and all these registers have been published by the Canterbury and York Society. Moreover, since the Welsh dioceses were within the province of Canterbury until the Welsh Church Act of 1914 became effective in 1920, the provincial archives of Canterbury contain scattered evidence for Welsh ecclesiastical life, in the episcopal registers as much as in the testamentary records discussed below.

The other main records produced by the bishops are visitation reports and the records of processes in diocesan courts. As far as I know there is in existence no visitation by a Welsh bishop investigating the morals and conduct of his parochial clergy or of religious houses not exempt from his jurisdiction. This should occasion no surprise, since the records of visitations are uncommon—even in English archives. It is rare to have a complete record of the proceedings during the investigation by a bishop or his official. There was no particular reason to copy all this into his episcopal register, although orders resulting from the enquiry might very well be enrolled.[1] Most of the detailed documents were no doubt kept separately, as indeed the register material was also kept on separate quaternions. When the time finally came to bind up the quaternions of the register, there was still little reason to include these full records of visitations, which were thereafter lost: the seventeen quires of the visitation records of bishop Alnwick in Lincoln between 1438 and his death in 1449 are very exceptional indeed.[2] The lack of Welsh visitation records should not surprise, although it may grieve. There is, however, one gleam of light. Since the Welsh dioceses came under

---

[1] See C. R. Cheney, *Episcopal Visitations of Monasteries in the Thirteenth Century* (Manchester 1931), chap. 1. Cf. R. M. Hill, *The Labourer in the Vineyard* (Borthwick Papers, xxxv, York 1968).

[2] *Visitations of Religious Houses in the Diocese of Lincoln*, ed. A. H. Thompson, ii (Canterbury and York Society, xxiv, London 1919) and iii (Canterbury and York Society, xxxiii, London 1927).

the jurisdiction of the Archbishop of Canterbury, he too could conduct a visitation. Thus in 1504 Archbishop Warham ordered the investigation of the diocese of Bangor, and the subsequent report, which survives, alleged various pluralities, accused forty-three clergy of keeping *de facto* wives, and listed other offences.[1] But this is a very rare survival. Certainly there were local visitations organised by the Welsh bishops. David Yale's commonplace book for the greater glory of David Yale, bachelor *utriusque juris*, records, for example, how the bishop of Bangor in 1501 appointed him to conduct a visitation of the deanery of Dyffryn Clwyd, an island dependency of Bangor surrounded by St Asaph's see. In this visitation Yale was to examine all religious who had not exemptions, including abbots, priors, wardens, provosts, rectors, vicars, curates and chaplains.[2] Cartularies too sometimes tell of otherwise unrecorded visitations. Thanks to the Llanthony cartularies, it is possible to know that the bishops of Llandaff, John de Monmouth, John de Eaglescliff and John Burghill, in 1301, 1329 and 1397, conducted visitations, at which they inspected the muniments supporting Llanthony's claim to two churches in the diocese.[3] Rare evidence of this sort helps perhaps to modify the opinion that 'in view of the fewness of the resident members of the chapters who had the necessary local knowledge and experience it may be doubted whether [visitation] functioned very smoothly'.[4] In general there is no valid way of ascertaining the regularity with which episcopal visitations were carried out, much less to know the scandals they uncovered.

The third class of diocesan archives comes from the hierarchy of ecclesiastical courts, from the archdeacon's, the official's and the bishop's courts within the diocese, to the provincial courts

---

[1] This is in Warham's unprinted archiepiscopal register. Only a digest of the names of clergy was printed by Price, *Diocese of Bangor*, Appendix A, 81–4. See Glanmor Williams, *Welsh Church*, 394–5.

[2] Cardiff Central Library, MS 2.2, fo. 73d. This is 'Cardiff MS 4' in Historical Manuscripts Commission 48, ii (1) (1902), 95–6.

[3] P.R.O., Chancery Masters' Exhibits, C. 115/A. 9/K. 1/6679 fo. 164; A. 1/K. 2/6683 section XIV, item xxxviij; A. 7/K. 2/6684 fo. 190d.

[4] Glanmor Williams, *Welsh Church*, 231.

beyond and, despite restrictions, the court of Rome as the ultimate court of appeal.[1] The records of these courts, interpreting canon law, are invaluable for insight into affairs of the clergy, into the intimacies of birth and death, marriage in its breach and in its observance, and the making and probate of last wills and testaments. The English testamentary records, recorded in separate registers, have survived in number, but the diocesan court books are uncommon in England before the sixteenth century and are characteristically non-existent in Wales.[2]

Courts were certainly held in Wales. A fragment of cases heard in St David's diocese, probably in 1349, survives as fly-leaves to that Hereford Cathedral manuscript which also contains a leaf of the *sede vacante* register.[3] It says much for our ignorance of ecclesiastical organisation in Wales that these fly-leaves are the only evidence that 'the rural deanery was a unit which had the power to hold its own court, at least for testamentary causes, and enjoyed a certain degree of autonomy in the sphere of ecclesiastical law';[4] or at least that Cemais was such a deanery. The other cases were not heard before the dean but, as might be expected, before the chancellor of the diocese.

There is little evidence of the regularity with which ecclesiastical courts met. Only odd scraps of information survive. We are dependent on stray documents[5] or the few registers to know even the names of vicars-general for absentee bishops, and on English registers or Chancery enrolments for the inadequate lists of deans,

[1] See I. J. Churchill, *Canterbury Administration* (London 1933); B. L. Woodcock, *Medieval Ecclesiastical Courts in the Diocese of Canterbury* (London 1952); C. Morris, 'A Consistory Court in the Middle Ages', *Journal of Ecclesiastical History*, xiv (1963), 150–9. Cf. D. M. Owen, *The Records of the Established Church in England excluding Parochial Records* (Archives and the User, i, 1970).

[2] The only ordinary entry-book for any ecclesiastical court which has yet been printed is *An Episcopal Court Book for the Diocese of Lincoln, 1514–1520*, ed. M. Bowker (Lincoln Record Society, lxi, 1967).

[3] Emanuel, 'Early St David's Records', *N.L.W.J.*, viii (1953–54), 258–63.

[4] *Ibid.*; cf. Glanmor Williams, *Welsh Church*, 253.

[5] E.g., Cardiff Central Library, D.D. Pembrokeshire 30 (or 1083), the commission of the bishop of St David's to Richard Caunton, his vicar-general, in 1415. Caunton is well known in other ecclesiastical capacities.

archdeacons and chancellors in the new edition of le Neve's *Fasti*.[1] As a result, we are unlikely to know much more of the archdeacon of Bangor who, in Henry VIII's reign, was criticised for keeping an alehouse which those attending the consistory court were obliged to patronise.[2] If David Yale had not been a vain and conceited man who kept a common-place book, noting down parts of documents which mentioned him and his university degree, there would be little information about the arrangements made by the bishop of Bangor for governing the deanery of Dyffryn Clwyd in Henry VII's reign.[3]

Testamentary records, which are discussed below, also give evidence of episcopal organisation, but systematic official court records simply do not exist. The nearest approach, other than the St David's fragment, is a jumble of medieval and Tudor copies of documents then in the archive of the bishop of Bangor. This unnumbered, unindexed volume of extracts, bound up in 1729, is known, mysteriously, as Acta 3.[4] Its contents seem to have been used by the ecclesiastical antiquary Browne Willis in the eighteenth century, and he may have been responsible for the table of contents added around that time.[5] The sort of rare evidence which can be found in this miscellany is the record of a case about tithes in the deanery of Dyffryn Clwyd. This case settled a dispute between the canons of Bangor Cathedral and the rector of Llanynys on the one hand and three other local rectors acting for all the rectors and vicars of Dyffryn Clwyd and the neighbouring commote of Ceinmeirch on the other hand. The right to receive all tithes, including the local variety about which dissension had arisen, was adjudged to the rectors.[6]

[1] J. le Neve, *Fasti*, xi, *The Welsh Dioceses*, compiled B. Jones.
[2] P.R.O., Special Collections, Ministers' Accounts, S.C. 6/Hen. VIII/7490.
[3] Cardiff Central Library, MS 2.2; H.M.C. 48, ii (1), 95.
[4] N.L.W., B/Misc. Vols/27. The register fragments for 1408–17 were removed from this volume to B/BR/1.
[5] Browne Willis, *A Survey of the Cathedral Church of Bangor and the Edifices Belonging To It* (London 1721).
[6] There is a note of a consistory court at Ruthin in 1502 held by David Yale as commissary of the bishop of Bangor (Cardiff Central Library, MS 2.2, fo. 74d).

Acta 3 includes not only extracts from diocesan legal records, but also copies of documents concerning temporalities, such as the important (and still unpublished) fourteenth-century extent of the episcopal lands[1] and a tantalising handful of extracts from the testamentary records of Bangor. Towards the end of the volume in the 'register of the vicar-general' are a few wills proved before Master William Capon in 1534. Acta 3 contains, too, a sixteenth-century transcript of the 1408–17 register; this transcript is important because it records what has become illegible on the original. The volume urgently needs an editor.

There is no comparable collection of extracts from records produced by the diocesan administration in any other Welsh see in the Middle Ages. The contrast with the superb, and under-used records of Hereford diocese is always forcible. The fifteenth-century consistory court-books of Hereford and its voluminous Tudor archives, together with the Dean and Chapter's accumulation of deeds, could be used to illuminate many corners of Welsh border history. Although the deed collection was deposited in the National Library of Wales for some years and a typed calendar is now available in Aberystwyth and in London, the diocesan records of Hereford, other than the registers, are much less familiar. But they are no less a source with which the historian of Wales should reckon. Professor Elton has emphasised that the records of the ecclesiastical courts of England should be tackled only by 'young scholars, still enthusiastic, physically strong, and possessed of a sound digestion' :[2] they should also be impervious to draughts and unaccustomed to bright lights. But valuable material on the realities of life in the medieval marches can certainly be extracted from the Hereford records, and the kind and scholarly welcome which the cathedral custodians give to the serious researcher is one of my happiest recollections of an antiquarian tour.

It should also be remembered that a small part of Flintshire

[1] See the valuable use of the Anglesey portion of this extent by G. R. J. Jones, 'The Distribution of Medieval Settlement in Anglesey', *Trans. Anglesey Antiquarian Society and Field Club* (1955).

[2] Elton, *England, 1200–1640*, 105.

and Denbighshire lay within the huge medieval diocese of Lichfield (until Henry VIII created the see of Chester in 1541), and fifteenth-century court books, together with a fine series of episcopal registers from 1297 onwards (all but one unpublished),[1] survive in the public library at Lichfield.

The marching dioceses are not, however, the only potential supplements to the deficiencies of Wales itself. The courts of appeal in the province of Canterbury (Audience and Arches) presumably heard appeals from Wales as from elsewhere in the province. But the medieval records of these courts no longer exist: even in 1666, when the Great Fire of London consumed most of the pre-Restoration records of the Court of Arches, nothing before Edward VI's reign still survived to be burnt.[2] The creation of the High Court of Delegates, after the 1532 Act in restraint of citations had restricted appeals to the provincial courts, changes the archival situation at the very end of our period, for the Act books of the new court exist for 1538 to 1544 (as well as for the seventeenth century).[3] Moreover, throughout England and Wales there were areas and religious houses which came under the direct jurisdiction of the appropriate archbishop, not the local bishop. Materials for these liberties and for various benefices in the Canterbury jurisdiction can be gleaned from the archbishops' registers. Unfortunately only the registers of Winchelsey, Pelham, Langham, Chichele and Bourgchier have yet been edited.

Finally, there are the records of the Roman curia itself. These are dealt with separately below, but it should be remembered that arising from appeals or petitions to Rome, significant evidence for Welsh ecclesiastical behaviour is found in the papal registers,

[1] The register of Bishop Stretton, 1358–85 (Staffordshire Record Society, new series viii, 1905, x (2), 1907).

[2] M. D. Slatter, 'The Records of the Court of Arches', *Journal of Ecclesiastical History*, iv (1953), 140. Some other fragments from the medieval archives of the Court of Arches survive at Lambeth: D. M. Owen, *A Catalogue of Lambeth Manuscripts 889 to 901 (Carte Antique et Miscellanee)* (London 1968), 7.

[3] A. M. Erskine, 'Ecclesiastical Courts and Their Records in the Province of Canterbury', *Archives*, iii (1957–58), 10–11. The Act books are in the Public Record Office, class Del. 4.

and a long series of calendars has made available the gist of many papal letters referring to England and Wales in the fourteenth and fifteenth centuries.

As well as these courts, the probate jurisdiction of the Church has created a huge bulk of records. Although only a few extracts from a Bangor register of 1534 survive from official Welsh records,[1] many Welshmen of substance came under the testamentary jurisdiction not of a Welsh bishop but of the Archbishop of Canterbury. Normally if the dying man held land in more than one diocese, his testament required probate from the Prerogative Court of the province, although there are anomalies. To find the will of a land-holder of substance who held Welsh or marcher property it is often necessary to search the records of the Prerogative Court of Canterbury. The testaments themselves, after grant of probate, were copied into great bound books, recently transferred from Somerset House in London to the Public Record Office.

These will registers, like those created by individual dioceses and archdeaconries, have never been indexed by their official custodians. Fortunately for the historian, the British Record Society has throughout this century been remedying this glaring omission. Since wills and testaments give information on social history, philanthropy, family structures, ecclesiastical organisation and so forth, medievalists should affectionately remember William Phillimore who, before founding the Scottish Record Society, the Thoroton Society and the Canterbury and York Society, created the Index Library in 1887 and in 1889 formed round it the British Record Society.[2] The publications and interests of the Society are not exclusively testamentary, but since 1940 it has published only will indexes.

The most important of these indexes for our purpose is one of the oldest, J. C. C. Smith's 1893 index to the will registers of the Prerogative Court of Canterbury from 1383 to 1558. Like the

[1] N.L.W., B/Misc. Vols/27. See above, 136–7.
[2] P. Spufford, 'The British Record Society—Eighty Years of an Index', *The Indexer*, vi (1968–69), 19–23.

Harleian Society's index to Early Chancery Proceedings, this index lists x ap y under ap. This has its convenient side, in producing four solid pages of Welshmen. In addition there are, of course, many less patronymic Welsh testators: there is, for example, half a page of Griffiths and more Howells. These lists extend, it must be noted, to the end of Mary's reign (and the series has been continued up to 1700), and those Welshmen listed may be resident in Wales or in England. One of the most recent Index Library volumes, edited by Mark Fitch, the patron of so many good historical works, indexes the testamentary records of the more localised Commissary Court of London from 1374 to 1488 with an admirable additional geographical index arranged under county. From Mr Fitch's index alone, one can find that among the fifteen men called Wallis, one William Waleys wished in 1407 to be buried in St Nicholas church, Pembroke; or that William Griffith, tailor and citizen of London, who died in 1479, had been born in Carmarthenshire. Small enough information, perhaps, but the gradual extension of indexing is making available more and more of these very personal records.

The wills of Welshmen are to be found elsewhere, but less frequently. The obvious dioceses are Hereford and Lichfield. There is a less than usually reliable Index Library calendar of the registers of Lichfield consistory court from 1516 to 1652 (edited by Phillimore himself in 1892) and there are no published lists of the Hereford wills (now in Aberystwyth). But in both dioceses, there is something to attract the searcher. Uncharacteristically, in both cases, original wills survive for a period substantially earlier than the first register, and the original wills have never been the subject of printed indexes. At Lichfield Public Library there are original wills from 1472, and the National Library of Wales has, among the Hereford records, a bundle of about eighty wills from the first forty years of the sixteenth century; the Hereford registers do not survive before 1663.[1]

[1] For this and other information about wills, see A. J. Camp, *Wills and their Whereabouts* (Bridge Place 1963). Lichfield appears *sub* Staffordshire, 67, Hereford *sub* Wales, 114. Such is the unrest among testamentary records that

Along with wills, inventories of the testator's goods were usually submitted to the ecclesiastical court, attested by the supervisors to assist the executors. These inventories are of quite outstanding interest, but were not copied into the will registers. Their survival has been less secure than that of the registers. For the Prerogative Court of Canterbury they do not exist before 1484 and are infrequent before 1524. There are none at all for Hereford before 1662 and none from any period for Lichfield. The P.C.C. inventories have for many years been scandalously unavailable, but they have recently been moved from Somerset House to the Public Record Office where they are being sorted, listed and cared for in the best traditions of that incomparable institution. Until the listing is completed, there is no ready means of knowing how much information of relevance to Wales before 1543 is contained in them.

It should also be remembered that part of the history of Wales consists of the careers of its people, and its people often left their homeland to work or settle elsewhere. Welshmen on the continent create problems for the researcher, but it should be remembered that many lived and died in England: their careers can partly be found in the records of every diocese in England and their wills may be in the great variety of local testamentary records which survive below the Prerogative Court of Canterbury. It would be an exercise less futile than many to consolidate a list of Welshmen's wills.

Finally, too, in considering wills, there is the other side of the process: the copy retained by the testator's family. These documents may turn up in any private archive in any of the two hundred repositories in England and Wales.[1] But they are not common and probably few Welsh wills are among them. If

Camp is already out of date in some of his information, e.g., over the Prerogative Court of Canterbury inventories (see below, 141).

---

[1] Most of these are listed in *Record Repositories: England and Wales* (4th ed. London 1971). For a very interesting will of 1463 preserved among Haverfordwest borough records, see F. Green, 'Early Wills in West Wales', *West Wales Historical Records*, vii (1917–18), 145–52.

they can be found, they fill a regrettable gap. The kind of information which can be obtained is exemplified by the will of Ithel Toua of Llanelidan in the lordship of Ruthin made in 1492 and proved in 1495. It supplies the name of the curate in the church of St Peter in Ruthin, a long list of debts owing to named local people often for specific purchases, a little genealogical data, and proof that probate of wills in the deanery of Dyffryn Clwyd was granted by the bishop of Bangor's commissary, who is named and whose university degree is recorded.[1] Or the grant of administration in 1447 by the dean of Cemais, in the archdeaconry of Cardigan, is evidence of decanal independence unlike the post-Reformation situation.[2] Or the probate of the will of John Gwyn, blacksmith of Newport on Usk, granted by Thomas Jankyns, commissary-general, in May 1471, is rare evidence of the Llandaff diocesan administration.[3] This sort of information can be confidently expected in England: it has to be fought for in Wales.

To return to the actual records of the Welsh dioceses, there are, in addition to the scanty register, court and testamentary remains, records of the temporalities which properly belong under estate administration. All religious institutions were landowners, many of them great landowners, and their records differ little from those of lay estates. The monasteries' records of estate management came first to the Court of Augmentations on the dissolution in the 1530s: thereafter many of the records were handed over to the new lay owners and have been discussed in the previous chapter. But the records of the diocesan landholdings were relatively undisturbed by the Reformation, except to the extent that the creation of new dioceses made some reorganisation of boundaries necessary. The Welsh dioceses and chapters must, therefore, have had a typical archive of seigneurial records—ministers' accounts, court rolls, rentals, extents, conveyances and extracts from court judgments. A little, but only a very little, remains.

[1] N.L.W., Wynnstay MSS (second deposit, 1952), box 104, no. 61.
[2] N.L.W., Bronwydd MSS (second deposit), 800: cf. Emanuel, 'Early St David's Records', *N.L.W.J.*, viii (1953–54), 260.
[3] Glamorgan County Record Office, Fonmon Castle deposit, D/D F. 2870.

The oldest and most notorious of Welsh ecclesiastical compilations belonging to this general category is the Book of Llandaff. The main portion of this book is written in a number of hands of the twelfth and thirteenth centuries. It contains two clearly identifiable groups of material, with no overlap of scribes. On the one hand there is a collection of sources, including papal bulls, which in one way or another relate directly to the episcopal powers claimed by the bishops of Llandaff in the twelfth century and particularly the disputes between Llandaff and St David's and between Llandaff and Hereford, in the years from 1119 to 1134. On the other hand there is what is in effect a historical account of the way in which these powers were allegedly exercised and developed over the previous six centuries. This latter part, written in one hand only, contains both narrative and a record of grants purporting to date from the time of Dyfrig, Teilo, Oudoceus and subsequent bishops. The purpose of the entire book is clearly connected with the disputes which ended with the death of Bishop Urban in 1133 or 1134 and it seems certain that this compilation was made in Urban's lifetime.

An edition of Robert Vaughan's transcript, with translation, has been available since 1840 and a splendid further edition, after the rediscovery of the original manuscript at Gwysaney, was produced by Gwenogvryn Evans and John Rhŷs in 1893, yet there has been surprisingly little rigorous examination of the text. The Book of Llandaff is of fundamental importance and it bristles with problems, coming as it does in the heyday of ecclesiastical forgers. Geoffrey of Monmouth himself, the high-priest of early British fiction, was suggested as the author by scholars as different as Dr Evans and Professor Christopher Brooke; Dr Conway Davies and Mr E. D. Jones marked it 'to be used with caution', while some Welsh scholars today, such as the former Chancellor of Bangor and Mr P. C. Bartrum, minimise the likelihood of forgery and use the book as a quarry for a wide range of pre-Norman topics.[1]

[1] Evans (firmly) in the introduction to the 1893 edition; C. N. L. Brooke (very diffidently) in 'The Archbishops of St David's, Llandaff and Caerleon-

In fact, it must be recognised that none of these opinions has any solid foundation, for the spade-work on the diplomatic of the book, which is a necessary preliminary to any proper assessment of its historical value, was not available. Dr Wendy Davies has, however, recently completed a thesis which in some measure fufills these preliminary tasks.[1] To write a full and authoritative monograph on the *Liber Landavensis* as a whole would require a combination of Père Grosjean, Dr Chaplais, Professor Melville Richards and Professor Brooke, but Dr Davies's study of the charters is an important beginning: it is an indictment of Welsh scholarship that this basic work should be so long delayed and that it should be achieved at the University of London under the supervision of an ancient historian. Welsh historians have not built on the pioneering work of Dr Conway Davies in demonstrating the importance of the study of document forms in the twelfth and thirteenth centuries:[2] Dr Wendy Davies has very percipiently extended this study into the pre-Norman period. It never ceases to surprise someone like me, coming late to Welsh history from English history, that technical expertise which has long been commonplace in English medieval studies has so infrequently been applied to the relatively small number of comparable Welsh texts: their rarity and their difficulty combine to make a diplomatic approach peculiarly appropriate.

The conclusions reached by Dr Wendy Davies are important. The charters as they now appear in the Book of Llandaff were

on-Usk', *Studies in the Early British Church*, ed. N. K. Chadwick (Cambridge 1958), 201–42, esp. 232–3; *Episcopal Acts*, ed. Davies, i, 163–77; E. D. Jones, 'The Book of Llandaff', *N.L.W.J.*, iv (1945–46), 123–57; J. W. James, 'Chronology in the Book of Llan Dav', *N.L.W.J.*, xvi (1969–70), 123–42 and earlier articles in *Journal of Historical Society of the Church in Wales*, v (1955), viii (1958) and ix (1959); P. C. Bartrum, 'Some Studies in Early Welsh History', *Trans. Hon. Soc. Cymm.* (1948), 279–302.

---

[1] W. E. Davies, 'The Early Charter Memoranda of the Book of Llandaff'. London Ph.D. thesis (1970). I am indebted to Dr Davies and the University of London for permission to cite this thesis. It should be noted that Dr Davies now regards the documents as charters rather than as charter memoranda.

[2] See in particular *N.L.W.J.*, iii (1943–44), 29–32, 158–62.

edited, brought into a uniform framework by an editor in the early twelfth century. Although in many cases there are no parallels at all, other formulae used in these edited charters have multiple affinities and associations, Anglo-Saxon, Celtic, papal and continental, but the predominant source for parallel formulae is the group of diplomas compiled and fabricated at Worcester in the late eleventh century. Urban was probably a priest of Worcester before he became bishop of Llandaff in 1107. This likely contact between the Llandaff and Worcester scriptoria early in the twelfth century explains the diplomatic affinities between the *Liber Landavensis* and the Worcester charters, most notably those in Hemming's Cartulary.[1]

But the charters in the Book of Llandaff are not forged in the way that charters were forged at Worcester, Westminster, Canterbury, Durham or Wix:[2] for, unlike all these others, the Llandaff charters are useless (except for bolstering claims to the antiquity of the diocese). The Llandaff charters do not simulate early charter forms, and, even more important, they do not contain the details about property, income or privileges, which are essential features of twelfth-century title-deeds. In short, it is impossible to regard the Llandaff charters as anything remotely comparable to the Anglo-Norman forgeries.

What then are they? The connection between Llandaff and Worcester explains why the predominant influence on Llandaff formulae which can be paralleled is Anglo-Saxon. But the Anglo-Saxon parallels are only part of the story, for there are many formulae for which no parallels at all can be found. Most of these formulae must stem from the Celtic charter tradition,

[1] W. E. Davies, 'St Mary's, Worcester, and the *Liber Landavensis*', *Journal of Society of Archivists*, iv (1970–73), forthcoming.

[2] Cf. P. Chaplais and C. N. L. Brooke in *A Medieval Miscellany for Doris Mary Stenton*, ed. P. M. Barnes and C. F. Slade (Pipe Roll Society, new series xxxvi for 1960, London 1962), 45–64, 89–110; W. Levison, *England and the Continent in the Eighth Century* (Oxford 1946), Appendix 1; G. V. Scammell, *Hugh du Puiset, Bishop of Durham* (Cambridge 1956), Appendix 4; R. W. Southern, 'The Canterbury Forgeries', *English Historical Review*, lxxiii (1958), 193–226.

which is quite separate from the Anglo-Saxon or Frankish. The witness-lists in the Llandaff charters contain names so consistently inter-related that they, and the documents of which they formed a part, must indeed date from the sixth and subsequent centuries, although their chronological order has been disturbed as the twelfth-century editor fitted them into his list of successive bishops 'of Llandaff'. Accordingly in the Llandaff charters there is a genuine core of information drawn from extraordinarily early documents. Used in conjunction with surviving Celtic documents, such as the marginalia of the Lichfield Gospels or the Bodmin Gospels or the Breton 'cartulary' of Landévennec, they form a vital part of the evidence for the independent development of the Celtic charter. Judiciously used, they contain a great deal of information about the darkest age of Welsh history.[1] Dr Davies, furthermore, has compiled a critical list of the charters up to the ninth century, giving a preliminary guide to the 'potential validity' of each. In default of the critical edition of all the charters which, I hope, she will produce, this appendix to her thesis is a convenient introduction to individual charters.[2]

The investigation of pre-Conquest South Wales has been put on a new footing by Wendy Davies. The Book of Llandaff can now, for the first time, be used with some properly established criteria of criticism. The implications for Celtic scholarship as a whole are very extensive.

Besides the Book of Llandaff other episcopal compilations seem rather unexciting, but there are three of importance. The 'Black Book of St David's' is the most significant of these. Like the 'Red Book of St Asaph', it no longer exists in its medieval form with coloured binding: unlike the Red Book, its text survives intact and it has been printed, with a facing translation, by J. W. Willis-Bund in the Cymmrodorion Record Series in 1902. Unfortunately, Dr Conway Davies has shaken the faith of anyone using only the printed version by pointing to inaccuracies and corruptions both in the Latin and in the translation. Like so many important projects, the necessary new edition shows no sign of

---

[1] W. E. Davies, thesis, sections 2 and 3.    [2] *Ibid.*, Appendix 1, 347–80.

being accomplished. It is questionable whether one is better off with no edition of the Red Book, and necessary recourse to the manuscripts, or with an untrustworthy edition of the Black Book, which drives one to the manuscripts to check everything. In fact probably only one manuscript requires to be compared with Willis-Bund's edition, British Museum Additional MS 34135 which he used. The Welsh Church's copy, now in the National Library, seems to be a copy of the British Museum manuscript.[1]

The Black Book is of prime importance to Welsh medieval historians, not simply ecclesiastical historians but everyone interested in the survival of Welsh law and custom after the Norman invasion of South Wales. For this superbly detailed extent of the temporalities of St David's, compiled in 1326, is a comprehensive survey of episcopal rights over the tenants of the largest, most ancient and least disrupted of Welsh dioceses. It is indeed 'a miniature Domesday Book':[2] and it offers rewards and difficulties of a range very similar to those offered by Domesday. But whereas scholars such as Round, Ballard, Eyton, Maitland, Galbraith, Darby and Finn have made possible highly sophisticated use of Domesday, there are no studies of the Black Book in any sense comparable.

The most important of the remaining documents is a collection made in the fifteenth century for the bishop of St Asaph.[3] This volume of twenty-four folios, like the much larger Acta 3 of Bangor, is in need of an editor: at present there is no available guide to its contents, much less an analysis of them. It begins by quoting from 'an old book of customs at London, of liberties and privilege granted to St Kentigern and his successors', proceeds with a description of the lands of St Asaph, and records six cases from the secular pleas at Flint in the reigns of Edward III and Richard II. But the most substantial part of the book is taken up with a very detailed rental of Llanelwy arranged under *gwelyau*, listing each member of each *gwely*, his holdings with the acres and rods in

[1] J. C. Davies, 'The Black Book of St David's', *N.L.W.J.*, iv (1945–46), 158–76.
[2] *Ibid.*, 162.    [3] N.L.W., SA/MB/22.

each and his total rent for his total acreage. This rental extends from fos. 6 to 18. At the end of fo. 18d an eighteenth-century quill, doubtless guided by Browne Willis,[1] noted 'desunt harum Rationum circa 5 folia': this is presumably based on the observation in the memoranda copied on fo. 19r that there are seven named *gwelyau* in Llanelwy, whereas the rental accounts for only five of these.

The next four pages (fos. 19d–21r) contain detailed extents of the bishop's rents and demesnes, and the remainder of the book contains miscellaneous transcripts. Memoranda on fo. 21d relate matters about Rhuddlan in Henry III's reign and give a brief recital of an arbitration in 1260, between Prince Llywelyn and the bishop, over Henllan in Denbighshire. Another copy of a case recorded on fo. 4 is given. This arose from an enquiry into the township of Vaynol and its six *gwelyau*, heard at Flint on 24 May 1350 following an inquisition by the justices of Chester at Rhuddlan on 1 April.[2] The volume ends with some partly mutilated material from early in Richard II's reign.

I have outlined the contents of this *Liber Antiquus* simply because it is so rare to find such a thing still among Welsh episcopal records, and because there is at present no way for anyone not actually in Aberystwyth to assess its relevance to his own interests (unless he has access to the brief description in the schedule of the Church's deposit, which can be seen at Bangor, Cardiff and other Welsh cathedral registries).

Bangor's Acta 3 is of the same genus. It contains *inter alia* an extent of the lands of the bishop of Bangor and copies of documents about episcopal rights: for example, the deposition of twelve Welsh jurors in 1325 about the payment of *amobyr* in Llanelidan, or the important *inspeximus* of the arrangement made on 27 November 1286 between Bishop Anian and Reynold Lord Grey of Wilton, the new master of Dyffryn Clwyd, over the ecclesiastical organisation of the deanery-lordship.

[1] Browne Willis wrote a *Survey of St Asaph* as well as of Bangor.
[2] A translation of this record, made in the eighteenth or nineteenth century, is also preserved in the St Asaph archive, N.L.W., SA/Misc./196.

Evidences of the temporalities and their administration can be found elsewhere among the archives of other individuals and institutions on whom the activities of the Welsh bishops impinged. But the tally does not seem to be very large. Even in the records of the Archbishop of Canterbury, who must at some time have received copies of many Welsh diocesan records, particularly during vacancies, there are few remaining. It is very unfortunate that, for example, among all the Carte Miscellanee at Lambeth there appears to be only one Welsh episcopal account, for St David's in 1415,[1] or that the only Llandaff document is a list of procurations payable to the archbishop after the death of Bishop Miles Salley in 1516/17,[2] or that the only Bangor document is a sixteenth-century valuation of spiritualities in the deaneries of Ceinmeirch and Dyffryn Clwyd which do not add much to knowledge.[3]

Throughout almost the whole of the period covered by this book, Wales was part of the Church universal. The long arm of Rome was felt in Wales as the ultimate ecclesiastical power. Papal provisions to benefices, judgments on legal appeals to the curia, answers to petitions of varied types, instructions to papal legates, arrangements for the collection of papal revenues and such things affected Wales as they affected other parts of Christian Europe. The problems of the schism also touched Wales, for Owain Glyndŵr sought to recognise the anti-pope Benedict XIII. Fortunately for the student, generations of work by British scholars at the Vatican and the enlightened publishing policy of Her Majesty's Stationery Office have much reduced the need for a visit to Rome. They have reduced it but not eliminated it. Although the publication of adequate calendars of documents touching on Great Britain and Ireland now covers the Vatican

[1] Lambeth Palace, Carte Miscellanee, xiii, 43. See D. M. Owen, *A Catalogue of Lambeth Manuscripts 889 to 901* (London 1968), 146.

[2] Lambeth Palace, Carte Miscellanee, ii, 82 (Owen, 38). The date must be 1516/17 since this was the only vacancy in Llandaff while Warham was archbishop.

[3] Lambeth Palace, Carte Miscellanee, vi, 35 (Owen, 81).

registers from 1198 to 1492 and the registers of petitions from
1342 to 1419, they do not regularly include documents about
English possessions overseas. Much more important, the separate
series of 'Avignon' registers covering 1316 to 1418 has not been
included in the British calendars: yet only forty-five out of 349
'Avignon' volumes are duplicates of Vatican registers in the so-
called Secret Archives. In particular most of the letters of Innocent
VI, Urban V and Gregory XI were not transcribed into the
Vatican registers from the Avignon registers and, of course, the
letters of the schismatic anti-popes were not copied at all save in
their own ('Avignon') registers.

The calendars of petitions stop short in 1419, but the series of
registers of supplications extends on majestically in Rome.
Students of Scottish history are much in the debt of Mrs Annie
Dunlop who has culled the supplications relevant to Scotland
up to the late fifteenth century; Irish scholars have access to
microfilms of British as well as Irish extracts for 1342 to 1421 and
1469 to 1472 held by the National Library in Dublin; but Welsh
historians have no such aids, although, for example, the potential
relevance of the register of Benedict XIII to Welsh studies is
obvious and the later fifteenth-century supplications would
certainly cast light on dark, unregistered Welsh dioceses.

As it is, the calendars available, supplemented by publications
of French and German scholars, supply a great deal of information
about the state of the medieval Church in Wales: in the absence of
most episcopal registers, the records of institutions and provisions
contained in the papal registers is of basic importance.[1]

The financial needs of the papacy also created documents
containing essential information about Wales. Valuations of
England and Wales were prepared as the basis for the assessment
of papal taxation of the clergy, and three fairly comprehensive
valuations survive. The earliest was organised by Walter Suffield,
bishop of Norwich, and two other leading clerics, in 1254, and

[1] The essential introduction is L. Macfarlane, 'The Vatican Archives, with
Special Reference to Sources for British Medieval History', *Archives*, iv (1959-
60), 29-44, 84-101.

revised in 1255 and 1256: it is known, rather misleadingly, as the Valuation of Norwich. This was superseded, both for papal and royal taxation of the clergy, in 1291 by the better-known valuation compiled on the order of Nicholas IV; so, lacking subsequent practical use, copies of the 1254–56 valuation became rare and only the labours of Professor Lunt half a century ago reassembled the scattered copies for eight dioceses, including Llandaff, St Asaph and Bangor, as well as some religious houses, including all the churches held by Brecon priory.[1]

Although the values put on temporalities and spiritualities by the bishop of Norwich and his colleagues were certainly too low, this was true of most medieval assessments. It was, however, less true of the next major valuation of clerical incomes, for the *Taxatio Nicholai* in 1291, was compiled by methods which 'should have produced a closer approximation to the desired standard of estimation than the machinery employed in 1254'.[2] The *Taxatio* of 1291 contains all four Welsh dioceses: but it excludes all benefices worth less than six marks ($£4$) a year.[3] Many small Welsh churches are not included as a result. There are, for example, seventy-two churches listed in Anglesey in the Valuation of Norwich, but only twelve in 1291, although Caer Gybi and its chapels were omitted in 1254 and included in 1291.[4]

The *Taxatio Nicholai* remained the basis for clerical taxation until the Reformation, when Thomas Cromwell, in one of his 'most remarkable administrative exploits', organised the compilation of the *Valor Ecclesiasticus*, 'the most informative single source on the economic history of the Tudor Church'.[5] If the Black

---

[1] *The Valuation of Norwich*, ed. W. E. Lunt (Oxford 1926).

[2] *Ibid.*, 155.

[3] *Taxatio Ecclesiastica Angliae et Walliae Auctoritate P. Nicholai IV circa A.D. 1291* (Record Commission, London 1802).

[4] Cf. G. R. J. Jones, 'The Distribution of Medieval Settlement in Anglesey', *Trans. Anglesey Antiquarian Society and Field Club* (1955), 51, 53.

[5] A. G. Dickens, *The English Reformation* (London 1964), 121. The *Valor* was published by the Record Commission in six huge volumes between 1810 and 1834.

Book of St David's was bishop Martin's Little Domesday, then the *Valor Ecclesiasticus* was Cromwell's Great Domesday.

The *Valor*, unlike the earlier assessments, was not, of course, under papal auspices: and, although papal initiative created the valuations of 1254 and 1291, these valuations were of such utility to the English king that they belong to the ecclesiastical and public records of England as much as to those of Rome. The Valuation of Norwich in fact survives only in scattered fragments, sometimes in cartularies and chronicles of monastic houses, and only one section (for the archdeaconry of Northumberland) exists among the taxation records in the Public Record Office. But the *Taxatio Nicholai*, as the basis of clerical taxation for over 240 years, survives more or less complete in the Public Record Office, copied in the Exchequer in 1294 from the collectors' rolls, and copies, complete or selective, exist all over England. But both assessments are essentially documents created by the papacy, and the records of the papal collectors, kept among the archives of the apostolic Camera in the Vatican, should be used in conjunction with them and the English clerical subsidy rolls. The collection of papal tenths, subsidies and annates all depended on the valuations, although other revenues such as Peter's pence, census (a payment by a religious house in return for papal protection or exemption) and visitation tax (payments required for each obligatory triennial visit by the bishops and some abbots to the tombs of the apostles, usually done by proxy) were independently assessed.[1] In the *collectoriae* section of the cameral archives, there are over five hundred volumes of reports and accounts from papal collectors throughout Europe between 1274 and 1447: those relevant to England and Wales have been posthumously printed in full transcription by Professor Lunt,[2] who also made

[1] W. E. Lunt, *Financial Relations of the Papacy with England to 1327* (Cambridge, Mass., 1939), and *Financial Relations of the Papacy with England, 1327–1534* (Cambridge, Mass., 1962).

[2] *Accounts Rendered by Papal Collectors in England, 1317–1378*, transcribed, annotated and introduced by W. E. Lunt, ed. E. B. Graves (Memoirs of American Philosophical Society, lxx, Philadelphia 1968).

available a great deal of the English material in the separate collection of *Quindennia* records of the fifteenth century. Largely unpublished and untapped, however, is the collection known as *diversa cameralia*, beginning in 1389, containing the administrative correspondence of the financial department of the papacy: the Scottish material was made available in 1934 by the future Mrs Dunlop, but the English references are too little known. An inventory of the *diversa*, volume by volume, is available in the Index Room of the Vatican Archives.[1]

There is more than simple financial information to be gleaned from these taxation records. Mr G. R. J. Jones, for example, has found the Valuation of Norwich very valuable for settlement studies: since it includes the small churches omitted in the *Taxatio* it allows parochial plotting which gives a settlement pattern coinciding 'in almost every detail' with the independent plotting of settlement *nuclei*.[2] The accounts of Arnald Garnerii, papal collector from 1371 to 1379, give a wealth of information about provisions to benefices, extending back beyond his period of accountancy.[3] But they are basically financial documents, and on the papal valuations royal taxation of the English and Welsh clergy was assessed: and royal taxation produces government records.

The clerical subsidy records for Wales are even more sparse than the lay. Only the diocese of Llandaff, so ill-served by its own records, is adequately documented. Collectors' certificates for parts of the diocese exist off and on from 1370 to 1445, with a more substantial series from 1461 to 1517.[4] These should be used in conjunction with the *Taxatio Nicholai*.

Those who wish to pursue taxation should bear in mind that the royal collectors had difficulties, just as papal collectors did,

[1] Macfarlane, *Archives*, iv (1959–60), 40–3. Mrs Dunlop published the Scottish extracts from the *quindennia* as A. I. Cameron, *The Apostolic Camera and Scottish Benefices, 1418–1488* (Edinburgh 1934).

[2] G. R. J. Jones, *Trans. Anglesey Antiq. Soc. and Field Club* (1955), 51–3.

[3] *Accounts Rendered by Papal Collectors*, trans. Lunt, 363–541; e.g., St Asaph's, 386.

[4] P.R.O., Exchequer, Subsidy Rolls, E. 179/33/1–18; 279/67–9.

and that evidence for these difficulties lies in very diverse places: chronicles, Early Chancery Proceedings, the Rolls of Parliament, Ancient Petitions, Chancery enrolments and the like. For example, the story of the wretched abbot of Tintern, collector of clerical subsidies for the bishop of Llandaff in Richard II's reign, is a necessary part of the history of taxation and Church life in Wales, but it cannot be guessed at from the formal subsidy records, or from any of the ecclesiastical archives. Instead it has to be pieced together from a wide variety of sources.

The abbot faced the problem that Margam, Neath and Llantarnam were all exempt jurisdictions: the bishop of Llandaff could not coerce them nor did the royal writ run in these parts. It is a test case for ecclesiastical liberties in the march. The king asked the appropriate marcher lords to arrange for the collection of taxation, but nothing happened. The Exchequer, perturbed at the non-arrival of the money, blamed the abbot, who had technical responsibility as collector, and issued writs of distraint against the English lands of Tintern to make up the deficit. This was unfair to the abbot, perhaps, but the Exchequer had its duty to perform too. The abbot petitioned King Richard in 1380 and the King asked the Treasurer to discharge the abbot and turn screws on Margam, Neath and Llantarnam instead. This was the end for the moment, but the abbot of Tintern was again appointed collector for successive clerical subsidies in Llandaff between 1383 and 1389. By 1386 about one hundred clergy of the diocese were in arrears. They suffered the ecclesiastical penalty of excommunication, Chancery issued the writs of *significavit*, making their state public, and the Exchequer issued writs asking the lords of the march to put them into prison. Nothing seems to have been done, and by 1391 the payment of the subsidies was even more in arrears. The Exchequer tried again to distrain on the property of Tintern and the abbot petitioned parliament. He was allowed a respite from distraint until the next parliament and was exempt from the need of accepting a position as collector for seven years. The council examined the position and decided that the bishop of Llandaff must signify to the lords marcher the names of the clergy who had been excommunicated for refusal to pay, and the sums which they owed to the government (figures which the bishop had to obtain from the abbot). To ensure success, letters under the privy seal were addressed both to the bishop and to the lords marcher setting all this out. But the letters were all sent to the bishop, who would be expected to send on the privy seals to the relevant magnates. Unfortunately, the government did not enclose a covering letter ordering the bishop to send them on and the bishop cleverly evaded this unpleasant task by sending the bundle of letters on to the abbot of Tintern. The abbot said that he dared not deliver the letters to the tough lords of the march: it was as much as his life was worth. So the abbot asked the bureaucrats in Westminster to instruct the bishop specifically to do it himself. By the time action had been taken it was 1396 and bishop Barret was on his death-bed, so again action lapsed. The Exchequer kept on grimly trying to distrain on Tintern lands and the abbot had to petition against it in 1399 and again in 1401. By this date the personnel in the march had, of course, changed dramatically, and a good deal of land in the diocese of Llandaff was in the hands of Henry IV. Even so, the royal orders to his ministers to levy the arrears of the clerical tenths were still unsuccessful. Since the money was still owing, the Exchequer attached Tintern yet again. Not until November 1407 did the abbot of Tintern finally gain release, when King Henry pardoned him all arrears from tenths due to Richard II: but since the ostensible reason for this clemency was the damage done to Tintern by the Welsh during the Glyndŵr revolt, the abbey did not gain materially; it merely avoided still further loss.[1]

I have told this story simply to demonstrate the interdependence of medieval records. The references in the footnote speak loudly enough without further comment.

[1] *Calendar of Close Rolls, 1377–1381*, 297–8; *1389–1392*, 507; *Calendar of Patent Rolls, 1389–1392*, 511; *1405–1408*, 378; *Rotuli Parliamentorum* (London 1783) iii, 481, 521; P.R.O., Special Collections, Ancient Petitions, S.C. 8/143/7124, 7126–7, 7136; 144/7160, 7162, 7166; 216/10778; 217/10839; 22/1074, 1100.

As well as valuations for taxation purposes or for the information of Thomas Cromwell's administration, there are scattered official valuations of individual religious houses or accounts of episcopal temporalities. The valuations were made at the time of the dissolution or confiscation of alien priories during the Hundred Years' War. Since there was a strong feeling that monastic establishments in England which were legally cells or dependencies of abbeys in enemy France should not retain their liaison (which implied that English revenues might be sent to 'the adversary of France'), the governments of Edward III and, more especially, Henry V, took into the king's hands or actually dissolved many such houses. As a result, accounts and valuations of these alien priories appear in the public records. Few, however, were in Wales, and fewer still are documented.[1]

The dissolution of the monasteries under Henry VIII brought into crown hands many of the archives of religious houses throughout England and Wales, and the further dissolution of chantries by Edward VI produced the so-called 'Chantry Certificates'. Although these documents and the investigations they record lie outside the period of this book, they should not be ignored, because they give the best systematic survey available of late medieval chantries. No new chantries had been created in the years between 1543 and their dissolution, and the certificates are as a result a necessary source for these pious endowments in the late Middle Ages. The certificates themselves, produced by the royal surveyors, give valuations and information about chantry priests and collegiate clergy: since chantry priests often had cure of souls, the certificates may also give evidence for parochial life. Since, moreover, the existing priests might be re-employed on a different basis once the chantry endowments had been extinguished, there is often comment about the quality of the priest, the needs of his congregation, and the emoluments available from

---

[1] An early example, however, is the valuation of Pembroke Priory (which was not dissolved), made on 28 April 1339, at the very beginning of the war (P.R.O., Chancery Miscellanea, C. 47/10/33/5).

other local sources.[1] Such certificates relate, for example, how a chantry priest was maintained 'chiefly upon the increase of a little stock of cattell preysed to be sold at £11, of all whiche commonly toogether with 3 kynne, 2 heifer & 6 shepe beinge dead this laste wynter by th'othes of the presenters there did acruue in 7 yeres last passed unto Robert Apryse stipendarye there by till the said tyme a clerk yerlie gaine & encreas of 53s 8d'.[2] Or the same certificate for North Wales describes how Ruthin College was 'allso a personage, of bothe whyche the said late warden was incumbent and the towen & paryshe conteynynge in circuyt about five myles wherein be of all sortes 700 houselynge people', and the surveyor recommended that Edward VI endow a vicar and find another priest for Llanrhudd church, suggesting that two of the 'late incumbents maie well serve, of whome Thomas Hughes above named, a man noted to be bothe of good conversacioun & indyfferent lernynge, maie be one'. The tithe and oblations of the collegiate church are rated at twenty marks a year (£13 6s 8d), 'the tenthe not deducted', and might usefully 'be assigned & ther penciouns therbye salved'.[3]

More economic information can be obtained, as for monasteries, from the records created by the purchase of these dissolved chantries and colleges from the crown,[4] from the ministers'

[1] The Chantry Certificates are class E. 301 in the Public Record Office. J. T. Evans published some, for Radnor in *The Church Plate of Radnorshire* (Stow-on-the-Wold 1910), for Carmarthen and Brecknock in similar books in 1907 and 1912. E. D. Jones published a copy of the survey of South Wales chantries which reached the National Library in the Milborne deposit, *Arch. Camb.*, lxxxix (1934), 135–55. A bibliography of such record publications is a major *desideratum*: none of Evans' books, for example, is recorded in *A Bibliography of the History of Wales* (2nd ed. Cardiff 1962).

[2] P.R.O., E. 301/76 rot. 1r.

[3] *Ibid.*

[4] P.R.O., Exchequer, Augmentation Office, Miscellaneous Books, E. 315/67, 68, are great volumes containing information on these sales. An eighteenth-century manuscript index is available in the Round Room (bay 9/3), arranged under the parishes in which the lands (not the chantries) lay. The Welsh certificates in E. 301 are, however, brought together on pp. 519–36 of the old manuscript index (Round Room, bay 9/2). The particulars for grants

accounts while they remained in royal keeping,[1] and from the archives of their new owners.

There is a total absence of parochial records for our period. Registers in any case were only kept from 1538 onwards, and not universally then.[2] It is thought that about one in eight of English parishes has registers of any sort (marriage, baptism or burial) or copies of registers, going back to 1538. The earliest register surviving from any parish in the diocese of Llandaff dates only from 1565 (the marriage-register for Matharn) and only twenty out of the 220 or so parishes in the diocese have registers which start in the sixteenth century at all.[3] In the diocese of Bangor only Conway goes back into Henry VIII's reign, beginning in 1541.[4] By contrast, in the neighbouring county of Hereford, nine parishes have some or all registers beginning in 1538, 1539 or 1540. Shropshire, where five begin in 1538 and seventeen more before 1558, has been vigorous in publication.[5] For basic data about the christenings, marriages and funerals of the Welsh-speaking areas in the marcher counties of England, these registers are indispensable, however far short of a statistical survey they may fall.

Churchwardens' accounts are rare enough in England before the seventeenth century. The earliest of all is the set for St Michael's church in Bath which starts in the year of the Black Death. But

are class E. 318: there is an alphabetical index of grantees in *D.K.R.*, ix (1848), Appendix 2, 148–232, and x (1849), Appendix 2, 223–309.

---

[1] P.R.O., Special Collections, Ministers' Accounts, S.C. 6/Ed. VI.

[2] For parish registers in general, see W. E. Tate, *The Parish Chest* (3rd ed., Cambridge 1969), and F. G. Emmison, *Archives and Local History* (London 1966).

[3] *A Digest of the Parish Registers within the Diocese of Llandaff previous to 1836, together with a table of the Bishops' Transcripts to 1812, now in existence in the bishop's registry, with inventories of the Act Books of the Bishops of Llandaff since 1660 and those of the Dean and Chapter since 1575* (Cardiff 1905).

[4] E. G. Wright, 'A Survey of Parish Records in the Diocese of Bangor', *Trans. Anglesey Antiquarian Society and Field Club* (1959), 45.

[5] *National Index of Parish Registers, v, South Midlands and the Welsh Border*, compiled D. J. Steel, A. E. F. Steel and C. W. Field (London 1966), 75–92, 146. Volumes x and xi, on Wales, have not yet appeared.

J. C. Cox's bibliography of over four hundred such accounts up to 1700 does not include any Welsh examples at all, nor does Dr Blair's substantial addendum to Cox.[1] It is a great pity, for these accounts of building costs, offerings, plate, books, vestments, bequests, and all the miscellaneous costs and income of a parish church put some meat on the bones of local ecclesiastical history.

For parochial life the researcher has to look around, not only among the records described earlier in this chapter, but also among the records of the secular landholders. The court rolls discussed above as 'private records' contain a wealth of information about the parishes of medieval Wales, if one has the patience and imagination to extract it. Whereas in most English parish churches some past antiquary has compiled a list of incumbents from very early times, and right-thinking congregations have had these names inscribed in gold upon a wooden board, this is not possible in most Welsh churches, since the episcopal registers, the basic source of the English lists, are virtually non-existent. To remedy this basic deficiency, one must ransack the seigneurial records of Wales and the marches and combine this incidental information with the calendars of papal letters and petitions and the many-sided records of the English secular government. It is all too possible that such a search may be fruitless for any individual parish (or monastery), but my experience of the Ruthin courts is that a comprehensive series of secular records can shed much light on local ecclesiastical history. Sometimes cases are heard between clerks in the lordship, or between layman and clerk; some clerks enter on property; others stand pledge or witness documents; cases are withdrawn to the episcopal court; the local college figures consistently; records of courts held by

[1] J. C. Cox, *Churchwardens' Accounts from the Fourteenth Century to the Close of the Seventeenth Century* (London 1913), 15–52; L. Blair, *A List of Churchwardens' Accounts* (Ann Arbor 1939). It is possible, though neither Cox nor Blair says so, that Welsh counties were excluded. Some Welsh accounts, unrecorded in these lists, do exist: e.g., Cardiff Central Library has seventeenth-century churchwardens' accounts for Newtown in Montgomery (MS 5.23), Llantwit Fardre (MS 4.1108) and Llangynwyd (MS 5.52), both in Glamorgan.

episcopal officials on the bishops' lands in the lordship are sometimes enrolled with the secular courts.[1]

It is a grave comment on the ecclesiastical archives of Wales
that a survey of them ends with secular court rolls. The lack of
ordinary, straightforward record material is a constant impedi-
ment. Welsh ecclesiastical historians must combine with their
sympathetic understanding of the pre-Reformation Church
superb physical fitness, a love of travel and limitless resourceful-
ness: they are true athletes of Christ.

[1] E.g., P.R.O., S.C. 2/215/71 mm. 3r, 9d; 72 m. 8d (episcopal courts, 1311
to 1313).

# CHAPTER 6

# *The Antiquaries*

The English antiquarian tradition has attracted modern scholars, partly because of the intrinsic worth of the characters concerned, partly because of their place in intellectual history, partly because medievalists (who must use their collections) have developed a proper curiosity. Scholars with interests as diverse as Professor Piggott, Sir Thomas Kendrick, Professor Douglas and Miss McKisack have all found in the antiquaries subjects of absorbing interest and historical value.[1] To study antiquaries is no longer antiquarianism. But, although this is abundantly true of England, Wales lags behind.

Welsh scholars of history, language and literature all use the work of the antiquaries extensively, yet there are no general surveys and few biographical studies. When in 1963 the Board of Celtic Studies prepared a survey of these studies in Wales, it chose the five heads of archaeology, history, the laws, literature and language. There was no sixth category drawing attention to the collectors and antiquaries whose zeal in preservation and transcription made possible modern Celtic studies. Moreover, Professor Dodd took a very limited view of his brief: 'To write of Welsh historiography in the present century is virtually to cover the whole subject, for it is only here that the serious writing of Welsh history begins.' Only Sir John Price (the sixteenth-century defender of Geoffrey of Monmouth) and David Powel gained a mention and there was no attempt at evaluation of anything but

[1] S. Piggott, 'Antiquarian Thought in the Sixteenth and Seventeenth Centuries', *English Historical Scholarship in the Sixteenth and Seventeenth Centuries*, ed. L. Fox (Dugdale Society, London 1956), 93–114, and numerous books and articles; T. D. Kendrick, *British Antiquity* (London 1950); D. C. Douglas, *English Scholars, 1660–1730* (2nd ed. London 1951); M. McKisack, *Medieval History in the Tudor Age* (Oxford 1971).

their 'propagandist' printed work.[1] Nowhere in the entire book is the name of Robert Vaughan even mentioned, although his manuscripts are cited. Such treatment is ungenerous. I am not qualified to write an appreciation of Vaughan and his fellow enthusiasts, but it is high time that those who are qualified were stimulated into doing for the Welsh antiquaries what has been done for the English. My limited purpose in this chapter is to talk briefly about some of the antiquaries whose work I have found significant, and I hope that those whose knowledge and experience are far wider than mine will feel moved to embark on a proper survey.

The two towering figures are George Owen and Robert Vaughan. Owen and Vaughan made very different contributions to our knowledge of old Wales, each in its own way of cardinal importance. George Owen is the principal Welsh representative of Elizabethan topographical scholarship. At the same time as Richard Carew was writing his *Survey of Cornwall* (finally published in 1602), Owen, Pembrokeshire born and bred, the second Owen to be lord of Cemais, was collecting materials for the history of his lordship and his county.[2] The link between Carew and Owen was the author of *Britannia*, William Camden. Although the original purpose of Camden's *Britannia* was to give an account of the island as it was under Roman occupation, with some indication of its medieval development, 'to restore Britain to antiquity, and antiquity to Britain',[3] it was the English 'flesh and blood' which Camden added to the Roman bones that made his work survive as a best-seller in Latin and English into the nineteenth century.[4] The *Britannia* was first translated into English by Philemon Holland in 1610, twenty-

[1] *Celtic Studies in Wales: A Survey*, ed. Elwyn Davies (Cardiff 1963), 49–50.

[2] Cf. *D.W.B.*, *sub* Owen, George. For the destruction of Owen's claim to be descended from the Martins, the medieval lords of Cemais, see J. H. Round, 'The Lords of Kemes', *Family Origins and Other Studies*, ed. W. Page (London 1930), 73–102.

[3] Preface to *Britannia*, translated under the editorship of E. Gibson (London 1695 and 1722). Cf. S. Piggott, 'William Camden and the *Britannia*', *Proceedings of British Academy*, xxxvii (1951), 207–8.    [4] *Ibid.*, 206.

four years after the original Latin version had been printed: the impact of the English translation on Stuart antiquarian tastes was enormous, but the original Latin was no less influential on a smaller circle in England and on a European audience. Long before Holland produced his translation, Camden's influence was felt through his letters and his tours as much as through his printed work. Among his languages was Welsh, among his itineraries was Wales, among his friends was George Owen.

Camden was not the only influence on Owen. Owen was at the centre of a strong group of like-minded men in South Wales. He was a friend of the herald and genealogist Lewys Dwnn. His antiquarian contacts extended to London. When he went there in 1589 to hunt for Pembrokeshire records, Owen met Arthur Agarde, the learned Exchequer official, and Mr Fenton of the Tellers' Office who 'hadd a grete canvas bagg full of Recordes for south wales wherein were bundells Indorsedd com' penbr' cardigan Carmardyn w$^{ch}$ I am promised to have the perusall of'.[1] But the major work which Owen partially completed in 1603 owed more to Carew and Camden than to Agarde: this remarkable antiquarian description of the county which he knew and loved so well was not published in his lifetime, nor did he live to complete the second, topographical, book, describing the county place by place.[2] His materials for the history of Cemais include transcripts of accounts now lost; his 'Treatise of Lordshipps Marchers in Wales' is still quarried by medievalists and Tudor historians; and his treatise discussing where marl is to be found in Wales and how it should be used and has been used is of unique interest to agrarian historians.[3] Scholars still dip into

[1] *The Description of Penbrokshire*, ed. H. Owen (Cymmrodorion Record Series i), ii (1897), 371.

[2] Twenty folios of this uncompleted second book survive, edited and introduced by B. G. Charles, 'The Second Book of George Owen's *Description of Pembrokeshire*', *N.L.W.J.*, v (1947–48), 265–85.

[3] All of these except the treatise on marl are in print, either in Henry Owen's edition of George Owen's work for the Cymmrodorion Record Series, i (4 vols. London 1892–1936) or in *Baronia de Kemeys*, a supplementary volume to *Arch. Camb.* (London 1862). The treatise on marl survives in a century-later

his book of miscellaneous information, 'The Taylors Cussion', and pull out useful snippets:

> 'The Taylors cussion made of shreedes
> of divers peeces hath a patch
> so he that all this volume reedes
> of divers thinges shall finde a snatch
> Therefore this booke of others all
> the taylors cussion do I call.'[1]

But despite this considerable achievement of description and transcription, of antiquarian and genealogical research, Owen published nothing except the charming map of Pembrokeshire which, at Camden's request, he drew in 1602. This map was engraved by William Kip and published in the 1607 edition of the *Britannia*, the first edition to contain county maps. Although Camden could have used the Pembrokeshire map prepared by Christopher Saxton in 1578, he preferred his friend's map in 1607: and, although Owen's map is worthy of the company it keeps, it must be admitted that his representation of the coast from St David's to Cardigan is notably inaccurate.[2]

Despite this virtual failure to publish, Owen's manuscripts were seen, copied and distributed among Welsh antiquaries. Richard Fenton's edition of the *Description* and his use of Owen's manuscripts in his *Historical Tour through Pembrokeshire* brought Owen a wider audience in the nineteenth century, but several of the treatises would not have survived so long had it not been for the circulation of manuscript copies: the autograph of the work on marl, for example, cannot now be found.

Among those who used Owen's manuscripts was Robert

transcript in the Vairdre Book (N.L.W., Bronwydd MSS (first deposit), 3, fos. 218r–222d) and in a transcript of that transcript in Cardiff Central Library, MS 4.35.

---

[1] *The Taylors Cussion*, ed. in facsimile E. M. Pritchard (London 1906), fo. 1.
[2] Cf. F. J. North, 'Humphrey Lhuyd's Maps of England and of Wales', *Arch. Camb.*, xcii (1937), 35–6.

Vaughan. Vaughan belonged to the next generation of antiquaries. Born about 1592, he was at Oxford when Owen died in 1613, he married soon after Camden's death ten years later, and on marriage settled at Hengwrt, a country estate in Merioneth. The rest of Vaughan's seventy-five years were spent in accumulating the collection of manuscripts which has made the name of Hengwrt famous. Vaughan is the Robert Cotton of Wales, as Owen was the Camden of Cemais. Without Vaughan most of the major manuscripts of medieval Wales would almost certainly have perished. Like Owen, Vaughan published virtually nothing, only a small, but learned, book called *British Antiquities Revived*.[1] Like Owen, too, Vaughan was a tireless transcriber and a vigorous correspondent. But his tastes and interests went far beyond those of Owen. Vaughan shared an interest in local history, but indulged much wider literary pursuits, in the chronicles and the poetry of Wales, while also being a first-rate genealogist. As a result, he acquired many of the manuscripts which are now foundation texts for medieval Welsh history and culture. Without the Hengwrt collection, Celtic studies would be immeasurably stinted, yet the Celticists have done Vaughan little honour. There is still no detailed study of this apolitical, scholarly, country gentleman, no analysis of his correspondence (or even any attempt to produce a list of surviving letters by him, to him and referring to him),[2] no examination of his library such as has been accorded the library of his correspondent, Sir Simonds D'Ewes.[3] The tercentenary of Vaughan's death in 1967 passed without any memorial volume, and up to that time the only national attention paid to him had been as an essay topic for the 1948 Eisteddfod.

[1] Oxford 1662; reprinted Bala 1834.
[2] E. D. Jones, 'Robert Vaughan of Hengwrt', *Journal of Merioneth Historical and Record Society*, i (1949–50), 28–30, prints four letters by Vaughan, but there is an unpublished file of his correspondence at Cardiff Central Library, MS 4.76, and letters to or about him are widely scattered.
[3] A. G. Watson, *The Library of Sir Simonds D'Ewes* (London 1966). Cf. the preliminary study of the important library, particularly of manuscripts, made immediately after the Dissolution by Sir John Price (N. Ker, 'Sir John Prise', *The Library*, 5th series, x (1955), 1–24.

Perhaps if someone started now, a suitable tribute could be prepared for 1992.

Even the name of Hengwrt, although familiar, has been obscured by the name of Peniarth on the palimpsest of library notation. The manuscript collection was for two centuries miraculously preserved at Hengwrt without disastrous losses. The good fortune of the manuscripts in remaining together is emphasised by the fate of Vaughan's printed books. 'I am told,' Evan Evans wrote to his fellow-antiquary Lewis Morris in 1764, 'some of the printed books were sold lately for a penny a pound. As the owner is dead, and the small remains of this unlucky library subdivided amongst the deceased's relations, probably some very valuable pieces may be lapt about tobacco and snuff.'[1] The printed books were all dispersed over a period, and some of the manuscripts also disappeared into the hands of acquisitive individuals like Dr Roberts of Dolgellau or John Lloyd of Wigfair, and, as early as 1697, Edward Lhuyd had told one of his correspondents that the Hengwrt manuscript collection 'has been much rifld'.[2] Since Vaughan's own catalogues of his manuscripts survive, it is possible to discover just how many remained at Hengwrt, how many strayed and how many of these strays have survived elsewhere. Those which remained were not well cared for and not easily accessible. When the lexicographer William Owen Pughe managed, with difficulty, to see the library at Hengwrt in 1800 he found 'a vast collection . . . all in confusion and mouldy',[3] but the condition and ultimate fate of the public records at Caernarvon should be remembered to put the mould of Hengwrt into

[1] 'Unpublished Letters of the Rev. Evan Evans', *Arch. Camb.*, 4th series, iii (1872), 61–3. Vaughan's notebook contained an interesting short list of manuscripts and their owners in South Wales, where he had been travelling.

[2] R. T. Gunther, *Early Science in Oxford*, xiv, *Life and Letters of Edward Lhwyd* (Oxford 1945), 348. Lhuyd visited Hengwrt briefly in September 1696 and 'took a catalogue' (309): he had still not had 'recourse to Hengwrt study' in October 1697 (348), but talked more knowledgeably of Vaughan's library in May 1698 (371).

[3] G. Tibbott, 'A Brief History of the Hengwrt–Peniarth Collection', *Handlist of Manuscripts in the National Library of Wales*, i (Aberystwyth 1943), ix, xi.

perspective. A major portion of Vaughan's manuscripts remained intact. The dispersion of the printed books is as much to be regretted as the sale of the printed section of the Harley library, but it is of greater consequence that the Hengwrt manuscripts, like those of the Earls of Oxford, remained together.

Whereas the Earl of Oxford's manuscripts were purchased by the nation in 1753, Vaughan's manuscripts were bequeathed in 1859 to that kindred spirit, W. W. E. Wynne of Peniarth in the same county of Merioneth.[1] So the Hengwrt collection joined Wynne's own important library at Peniarth and Vaughan's manuscripts were renumbered. In due course, Sir John Williams, whose own library at Llanstephan in Carmarthenshire was second only to that at Peniarth, purchased the reversionary interest in the Wynne collection on the condition that it would pass to the proposed National Library of Wales if—and only if—it were built at Aberystwyth. The sheer weight of the monopoly thus created by Sir John Williams produced the royal charter for the National Library two years later in 1907, and in 1909 the death of the last of the Wynnes brought the library its greatest collection.[2] Not only does the National Library owe an incalculable debt to Robert Vaughan, but it also owes its very existence at Aberystwyth to him.

The Peniarth-Hengwrt manuscripts, now in their last resting-place, contain, as well as the spectacular literary manuscripts, many transcripts of lost archives. It is from Peniarth 236, for example, that Mr Carr printed the only surviving Edeirnion inquisition; the charter which Hugh Burgh granted to his borough of Mawddwy in 1423, inspecting another charter of

[1] Cf. G. Tibbott, 'William Watkin Edward Wynne', *Journal of Merioneth Historical and Record Society*, i (1949–50), 69–76. Wynne had already been acquiring Vaughan manuscripts: he purchased one from Fenton before the bequest (D. L. Evans, 'Llyfr Coch Asaph', *N.L.W.J.*, iv (1945–46), 181).

[2] National Library of Wales, *Charter of Incorporation and Report on the Progress of the Library* (Oswestry 1909), 33; *D.W.B.*, *sub* Wynne family and Williams, Sir John; G. Tibbott, 'The National Library of Wales and its Charter', *N.L.W.J.*, v (1947–48), 89.

1394, survives only in the same manuscript;[1] the 'Redd Booke of Caures Castle', which was that rare bird, a baronial commonplace book of the fifteenth century, was copied into Peniarth 280: and these are casually chosen instances.

Owen and Vaughan have, in different ways, influenced Welsh historiography very deeply, but they are only the best known and most superficially accessible of their kind. They require a context. Their English context, the world of Leland, Camden, Cotton, Selden, Ussher, is tolerably familiar, but Owen and Vaughan have been insufficiently related to it. Even more serious, there is very little secondary literature about their Welsh contemporaries and successors. The English predecessors of Camden, who touched Wales on their travels, have had more appreciation, even in Wales, than the native Welsh transcribers and collectors to whom the debt of scholarship is no less. The *Itineraries* of the retired fifteenth-century steward, William Worcestre, the earliest English antiquary, contain very interesting descriptions of the fauna on Welsh islands, lists of Welsh casualties at battles during the Wars of the Roses and notes on Welsh religious houses.[2] John Leland's far more important *Itinerary in Wales*, too, is available still in an admirable annotated edition:[3] it is an indispensable source of curious information and description of early Tudor Wales, although Leland was not Welsh and not primarily concerned with Wales. The very volume edited by Miss Toulmin Smith is her compilation of a Welsh itinerary from the less

---

[1] A. D. Carr, 'An Edeirnion Inquisition, 1390', *Journal of Meroneth Historical and Record Society*, vi (1969–70), 1–7; B. G. Charles, 'Merioneth Records: Court Rolls and other Records of the Borough of Dinas Mawddwy and the Manor of Mawddwy', *ibid.*, i (1949–50), 44–7. Cf. the small book of notes from Merioneth inquisitions of the fourteenth and fifteenth centuries in Peniarth MS 279, ed. W. W. E. Wynne in *Arch. Camb.*, orig. series, i (1846), 396–403.

[2] William Worcestre, *Itineraries*, ed. J. H. Harvey (Oxford Medieval Texts, Oxford 1969); C. Z. Hulbert-Powell, 'Allusions to the Isle of Anglesey in the Itinerarium of William Worcester', *Trans. Anglesey Antiquarian Society and Field Club* (1949), 25–37.

[3] *The Itinerary in Wales of John Leland In or About the Years 1536–1539*, ed. L. T. Smith (London 1906, vol. iii of *Itineraries in England and Wales*).

systematic entries in Leland's manuscripts. It is right that Leland's collection should be used extensively for Welsh Tudor and medieval studies: modern scholars recognise the value of Leland, just as Robert Vaughan did (Vaughan borrowed John Stow's copy of Leland's autograph and in turn copied it for himself).[1] But the extensive sources for antiquarian scholarship inside Wales are still largely unexploited.

A certain amount of interest has been shown, however, in genealogists, mainly by other genealogists: Owen's younger friend George William Griffith of Penybenglog;[2] George Owen Harry, who held a Cemais living which was in George Owen's gift and visited Henllys regularly for some thirty years;[3] Lewys Dwnn, whose 'visitations' were published after two hundred years by Sir Samuel Meyrick;[4] John Williams, whose *Llyfr Baglan* deserves study as a glorification of the Herberts;[5] and many others commemorated through the pages of the *Dictionary of Welsh Biography* and the work of the Wales Herald Extraordinary.

For many of these scholars there may be insufficient materials for extensive study, but until more information is available not just about individuals but about contacts between them by letter and visit, about the descent and transcription of manuscripts, genealogical, literary and historical, the context of Owen and Vaughan remains ill-defined. Sometimes centenaries will assist, although Vaughan's was ignored. Sir John Wynn's *History of the Gwydir Family* was last edited in 1927, on the tercentenary of his death. Humphrey Llwyd, who was one of the vital links in the creation of Powel's *Historie of Cambria* and whose map of Wales was published in the 1573 edition of Ortelius' great atlas, the *Theatrum Orbis Terrarum*, was celebrated in his native Denbigh

[1] N. L. W., Peniarth MS 273.

[2] Francis Jones, 'An Approach to Welsh Genealogy', *Trans. Hon. Soc. Cymm.* (1948), 407–9; *D.W.B.*

[3] Jones, 382–3; *D.W.B.*

[4] *Heraldic Visitations of Wales by Lewys Dwnn*, ed. S. R. Meyrick (Llandovery 1846); Jones, 375–7; *D.W.B.*

[5] John Williams, *Llyfr Baglan, 1600–7*, ed. J. A. Bradney (London 1910); Jones, 377–8; not in *D.W.B.*

in 1968.[1] But scholarship cannot be wholly dependent on centennial piety.

The age of Owen and Vaughan bristles with absorbing problems, particularly about the ownership and accessibility of manuscripts. Part of the history of the gentry is their attitude towards learning. But this does not simply enlarge the horizons of social historians: it also supplies essential information about the descent of texts, the reliability of transcripts, the libraries in which manuscripts survived three or four hundred years ago. There is a strong *prima facie* case for thinking that until more comprehensive and inter-relating studies of the heroic period of antiquarianism are published the historian is denied something that may be of service to him.

This is perhaps most true of the sixteenth and seventeenth centuries, but knowledge of the more recent antiquaries has also more than pious interest. The learned archdeacons, Henry Thomas Payne of Carmarthen, Edward Yardley of Cardigan and, much less significantly, Richard Newcome of Merioneth, are worthy of study, and ecclesiastical historians have good reason to be grateful for their efforts. Both Yardley and Payne were concerned primarily with the see of St David's, Yardley, a Londoner, moving to St David's in 1739, Payne going there from Brecknock in 1814. Yardley's manuscript collection of biographies covering all officials of the diocese, bishops, precentors, chancellors, treasurers, archdeacons and prebendaries, was not printed in his lifetime, although as early as 1746 Browne Willis wrote to him urging publication: 'Tis a debt you owe the World & will be the greatest act of gratitude you can shew y[t] worthy & generous Patron; & so pray by no means delay it.'[2] But Yardley did not discharge this debt and his *Menevia Sacra* survived only by finding its way into the Earl of Cawdor's library at Stackpole.

---

[1] R. Geraint Gruffydd, 'Humphrey Llwyd of Denbigh; some Documents and a Catalogue', *Trans. Denbighshire Historical Society*, xvii (1968). Llwyd died in 1568. Cf. *D.W.B.*, *sub* Llwyd.

[2] E. Yardley, *Menevia Sacra*, ed. F. Green (Cambrian Archaeological Association, supplementary volume, London 1927), iv.

The fifteenth-century registers of Bishops Nicholls and Rodburn
which he cites were less fortunate, so Yardley's precise references
to them have an especial value. But his description of the buildings
and Lord's plan of the cathedral close are also useful.[1]

Payne, who was a boy of eleven when Yardley died in 1759,
was one in a line of collectors and arrangers of the cathedral
statutes. In his two large volumes of 'Collectanea Menevensia',
however, he gave many extracts from documents then (1820 to
1825) in the capitular archives. Not all of these records survive
and Payne's collections will supplement work on the existing
St David's records in Aberystwyth, just as the Bangor and St
Asaph archives can be supplemented from Browne Willis's
appendices to his surveys. In his later years Payne concentrated
on his native Brecknock, and his collection, as he complained,
was 'shamefully used by Theophilus Jones to whom I lent it for
his history of Brecknockshire'. Since Jones's work was the first
of the Welsh county histories, and since old-fashioned county
histories are still basic tools of trade, however deficient their
vision and execution may be, Payne deserves to be remembered
for more than his early manuscript book, written in 1785, describing in words and drawings the topography and customs of
the deanery of the third part of Brecon.[2]

Archdeacon Newcome was a Denbighshire man, born in
Wrexham in 1779, educated at Ruthin and Cambridge, and
warden of Ruthin for forty-seven years from 1804. His con-
tribution to local history was modest, but his account of Ruthin
Castle is still the only one of any value after 142 years and his
*Memoir of Dr Gabriel Goodman* contains useful transcripts.

---

[1] Yardley is ill-served by biographers, but it is plain from Bridget Jones's
introduction to J. le Neve, *Fasti Ecclesiae Anglicanae, 1300–1541*, xi, *The Welsh
Dioceses* (London 1965), v, that he would repay research.

[2] See B. G. Owens, 'Biographica et Bibliographica: Archdeacon Henry
Thomas Payne (1759–1832)', *N.L.W. J.*, iv (1945–46), 210–14. The 'Collectanea'
are in the St David's archive in the National Library, the Brecknock manuscripts are also deposited there as Crickhowell MSS 3, 4 and N.L.W. MS 4278.
Cf. J. C. Davies, 'The Records of the Church in Wales', *N.L.W. J.*, iv (1945–
46), 3.

Newcome is a far more representative figure than Yardley or Payne, but such men, writing the history of their parish, or their archdeaconry, or their diocese, or their county, have nourished the British antiquarian tradition, preserved texts, oral traditions, views of vanished buildings and created the climate out of which the historical discipline could emerge in the later nineteenth century.

The churchmen are characteristically less mobile, however, than the secular tourists. These compilers of 'Tours' become, of course, very numerous in the eighteenth and nineteenth centuries. The tradition goes back to William Worcestre and John Leland, but in Wales the founding father is really Edward Lhuyd. William Camden was as dominating an influence on Lhuyd as he had been on George Owen, although Lhuyd set out on his tour more than seventy years after Camden's death. It was the new translation and edition of the *Britannia* organised by Edmund Gibson that directed Lhuyd's energies in the 1690s. He contributed new Welsh sections to the text printed in 1695 and spent much of the three years from 1697 onwards touring systematically in Wales with a well-trained entourage. Lhuyd's particular interests, outside his scientific and philological work, were archaeological rather than historical, but his position in the history of British archaeology, 'at the end of the first period, at the move from the speculative to the formative', is critical.[1] He began that factual interest in material remains which is essential to any archaeological progress, and archaeology is no less a source for medieval Wales than the written word.

Lhuyd also pioneered the questionnaire and the protracted antiquarian tour in Wales. In 1697 Lhuyd distributed four thousand copies of his 'Parochial Queries', thirty-one questions on antiquities, place-names, manuscripts, customs and natural history, on a printed sheet with space for replies. With 'a sufficient Encouragem[t] from the Gentry of the Country, & several others, Lovers of such Studies', Lhuyd solicited them not to 'omit

[1] Glyn Daniel, 'Edward Lhwyd: Antiquary and Archaeologist', *Welsh History Review*, iii (1966–67), 345–57; *D.W.B.*, *sub* Lhuyd.

such Informations as shall occur to their Thoughts, upon Presumption, they can be of little Use to the Undertaker, or the Publick . . . Seeing that what we sometimes judge insignificant, may afterwards upon some Application unthought of, appear very useful.'[1] The grand scheme was not a complete success, but the notebooks resulting from Lhuyd's tours, in conjunction with the responses of informants, contain a good deal of value, nowhere else recorded. His only published volume of the projected *Archaeologia Britannica* was devoted to comparative philology and the rest remained in manuscript.

Some of these manuscripts of Lhuyd are lost. The bulk of them remained in the possession of the Sebright family for most of the eighteenth century. The Irish section was presented to Trinity College, Dublin, in 1786; some Welsh volumes were bequeathed to the Earl of Macclesfield and ultimately came to the National Library via Llanstephan; the remainder were dispersed at the Sebright sale in April 1807. The two major purchasers were both plagued by fire, but whereas Thomas Johnes of Hafod had lost most of his famous library in the previous month and the Sebright sale was the beginning of his new collection, Watkin Williams Wynn of Wynnstay lost most of his Lhuyd manuscripts when he sent them for rebinding in a Covent Garden shop which was gutted. Johnes's manuscripts were sold after his death and the three volumes published as the first part of *Parochialia* had been at Hafod. The actual returns of his informants together with much of his correspondence had never been in the hands of the Sebrights, but had remained among the Ashmolean manuscripts in Oxford, since Lhuyd, from 1684 until his death, was successively under-keeper and keeper of the Ashmolean Museum.[2]

The surviving manuscripts from Lhuyd's collection show only a part of his polymathic achievement, but his influence was felt widely. One of the activities which he did much to encourage

[1] *Parochialia, being a Summary of Answers to 'Parochial Queries' . . . issued by Edward Lhwyd*, ed. R. H. Morris, 8 (Supplement to *Arch. Camb.*, 1909), ix–x.
[2] The 'Reliquiae Lhuydianae' are now Bodley, Ashmolean MSS 1814–1821, 1825.

was the antiquarian tour. The century after his death produced a spate of published tours. Many of these aspired to no intellectual eminence, but some are useful still.

The most widely read was probably Francis Grose's *Antiquities of England and Wales*, with companion sets for Scotland and (posthumously) for Ireland. These lavishly illustrated books (seven volumes on England, one on Wales) are rather on the level of Sunday colour supplements; the text has little to offer which cannot be better got elsewhere, but the engravings preserve views of castles and abbeys as they were in the eighteenth century. The artists took some licence, particularly in the background environment, but the plates give substance to our visual reconstruction of the present remains of sites like Cardiff Castle.

The slightly earlier tourist, Thomas Pennant, on whose work Grose relied heavily in his Welsh volume, was of much sterner mettle, and for intimate touches of the local scene with well enough informed historical comment he is very useful. Like Lhuyd, though on a lower level of attainment, Pennant was a scientist as well as an antiquary, so birds and geology vied in his enthusiasm with remains of the past. The value of Pennant's popular literary work was sufficient to encourage Sir John Rhŷs to edit the *Tours in Wales* in 1883, just over a century after their first appearance. Moreover, Pennant is linked to Edward Lhuyd and George Owen through Camden's *Britannia*, for, like them, he contributed to the current edition. Just as Lhuyd had collaborated with Edmund Gibson, so Pennant collaborated with Richard Gough, the last editor and translator of the *Britannia*. Wales was only one of Pennant's interests—he himself confessed that 'I am often astonished at the multiplicity of my publications'[1]—but whereas he alone 'overlooked the Northern counties of Wales' for Gough, in the Scottish section he played a subsidiary role to George Paton, the indefatigable and abstemious Edinburgh antiquary.[2]

[1] *The Literary Life of the Late Thomas Pennant, Esq., by Himself* (London 1793) 35.
[2] W. Camden, *Britannia*, ed. R. Gough (1st ed. London 1789, 2nd ed. London 1806), Gough's preface.

Pennant's sales, both for his Welsh and his Scottish tours, were considerable and he had followers, notably Wyndham and Gilpin, even before the French Revolution drove those who would have explored Europe to explore Britain instead. But among the many who wrote of Wales in the age of Napoleon, two inseparable companions stand out: Richard Fenton and Sir Richard Colt Hoare. Fenton was a part-time barrister on the Welsh circuit, with literary and antiquarian tastes, who had been a friend of Goldsmith and Garrick in London, and who was now an indefatigable traveller and transcriber in Wales. Colt Hoare, on the other hand, was one of the wealthiest of the English gentry. His grandfather, Henry Hoare, the banker, had pioneered Augustan landscape gardening at his Wiltshire mansion of Stourhead. This property, though not the bank, came to his only grandson Colt after Henry's death in 1785. Just before Henry's death, Colt's wife Hester had died too young and the double bereavement sent the heir to Stourhead travelling restlessly in Europe until he returned to his inheritance in 1791. From then until his death forty-seven years later two things dominated Colt Hoare's life: his reshaping of Stourhead, which is, as a result, the greatest surviving monument to the younger Thomas Chippendale, and his antiquarian explorations and writings about Wales and his own county of Wiltshire.[1]

Fenton played little part in Hoare's monumental *History of Wiltshire*, although he did stay at Stourhead occasionally. The collaboration which the two friends achieved was principally in riding together around Wales, writing descriptions, making drawings, tracing out the Itinerary of Gerald of Wales six hundred years before, copying inscriptions and 'cracking cromlechs'.[2] The

---

[1] The Hoares, grandfather and grandson, and their achievements in Wiltshire are delightfully portrayed in K. Woodbridge, *Landscape and Antiquity: Aspects of English Culture at Stourhead, 1718 to 1838* (Oxford 1970).

[2] This memorable phrase was coined, and the charge resisted, by Edward Laws in his review of Henry Owen's index to Fenton's *Pembrokeshire*, *Arch. Camb.*, 5th series, xii (1895), 159. Hoare published an edition of Gerald's Itinerary in 1804 and a sumptuous two-volume translation with valuable notes in 1806.

'rape of the barrows'[1] by Hoare, Fenton and their workmen was rather violent and the picnics held in the unstratified debris must appal modern archaeologists: at Everleigh, Fenton, one of his sons, William Coxe and Colt Hoare gave 'The Britons' as a toast while 'amidst the desert of fruit & the sparkling glass stood the rude relicks of 2,000 years'.[2] But Hoare's professional competence was a good influence on Fenton, whom Colt encouraged to collect and publish antiquarian material.

The two conceived the ambitious plan of a series of county histories. Pembrokeshire, which was completed, was to be followed by Caernarvonshire, to judge from the manuscript compilations. Fenton was not the only Welshman with an interest in county histories at this time. In 1805 Theophilus Jones produced the first volume of his *History of the County of Brecknock* (about which archdeacon Payne complained) and the second volume followed four years later. In 1808 Sir Samuel Meyrick published his *History and Antiquities of the County of Cardigan*, 'good enough to court comparison with Owen's [Pembrokeshire] and bad enough to suffer thereby'.[3] So both Brecknock and Cardigan had been dealt with before Fenton finally published his *Historical Tour through Pembrokeshire* in 1811. Just as Jones had used Payne's collections, so Fenton incorporated much of George Owen's work. This widespread interest, arising simultaneously in several counties, did much for Welsh historiography. The English county histories, from Dugdale's Warwickshire through Morant's Essex and Nichols' Leicestershire to Hoare's Wiltshire, are still fundamental reference books despite the Victoria County History, and Wales badly needed something comparable. In fact neither Jones nor Meyrick nor Fenton compares well with the best English county histories, but the effort was important.

More immediately valuable today are Fenton's manuscript collections. Although neither he nor Hoare collected old manu-

---

[1] A chapter-heading in Woodbridge, *Landscape and Antiquity*.

[2] Quoted *ibid.*, 217: 'Desert' equals dessert.

[3] R. E. M. Wheeler, 'Wales and Archaeology', *Proceedings of British Academy*, xv (1929), 328.

scripts like Vaughan—the superb library at Stourhead was entirely of printed books—Fenton was a great transcriber and diarist and his own sixty manuscript volumes survive intact. Sir Thomas Phillipps acquired them from Fenton's youngest son, Samuel, in 1858, and they passed with the major part of Phillipps' Welsh manuscripts to Cardiff in 1896. The journals have been edited as *Tours in Wales (1804-1813)* for the Cambrian Archaeological Association in 1917, but there does not seem to be any proper survey of the collection as a whole and its importance for Welsh history. Probably much of the material is available elsewhere, but much has been lost since Fenton died and some assessment might be rewarding, as well as being a useful archival exercise. One volume, for example, of transcripts from the Plâs Gwyn correspondence includes as well as seventeenth-century letters a very interesting long extract from the great sessions of Denbigh in 1461.[1] Another of his volumes contains an original Haverfordwest deed of 1286,[2] and, in general, one's instinct is that Fenton's collections require more scholarly attention than they have been given.

Probably, too, the extensive archives of Colt Hoare himself, preserved in the Wiltshire County Record Office at Trowbridge and the records of his principal excavator, William Cunnington, in the library of the Wiltshire Archaeological and Natural History Society at Devizes, would produce more information about the antiquities of Wales and their molestation about this time. The memory of Fenton deserves more than piety, and Colt Hoare's place in Welsh historiography still waits to be put beside Mr Woodbridge's treatment of Stourhead and Wiltshire, to round out our knowledge of a remarkable connoisseur and antiquary.

Collectors and patrons such as these were particularly important before public libraries were created. Sir Thomas Phillipps, the greatest bibliophile in English history, kept an interest in Wales. His seat, Middle Hill, was close by in Worcestershire. In 1850 Phillipps wrote to the recently formed Cambrian Archaeological

[1] Cardiff Central Library, MS 2.70, item 301.
[2] Cardiff Central Library, MS 3.20, unfoliated.

Association and said 'that he had noticed with regret the absence of public libraries in Wales, and that he intended to offer his own magnificent collection to be at some central place in the Principality'. Swansea tried to obtain this potential national library, but Phillipps preferred central Wales and suggested Llandovery if someone there would put up a suitable building. The correspondence between Phillipps and Harry Longueville Jones, the co-founder of the *Archaeologia Cambrensis*, is of importance in demonstrating the odds over which the antiquaries had triumphed and their failure to create any general historical appreciation. In January 1851 Longueville Jones wrote to Phillipps from Bangor:

> I do not wish to underrate the intellect of Wales but I do know that great apathy exists as to all that concerns literature, science, or the fine arts. I know of nothing in which my fellow countrymen shew any energy except in mining, drinking—writing half-drunken rhymes for prizes at Eisteddfodau—and embarking in polemical controversy without any theological knowledge.

Longueville Jones argued that the state of Lampeter library, where students were admitted only once a week, 'for fear of reading *too much*?', and where the rain came in on the books, strengthened his general feeling that Phillipps should give his library to the British Museum where it would be just as handy for most Welshmen.

Phillipps noted the advice and filed the letter, but after quarrelling with Panizzi at the Museum he made one of his many draft wills in 1862, returning to his first thought of Swansea. Two years later he toyed with the idea of fitting up the palace at St David's, then he thought of buying Manorbier Castle where Gerald of Wales had been born. Manorbier belonged to the Philipps family of Picton in Pembrokeshire, to which Sir Thomas mistakenly thought himself related, but he abandoned this notion in 1866. A building was erected at Llandovery, at Phillipps's expense, and although a great storm damaged it, repairs were carried out. The gentlemen of Llandovery, however, prevaricated about building a house for the necessary librarian, so Phillipps dismantled the iron building and re-erected it at Picton. The contraption proved damp, however, and he finally abandoned it, and Wales, in 1868.[1]

It is tempting to speculate what impact the successful transplantation of the Phillipps library would have had on intellectual life in Wales. Phillipps was the last and greatest of English bibliomaniacs: he belonged to the last period in which the accumulation of such a library was still a practicable proposition. Had his library been kept intact it would have provided a focus for research on the scale of the Harleian collection at the British Museum. This did not happen, but a large block of manuscripts obviously of interest to Wales was brought together after Sir Thomas's death and sold to Cardiff in 1896. The behaviour of Cardiff's Library Committee was extraordinarily enlightened. Its usual expenditure was around £650 a year and the cost of the seven hundred Phillipps manuscripts was more than five and a half times that, but private benefactors led by John Cory and handsomely helped by Lord Bute contributed or were guarantors, so that half the total was paid in cash and the remainder was spread over ten years.[2]

These seven hundred manuscripts (which seem to have become some four hundred and thirty Cardiff manuscripts, because of composite volumes, but an analysis is needed) might very well have been the basis for a national library in the capital. But it must be recognised that, important as this collection is, it does not contain much material of the fundamental importance of Robert Vaughan's library. Indeed the most valuable single item in the Cardiff purchase, the book of Aneirin, was itself a stray from Hengwrt which had fortunately been taken in at Middle Hill.[3] Sir John Williams was a small-time collector beside Phillipps, but he did bring into public ownership the richest private library ever amassed in Wales.

---

[1] A. N. L. Munby, *Phillipps Studies no. 5: the Dispersal of the Phillipps Library* (Cambridge 1960), 4–10.

[2] *Ibid.*, 31–2.

[3] Historical Manuscripts Commission 48, *Report on Manuscripts in the Welsh Language*, ii (1) (London 1902), 91.

These antiquaries and collectors are constantly inter-relating over the centuries. In one way and another they have provided or preserved a vital portion of the source-material on which Welsh history before 1543 is based. When Rice Lewis compiled his feudal history, the 'Breviat of Glamorgan', late in Elizabeth's reign, he wrote a charming foreword, spelling out the modest hopes of a run-of-the-mill antiquary:

> Gentle Reader no doubt but thou wilt laughe me to scorne, for bindinge up these bundell of papers, wherein thou shalt have occasions enoughe so to doe. But yet sith they were gathered out of many old peeces of paper, and with paines sought for of me in so many odd places, I hope thou wilt beare some thinge the more with me because I looke for no gaine but thy gentle takinge and to be silent, and this hande ready to amend all faultes, for I stande not to please or displease any, but those that have to doe with those Honourable service that hath taught me to knowe the countrey as nowe I doe.[1]

Too many of those old pieces of paper can no longer be found, even in odd places, and insufficient gratitude has been expressed to Lewis and his kin for binding up some of the bundles. The old antiquaries were proud of their work, their country and their predecessors. George Owen, Robert Vaughan, Thomas Pennant, Richard Fenton all belong one to another. Camden's *Britannia* remained a link and an inspiration over the centuries, but the Welsh antiquaries published little of their own in their own lifetimes. Because their notes and collections exist in manuscripts scattered throughout Britain, the task of surveying their achievement has been made harder.

Something of the sort might have been achieved by the Victoria History of the Counties of Wales, but this failed. The attempt was made during the formative period of the great project for England which is still vigorous, but the combined plans

[1] 'A Breviat of Glamorgan, 1596–1600, by Rice Lewis, Bute MSS Box 99D, National Library of Wales (formerly Phillipps MSS No. 13159)', ed. W. Rees, *South Wales and Monmouthshire Record Society Publications*, iii (1954), 95.

of Lord Kenyon, Sir John Williams, Henry Owen and Edward Owen produced no more than a prospectus, proposing two general volumes and forty-eight topographical volumes. By September 1904 all negotiations had been terminated and all Welsh subscribers released.[1] So, although Carmarthenshire produced a two-volume history under Sir John Lloyd's editorship in 1935 and 1939 and although Glamorgan has a County History Committee which produced a natural history volume in 1936 and has a medieval volume in the press now, no Welsh organisation exists to make any comprehensive survey of county materials in antiquaries' collections or anywhere else. The antiquaries should not have as high priority as the public records relating to Wales, but the Board of Celtic Studies might well consider some bibliographical aid, for, unlike the public records, the antiquaries shed equal light on literature and language.

[1] Victoria History of the Counties of England, *General Introduction*, ed. R. B. Pugh (London 1970), 5-6.

# CHAPTER 7

## Archaeology and Numismatics

The material remains of medieval Wales are essential comple-
ments to literary and archival evidence. In some areas of enquiry
they are more equal partners than in others, but there are few
topics which can be treated from exclusively written or exclusively material sources. Although coins are as much archaeological
as castles or barrows, the science of numismatics is so specialised
a part of archaeology that it is best treated separately, but its place
in the wider context of excavation, exploration and dating of
remains should not be forgotten.

## ARCHAEOLOGY

Welsh archaeology is characteristically the archaeology of the
living: Anglo-Saxon archaeology is dominated by the dead. The
grave-goods of so many pagan graves of early England[1] have no
counterpart in the Christian graves of contemporary Wales.
Instead the material evidences for early Welsh history are settlement sites and inscribed stones. The standing stones of still earlier
Wales have value, too, in giving a local habitation to some of the
heroic names in the *Mabinogion* and the 'Stanzas of the Graves',
but, although they allow fascinating detective work and hint at
the processes of rationalisation and connection which created
Welsh stories,[2] they do not really advance historical study very
dramatically.

The interpretation of the settlement sites is made difficult
because of the lack of datable pottery. Since pottery, as Dr Myres

[1] A. L. Meaney, *A Gazetteer of Early Anglo-Saxon Burial Sites* (London 1964),
*passim*.
[2] See T. Jones, 'The Black Book of Carmarthen "Stanzas of the Graves"',
*Proceedings of British Academy*, liii (1967), 112–16.

has recently demonstrated,[1] is a key element in Anglo-Saxon archaeology, the dearth in Wales is a serious handicap. Datable metal objects too are uncommon. As a result, the scanty written sources for the period before the Norman invasions are supplemented inadequately by material remains. It is difficult to make the necessary connections between the archaeological data and the writings of Gildas, Bede, Nennius and the anonymous annalists. The most exciting prospect from settlement excavations certainly arises from the thorough plotting of types of homestead over a wide area. A valuable beginning has been made in the three volumes of *The Inventory of the Ancient Monuments in Caernarvonshire* issued between 1956 and 1964 by the Royal Commission on Ancient and Historical Monuments in Wales and Monmouthshire. The data provided there and the brief analysis of enclosed homesteads and platform houses are basic source material for the vexed question of settlement patterns in very early Wales and for the transhumance up to the summer pastures and the *hafotai*.[2] The physical sites must be treated in conjunction with written sources and place-name studies, but this large-scale mapping of surveyed sites is essential. Unfortunately, it is unlikely to be possible on the Welsh mainland outside Caernarvonshire for a considerable time. The Royal Commission rightly pursued the policy after the last war of giving priority to the counties of Caernarvon and Glamorgan which had not been inventoried in the earlier series of volumes: but the old folio reports on Carmarthen, Denbigh, Flint, Merioneth, Montgomery, Pembroke and Radnor, published between 1911 and 1925, are seriously inadequate. Anglesey was properly treated in 1937, but the inventory of Glamorgan, though well advanced, has not yet

[1] J. N. L. Myres, *Anglo-Saxon Pottery and the Settlement of England* (Oxford 1969).

[2] The short analysis is in volume iii of the *Inventory*, clxxviii–clxxx. For discussion of these topics, see T. Jones Pierce's review of volume i in *Trans. Caernarvonshire Historical Society*, xviii (1957), 106–8, and Colin Gresham's reviews in *Arch. Camb.*, cvi (1957), 123–7, cx (1961), 157–62, cxiv (1965), 183–9. Cf. G. R. J. Jones, 'The Tribal System in Wales: a Re-assessment in the Light of Settlement Studies', *Welsh History Review*, i (1960–63), 111–32.

appeared. Analysis, therefore, outside Caernarvonshire, depends on the initiative of local archaeologists and the National Museum, whose important work cannot replace a Commission's inventory.

But Caernarvonshire is a fine beginning to the archaeological survey desperately needed for Wales as a whole. It is supplemented by the English Commission's report on Herefordshire, but Shropshire, Monmouth and Brecknock entirely lack an inventory. All this is very unfortunate, for modern farming and industry remove a substantial number of sites every year, and the various emergency operations mounted by the National Museum and by local societies are no substitute for normal excavation and systematic inspection. As the Caernarvon inventory demonstrates, however, a great deal does survive: the difficulty is basically one of dating early settlements, as the divergence of opinion between Mr Gresham and the Commissioners illustrates. In matters such as land utilisation, field organisation and the like, precise dating is not normally obtainable in any case without archival evidence, but the cultivation terraces and fields of Caernarvonshire still present ambiguous evidence because of the amount of arable farming in the Lleyn peninsula which has certainly obscured much earlier evidence. The welcome attention now being given to medieval archaeology of this sort in Wales is gradually building up a more impressive corpus of agrarian and settlement evidence, but the comparison with Roman and prehistoric Wales is still disturbingly unfavourable.

The ecclesiastical remains from the pre-Norman period are slender. The major centres of the age of saints are barely preserved: when foundations like those in the University College grounds at Bangor are revealed,[1] small cells in a group can be postulated but neither proved nor dated. The Anglesey sites associated with St Seiriol at Penmon and on Puffin Island are similarly meagre compared to the Irish monastic communities at Glendalough or at Clonmacnois.[2] The inscribed and carved monuments are, however, numerous, in contrast to England,

[1] *Inventory of . . . Caernarvonshire*, ii, no. 683.
[2] *Inventory of . . . Anglesey* (London 1937), 123, 141-4.

and the labours of Dr Nash-Williams on behalf of the National Museum have supplied a fully illustrated corpus of some four hundred pillars, slabs and crosses ranging over some eight centuries.[1] The value of this corpus is inestimable. It brings together the materials on Ogam, Latin, Welsh and mixed inscriptions; it supplies the data to compare with its Scottish counterpart by Romilly Allen and Anderson and with the extensive literature on Ireland. Through such comparisons, in conjunction with every other available discipline, some better understanding of the migrations, the development of Christianity and the spread of artistic influences is being reached.

In the same way a Celtic context needs to be sought for other types of medieval Welsh carving. For example, the three-headed carving in Llandaff cathedral suggests continuity with much earlier Celtic head-cults of which glimpses survive in pre-Christian carvings at Corleck in county Cavan or in a Romanesque doorway at St Brendan's cathedral, Clonfert.[2] Nor is the interest only personal, religious or artistic. The consular dating on one of the Penmachno stones, if used in conjunction with Procopius' *Gothic History*, gives elusive evidence of diplomatic relations between the Byzantium of Justinian and the Gwynedd of Maelgwn.[3]

The other main aspect of the early period with which archaeology can help is the encroachment first from Anglo-Saxons, then from Normans. Wat's Dyke and Offa's Dyke, which Sir Cyril Fox surveyed so magisterially, constitute a necessary part of the evidence for the Mercian frontier, while the numerous native dykes in Glamorgan, controlling 'movement along the ridgeways from the hinterland in the direction of the coast' are important evidence of internal economic and political divisions, probably fluctuating divisions: similarly Clawdd Mawr in Car-

---

[1] V. E. Nash-Williams, *The Early Christian Monuments of Wales* (Cardiff 1950). Cf. the review by Françoise Henry in *Antiquaries Journal*, xxxii (1952), 88–90. [2] N. K. Chadwick, *The Celts* (Harmondsworth 1970), 158–9. [3] *Inventory of . . . Caernarvonshire*, i, no. 646; J. O. Ward, 'Procopius, "Bellum Gothicum" II.6.28: the Problem of Contacts between Justinian I and Britain', *Byzantion*, xxxviii (1968), 464–5, 468–70.

marthenshire is probable evidence of Dyfed's eastern frontier.[1]

The principal Norman remains are, of course, castles, first wooden buildings usually on mottes, later the stone buildings which in their full evolution are the show-pieces of South Wales today. Wales has been fortunate in having G. T. Clark to pioneer modern castle-studies. Clark, who seems to be better known in Wales as the editor of the charters of Glamorgan, was also the author of *Mediaeval Military Architecture in England*. As a practising engineer, who had worked with Brunel on the Great Western Railway and, after a period in India, become the imaginative ironmaster of Dowlais in its heyday, Clark was eminently qualified to understand fortifications.[2] Since his basic work published in the *Archaeologia Cambrensis* throughout the second half of the nineteenth century, the Welsh castles have continued to attract antiquaries and scholars and, into the bargain, the enlightened patronage of the Ministry of Works.

As a result of a century's work, put into perspective by Dr R. A. Brown,[3] the Welsh castles can now be used as meaningful archaeological data. The early castles present dating problems still, but the old confusion in Glamorgan between castle mounds and Bronze Age mounds has largely been resolved. As a result, the Norman advance can be traced more accurately and its influence on native Welsh fortifications can also be suggested. Thanks to the labours of Mr Hogg and Mr King, any student requiring to find his way about castles has got ready access to current knowledge: Hogg and King produced lists of some six hundred castle earthworks and over two hundred stone castles, with bibliographical references.[4] There is still a great deal of

---

[1] C. Fox, *Offa's Dyke* (London 1955); A. Fox, 'The "Short Dykes" of Glamorgan', *B.B.C.S.*, viii (1935–37), 280–4; E. G. Bowen, 'Clawdd Mawr, Carmarthenshire', *ibid.*, 383–5.

[2] *D.N.B.*, *Supplement* (London 1909), 449–51.

[3] R. A. Brown, *English Medieval Castles* (London 1954).

[4] A. H. A. Hogg and D. J. C. King, 'Early Castles in Wales and the Marches', *Arch. Camb.*, cxii (1963), 77–124; 'Masonry Castles in Wales and the Marches', *ibid.*, cxvi (1967), 71–132; 'Castles in Wales and the Marches: Additions and Corrections', *ibid.*, cxix (1970), 119–24.

spade-work to be done, but the contrast with the situation even in 1946, when the Cambrian Archaeological Association took centennial stock,[1] is striking. Mr O'Neil's queries about Degannwy, a fascinating site on two volcanic outcrops, fortified since at least the ninth century and built in stone in the thirteenth, are now being resolved by excavation.[2] Hen Domen, the old castle at Montgomery, is now clearly from the first a motte and bailey, since Roger of Montgomery raised it in 1070–74.[3] And the work-in-progress section of the journal *Medieval Archaeology* shows a satisfying number of Welsh castle-projects.

The Edwardian castles have always attracted attention, of course, but it is pleasing to see, at last, an adequate record in print not only of their architecture, but also of the masons' marks which appear on many blocks. Although Edward Lhuyd had pioneered the study of masons' marks at Caerphilly in 1697—he thought that they might prove it to be '*Roman* or late *British* Building'[4]—only in the third volume on Caernarvonshire did the Royal Commission on Ancient Monuments tabulate facsimiles, identified by location, of these interesting marks on Edwardian castles.[5] The page of Beaumaris marks in the Anglesey inventory does not meet scholarly requirements.[6]

---

[1] *A Hundred Years of Welsh Archaeology: Centenary Volume, 1846–1946*, ed. V. E. Nash-Williams (Gloucester 1946). The section on castles is by B. H. St. J. O'Neil, 129–40.

[2] L. Alcock's reports in *Medieval Archaeology*, vi–vii (1963), 313; viii (1964), 261; x (1966), 193.

[3] P. A. Barker's report in *Medieval Archaeology*, xii (1968), 182. The royal castle at Montgomery, built 1223–27, has also been excavated recently (ibid., 182–3). Cf. R. A. Brown, H. M. Colvin and A. J. Taylor, *History of the King's Works* (London 1963), ii, 739–42.

[4] In a letter published posthumously in the Royal Society of London's *Philosophical Transactions*, xxvii (1712), 502: see R. T. Gunther, *Early Science in Oxford*, xiv, *Life and Letters of Edward Lhwyd* (Oxford 1945), 346, where the reproduction of Lhuyd's drawings of the masons' marks is less satisfactory than figure 1 facing p. 477 in the *Philosophical Transactions* (in H. Jones's abridgment, v (2), figure 59).

[5] *Inventory of . . . Caernarvonshire*, iii, cl–clviii.

[6] *Inventory of . . . Anglesey*, cxxii.

The evidential value of masons' marks is still to be properly appraised. The Commissioners suggest that some of the marks may have been intended to show where a stone was intended to be placed; this is a function quite separate from the usual one of identifying the individual mason. It has also been suggested that these identifying marks checked workmanship rather than pay, since they exist in buildings where the masons were paid by the day, not on a piece-work basis.[1] But the marks at Chartres are found only in periods when piecework was common[2] and the relationship of marks to men is only beginning to be considered. Until a corpus of marks made by mobile masons is completed not only for Britain but for Northern Europe as well, most remarks are speculative.

There are hints of interesting conclusions. S. W. Williams noted that masons' marks which he found while excavating Strata Marcella were identical with others found at Strata Florida some years previously, but he reproduced only a few of the Strata Florida marks and the matter requires complete reinvestigation.[3] It is, in any case, not sufficient to collect the marks in only one building, or even in one county. There is an obvious need, for a start, to continue the Commission's work in tabulating (and then to classify) all the marks in all the Edwardian castles, to compare not only Caernarvon and Conway but also to compare, for example, Harlech with Kildrummy, its Scottish counterpart. Such an experiment might fail, but scientific experiments are failing every day and this one ought to be tried. The results could be important, not only for supplementing the very full accounts of the royal works but also, because of these accounts, for establishing criteria in the use of these marks. Speculation can be controlled to a unique extent in studying the Edwardian castles.

[1] F. W. Brooks, *Masons' Marks* (East Yorkshire Local History Series i, York 1952), 9.

[2] Information from Mr J. James whose book on the stones of Chartres Cathedral is nearing completion.

[3] S. W. Williams, 'The Cistercian Abbey of Strata Marcella', *Arch. Camb.*, 5th series, ix (1892), 14; 'On Further Excavations at Strata Florida Abbey', *ibid.*, 5th series, vi (1889), 46–7.

Once valid critical data on these marks are available, their evidence could be used more confidently in other, less documented, contexts. Professor R. H. C. Davis has made a splendid beginning in the *Journal of the British Archaeological Association*, 3rd series, xvii (1954).

I have devoted space to these marks because they offer an exciting, indeed hazardous, form of research inside Wales. Is the assumption correct that marks were introduced for the first time into Wales under James of St George? What evidence is there in the seigneurial castles of the south and the march? Can groups of English masons be followed as Mr James has followed them round Chartres and the Ile de France?

Since mottes are hard to remove and stone fortifications hard to slight, castles remain very visible. Other habitations are less obvious. The halls of Llywelyn ap Gruffydd at Aberffraw and Ystumgwern were removed bodily by Edward I and re-erected, the one inside Caernarvon Castle, the other inside Harlech.[1] Neither survives in its new site, and the combination of geographical analysis, archival evidence and actual digging at Aberffraw failed to produce any conclusive information about the original site of the palace.[2] Other than the numerous *hafotai* sites which continued to be used into modern times,[3] there was little known about Welsh housing in the later Middle Ages until Sir Cyril Fox and Lord Raglan produced their survey of *Monmouthshire Houses*, of which the first part, published in 1951, covered the period c. 1415 to 1560. The sixty houses included in this first volume are a source for historians of the smaller medieval house generally: it remains a remarkable survey not just by Welsh but by British standards. The work done by the Welsh Folk Museum at St Fagans Castle near Cardiff has built on Fox and

[1] C. R. Peers, 'Harlech Castle', *Trans. Hon. Soc. Cymm.* (1921-22), 68-9.

[2] D. B. Hague, 'Some Light on the Site of the Palace of Aberffraw', *Trans. Anglesey Antiquarian Society and Field Club* (1957), 1-4; G. R. J. Jones, 'The Site of Llys Aberffraw', *ibid.*, 5-7.

[3] Cf. R. U. Sayer, 'The Old Summer Pastures: a Comparative Study', *Montgomeryshire Collections*, liv (1955-56), 117-45; lv (1957-58), 37-86.

Raglan. The restoration and re-erection there of Hendre'r-ywydd Uchaf, a late-fifteenth-century house originally at Llangynhafal in Denbighshire, shows what some of the Monmouthshire houses must have resembled before accretions of centuries concealed their nature from the casual eye. A fifteenth-century hoard from Merioneth, the Welsh laws and the Monmouthshire parallels were all used to assist in the restoration of Hendre'r-ywydd Uchaf, which in turn gives substance to the laws and the household finds.[1]

Although domestic and military architecture has attracted so much attention in Wales, urban archaeology (except in the Roman sites) has been relatively uninteresting. The appeal made by Mr O'Neil in 1946 for the study of town defences[2] has not been widely answered, yet the importance of earthworks or stone walls round seigneurial boroughs, or gates into market towns, is no less than the importance of Caernarvon Castle and the walls of its fledgling town.

As well as secular buildings, the monasteries of Wales have left material traces. Like the major castles, these have attracted much attention in the last century, but the damage done after the dissolution and subsequent quarrying activities and sheer neglect have reduced most of the monastic complexes to ruins and foundations. Thanks to the labours of Stephen Williams at Strata Florida, Cwmhir, Strata Marcella and Talley, his more scholarly successor Harold Hughes at Valle Crucis and Conway, and Sir Harold Brakspear at Tintern, a great deal of salvage excavation and recording had been done before the Ministry of Works took an interest in the Welsh monasteries.[3] It is obviously important to know ground plans, not only of the monastic churches but also of the conventual buildings, to date progressive

[1] I. C. Peate, *Hendre'r-ywydd Uchaf* (Cardiff 1967), reprinted from *Trans. Denbighshire Historical Society*, xi (1962).

[2] *A Hundred Years of Welsh Archaeology*, ed. Nash-Williams, 139. For descriptions of all currently recorded Welsh town defences; see H. L. Turner, *Town Defences in England and Wales* (London 1971), 210–24.

[3] Cf. A. J. Taylor, *ibid.*, 140–7.

building programmes and to assess the architectural features of the houses.

The architecture of parish churches and the cathedrals has also a good deal to offer the medievalist. As with all other material remains, the absence of up-to-date inventory descriptions for most of Wales is regrettable, particularly since so many old churches have been drastically restored or rebuilt over the centuries: in Anglesey alone twenty-seven 'old' churches were rebuilt in the nineteenth century and most of the other churches were in some measure restored.[1]

Archaeology extends beyond excavation of buried remains and study of surviving masonry: it includes, too, the roads and means of communication. Again the Romans have come off best, because Roman roads are in part solid material remains, whereas medieval roads, if they did not follow close to Roman lines (and this was in any case possible only in the marches of Wales), are less susceptible to exact study. The buildings, especially the castles, give some indication of probable road lines. Just as interesting are the routes used by the Welsh drovers in the later Middle Ages both within Wales and for driving cattle to England. This is part of the source-material for Welsh economic history. Unfortunately, the evidence is rather late and comes partly from written itineraries, from market records and from the recollections of drovers alive within this century:[2] but it can perhaps be tested by archaeology on the ground, on the old roads themselves where they are discoverable, on the history of hostelries called 'Drovers' Arms' and on the resting enclosures (how old are they?). There was evidently a droving profession in medieval Wales, moving around cattle and probably horses as well as sheep. Glimpses of this can be caught in the number of

[1] M. L. Clarke, 'Anglesey Churches in the Nineteenth Century', *Trans. Anglesey Antiquarian Society and Field Club* (1961), 53–68.

[2] Cf. R. Phillips, 'The Last of the Drovers—Dafydd Isaac', *Trans. Hon. Soc. Cymm.* (1968), 110–21, C. A. J. Skeel, 'The Cattle Trade between Wales and England from the Fifteenth to the Nineteenth Centuries', *Trans. Royal Historical Society*, 4th series, ix (1926), 135–58, and K. J. Bonser, *The Drovers* (London 1970), esp. 38–49.

men called *Porthmon* which turn up in lordship and borough records of the fourteenth and fifteenth centuries. Mobility of another kind is instanced in an Arundel valor, which shows the Earl moving ninety beeves to Sussex from Wales in 1349.[1] But archaeology of an untraditional sort should surely be able to make further contributions to this important subject of communications and mobility.

Archaeology is a means to an historical end. With the gradual assembly of a corpus of properly examined sites and artifacts, a more comprehensive understanding of medieval Wales will be possible.[2] But it is not so much the spectacular single find, like the brooch bearing Glyndŵr's princely arms found in Harlech Castle in 1923,[3] which advances knowledge: it is rather the systematic accumulation of evidence for ways of life, domestic, defensive, ecclesiastical, peripatetic, and despite the great achievements of the Cambrian Archaeological Association, many vigorous local societies, the National Museum of Wales and the Royal Commission on Ancient Monuments, this systematic herding has still need of many porthmen.

[1] Shropshire Record Office, Acton of Aldenham deposit, 1093/Box 1, unsorted.

[2] As well as the various printed guides and inventories of the Commission and the Ministry of Works, useful information on the castles of Caernarvon, Criccieth, Monmouth, Kidwelly and Ewyas Harold and the abbeys of Tintern and Basingwerk can be found in the records of the Ministry in the Public Record Office (Works 14/9–12, 58, 75–8, 1337, 1339–40, 1343, 1346, 1350, 1357, 1372–3). Most of this material is available since very little is less than thirty years old. The files of the Royal Commission on Ancient and Historical Monuments in Wales and Monmouthshire from 1908 to 1944 have now been received by the P.R.O. and form the new class unhappily titled Monwal 1.

[3] C. R. Peers, 'Harlech Castle: a Recent "Find"', tipped in to *Trans. Hon. Soc. Cymm.* (1921–22), opposite p. 70.

### NUMISMATICS[1]

Like Edward Lhuyd, 'I have been very inquisitive about Coyns of the Princes of *Wales* since I began this undertaking.'[2] Coins of the independent princes are not by any means the only interesting object of speculation, for the Norman and Angevin mints in Wales and deposits of coins 'hoarded' in Wales exert an equal fascination, but the numismatics of the princes take pride of place.

Only one existing coin is acceptably attributed to a Welsh ruler. Major Carlyon-Britton, a founder of the British Numismatic Society, bought it in June 1903 along with two Anglo-Saxon pennies for only thirty shillings in a Sotheby sale, where it was wrongly catalogued. He revealed his discovery to the Numismatic Society in 1905 and repeated the lecture to the Honourable Society of Cymmrodorion in January 1906.[3] The coin was sold to Spink's for £115 in the sale of the second portion of Carlyon-Britton's superb collection in November 1916 and was acquired by the British Museum in the following year after a public subscription had been raised. No other example is known, but there seems little doubt that the obverse legend HOWÆL REX was indeed struck for Hywel Dda in the mid-tenth century.[4] This is more than a curiosity, although Sir John Lloyd made little of the discovery.[5] It is the only tangible evidence of the elusive law-

[1] I am indebted for generous assistance to Miss Marion Archibald of the Department of Coins and Medals at the British Museum and to Mr Colin Pitchfork, a prominent Australian numismatist, but they have no responsibility for what follows.

[2] Letter from Lhuyd to Dr Richardson, 19 June 1698: Gunther, *Life and Letters of Lhwyd*, 376.

[3] P. W. P. Carlyon-Britton, 'The Saxon, Norman and Plantagenet Coinage of Wales', *British Numismatic Journal*, original series, ii (1905), 31–40, and *Trans. Hon. Soc. Cymm.* (1905–6), 1–13. The prices are known from the printed price-lists issued after the two sales.

[4] Cf. G. C. Brooke, *English Coins from the Seventh Century to the Present Day*, 3rd ed. (London 1950), 57; J. J. North, *English Hammered Coinage*, i, *Early Anglo-Saxon—Henry III, c. 650–1272* (London 1963), 20, 95.

[5] Lloyd, *History*, i, 337, n. 65.

giver, and in this small piece of silver there is a surprising amount of historical data.

For example, although the obverse legend was specially struck for Hywel, the coin itself is of a common Anglo-Saxon type, the penny struck for Athelstan (d. 939) and Edmund (d. 946). Contact between Hywel and the Wessex dynasty is well known from Hywel's appearance as a witness to several charters of Athelstan and Edred: this coin was struck by the moneyer Gillys, whose name appears on the reverse, and a Gillys, surely the same man (for the name is rare), was minting coins for Edred and Edgar at Chester in the later 940s. The coin is likely then to have been minted towards the end of Hywel's long reign, after he became, as he is styled in the laws, 'by the grace of God ruler of all Wales'. It demonstrates close relations with the English, it suggests a degree of sophistication, it may point to a more general money economy in Wales (although the National Museum of Wales regards it merely as a presentation piece), it may possibly indicate (as Carlyon-Britton thought) that Chester was Hywel's capital in the 940s, for, although Gillys may just possibly have gone to Hywel in Wales, the rosettes on the coin point to a Chester provenance.[1] The tribute of twenty pounds of gold and three hundred pounds of silver which the Welsh princes agreed to pay to Athelstan around 926 or 927 is the best documentary backing to the Hywel Dda coin.[2]

It is a unique survivor. Although Carlyon-Britton later announced his identification of a coin of a late eleventh-century 'king Llywelyn', this attribution is very doubtful.[3] But there have

[1] Rosettes 'seem to have been a Mercian privy-mark' in the tenth century and Mr Dolley ascribes a penny of Edred, *c*. 950, to Chester solely on these grounds (*Anglo-Saxon Pennies*, London 1964, 23–4, plate XIII, 39).

[2] *Willelmi Malmesbiriensis Monachi de Gestis Regum Anglorum Libri Quinque*, ed. W. Stubbs (Rolls Series 90, London 1887), i, 148. Cf. Lloyd, *History*, i, 335.

[3] P. W. P. Carlyon-Britton, 'A Penny of Llywelyn, son of Cadwgan, of the Type of the Second Issue of William Rufus', *Brit. Num. J.*, orig. series, viii (1911), 83–6; F. Elmore Jones, 'Thoughts on the Norman Coinage of Wales in the Light of two Additions to the Series', *ibid.*, xxviii (1955–57), 194.

been reports over the centuries of other princely coins. The most circumstantial of these reports comes characteristically from Edward Lhuyd. He reported from Narberth in Pembrokeshire in June 1698 that he had been told by the bishop of Bangor that one of his relations had possessed a coin issued by Llywelyn ab Iorwerth and kept it 'in his Pocket several Years, and shewed it to many of the Bishops Acquaintance, still living, who confirm it'.[1] This is adequate evidence: for the bishop of Bangor was Humphrey Humphreys who, Thomas Hearne attested, 'was reckon'd next to Mr. Edw. Lhuyd for knowledge in the British Language; but Mr. Lhuyd used to say, he was a greater Master of it'.[2] It is unfortunate that no more detailed description or rubbing of the coin survives, and Lhuyd implies that it was already lost by 1698.

The other accounts of princely coins are far less persuasive. Sir Samuel Meyrick was too late on the scene at a farm in Llanwnnen, Cardiganshire, where in the first years of the nineteenth century 'several curious silver coins were dug up in a field. They were all triangular, with a hole in the centre, and a circular inscription on each. These curiosities suffered the fate of many antiquities, being given to children as playthings, and were consequently lost.' Meyrick speculated, however, that if these and 'the coins found near the inscribed stone in the parish of Penbryn had been preserved, they might perhaps have settled the long doubted question, whether the Welsh princes coined money themselves, or used that of the English'.[3] Carlyon-Britton a century later was to settle part of that question, and Meyrick's earlier speculation ought not to be dismissed out of hand. For one M.R.R., a reader of his book, wrote at once to the *Gentleman's Magazine* to communicate his story.

---

[1] Gunther, *Life and Letters of Lhwyd*, 376. This letter is quoted in R. Ruding, *Annals of the Coinage of Great Britain* (3rd ed. London 1840), i, 195.

[2] *Thomae Caii Vindiciae Antiquitatis Academiae Oxoniensis, contra Joannem Caium, Cantabrigiensem*, ed. T. Hearne (Oxford 1730), ii, 646.

[3] S. R. Meyrick, *History and Antiquities of the County of Cardigan* (1808, Brecon 1907 ed.), 218; quoted in Ruding, *Annals of Coinage*, i, 195 n. 6.

According to M.R.R., coins 'exactly answering the above description' had been dug up at virtually the same time, 'in a leaden box, that was drawn out of the earth by the teeth of a harrow, in a field belonging to Green Castle, antiently called Castell Moel, about 4 miles from Caermarthen, on the river Towey'. But the two servants who found the coins sold some to a watch-maker in Carmarthen, who presumably melted them down, and the rest were sold in Swansea.[1] The appeal of M.R.R. to other readers who knew of similar triangular coins produced no apparent response.

There are strange things abroad in Wales: triangular silver coins and, as discussed later in this chapter, a concentration of leather coins. It is surprising that scant attention has been paid to these eccentricities. Even Hywel Dda's coin is overdue for re-examination, for Anglo-Saxon numismatics have advanced greatly since 1905.

The evidence amounts to one virtually certain coin, one very doubtful coin of a doubtful prince, one well-attested lost piece of Llywelyn the Great and some lost triangular curiosities. With Norman and Angevin mintings in Wales, the evidence, though still uncomfortably scanty, is much more substantial.

In some Welsh centre or another coins were minted during the reigns of all the English kings from William the Conqueror to Henry III. The importance of these pieces as historical evidence is considerable.

First of all, the coins can assist in dating English occupation of places such as Pembroke or Rhuddlan. The survival of coins is, however, chancy, and the non-appearance of coins is very weak evidence for non-occupation. Moreover, there is room for debate over the attribution of those Norman coins which do survive. Before the numismatic evidence can be used, careful consideration must always be given to the validity of attribution. The St David's mint, for example, to which coins of William the Conqueror and of Henry I have been assigned, depends for its very existence on the interpretation of 'Devitun'. For half a century

[1] *Gentleman's Magazine*, lxxx (2) (1810), 24; cited in Ruding, i, 195, n. 6.

after Carlyon-Britton in 1905 suggested that 'Devitun' was 'Dewi's town', and not Devizes or Downton in Wiltshire,[1] St David's was the orthodox translation of the mint-name, but F. Elmore Jones put 'Devitun' back into inverted commas thirteen years ago,[2] and today the National Museum's public exhibition, basing itself on Mr Dolley's subsequent suggestions,[3] says that 'Devitun was probably in the eastern marches'. Although very interesting suggestions about Rhuddlan have been made by Mr Dolley and Mr Brand,[4] Elmore Jones's hope that his note 'may be helpful as a starting point for more exhaustive research on this fascinating group of Norman coins, both the angle of the historical background and the validity of the existing attributions to St David's and Cardiff' has not yet been fully realised.[5] Mr Dolley has indeed recognised in two Henry I pieces unearthed at Llantrithyd in 1962 and 1963 not only the first coins of this reign struck at Cardiff but also the first coins 'that can be attributed with absolute confidence to the mint of Cardiff',[6] but no full examination of the William I piece formerly assigned to Cardiff and the relationship between CAIRDI and DEVITUN in the eleventh century has yet appeared. Coins, moreover, continue to appear. The Llantrithyd pieces were 'sensational', but they have since been joined in the National Museum by an isolated find of another Cardiff penny of Henry I, type x, chronologically between the Llantrithyd penny and halfpenny, which were type xi and type v respectively: and this new chance find, struck by the same moneyer, Walter, is important confirmation of the

[1] Carlyon-Britton, *Brit. Num. J.*, orig. series, ii (1905), 49.

[2] F. E. Jones, *Brit. Num. J.*, xxviii (1955–57), 192–4.

[3] R. H. M. Dolley, 'The 1962 Llantrithyd Treasure Trove and Some Thoughts on the First Norman Coinage of Wales', *Brit. Num. J.*, xxxi (1962), 74–9.

[4] R. H. M. Dolley, 'The Sequence of Moneyers at Rhuddlan in the Short-Cross Period', Spink's *Numismatic Circular*, lxxi (1963), 226–7; J. D. Brand, 'The Short Cross Coins of Rhuddlan', *Brit. Num. J.*, xxxiv (1965), 90–7.

[5] F. E. Jones, *Brit. Num. J.*, xxviii (1955–57), 194.

[6] Dolley, *Brit. Num. J.*, xxxi (1962), 74–9; 'Two Further Coins of Henry I from Llantrithyd', *ibid.*, xxxiii (1964), 169–71.

regular working of the Cardiff mint in the early twelfth century.

The recent re-examination of the Plantagenet coinage of Rhuddlan demonstrates the sort of results which may be obtained when a larger sampling of coins is available. Brand, building on Dolley's work, examined no fewer than 128 coins with forty-four different die-combinations to produce a fairly sophisticated classification of the class of penny, issued from 1180 to 1247, known as 'short cross', since the cross motif on the reverse did not reach the outer edge of the coin (unlike the 'long cross' current thereafter). The result of this work is knowledge that one moneyer at a time produced coins at Rhuddlan. First there was Halli, late in Henry II's reign. It is of historical importance that the dies were probably manufactured not by a blacksmith but by a goldsmith, and that these copies of the regular English coinage were 'not without technical competence and artistic merit', in contrast to the 'barbarous' work ascribed to the Cardiff and 'Devitun' mints of William I and in contrast too to the crudity of execution achieved at Rhuddlan itself by the fourth known Angevin moneyer, one Henry who was at work in the early 1240s. This recent work, using extensively an unpublished hoard which has been in the British Museum for more than thirty years, extends dramatically the history of minting in North Wales. Previously it was accepted that coins had been minted at Rhuddlan only for a brief period. There was disagreement about the date (either *c.* 1212–13 or *c.* 1240), but there had been unanimity about the brevity.[1] Now continuity of a sort has been established: Halli, followed by Tomas in the early 1190s, then Simon in John's reign. There is then a gap in the evidence until Henry appears in *c.* 1240, but 'none of the well-documented finds of Short Cross pennies that were deposited in the period between *c.* 1210 and *c.* 1240 contained any coins of the Rhuddlan mint'[2] and 'it would be dangerous to infer . . . that the fortress [of Rhuddlan] at any given time [early in Henry III's reign] was in the hands of the Welsh, if only because we know from other

---

[1] Dolley, *Numismatic Circular*, lxxi (1963), 226.
[2] Brand, *Brit. Num. J.*, xxxiv (1965), 94.

sources that royal policy was to concentrate minting at London and Canterbury.'[1]

Rhuddlan, therefore, serves both as an example of the evidence which can be obtained from the Welsh coinage, and as a warning against too ready acceptance of the value of negative evidence. Even Rhuddlan, a relatively productive mint, can be useful to the historian only when coins survive, not when they are absent, and useful moreover only when all surviving pieces are taken in conjunction. Welsh coins are, however, simply too rare for any meaningful quantification.

A second category of historical usage of numismatics is the study of place-names. On the whole the place-name specialist has more to offer the numismatist than the converse. This is because of the excessive abbreviations often used in coin-legends and because the written evidence for place-name forms is more substantial than the hammered evidence. But sometimes the knowledge that a place-name belongs to a mint-town can eliminate possibilities and add something to the scanty written evidence for the eleventh century. PEI and PAN are thought to represent Pembroke: they cannot represent Painswick or Paignton or Pangbourne, for these are unacceptable mint-sites.[2] The forms CAIRDI, CIVRDI or CARITI on coins of William the Conqueror are no longer thought to refer to Cardiff, although a question-mark about their true significance remains. What has the place-name specialist to contribute to this question-mark? and what light does the coin-legend throw on Anglo-Saxon language, since one of the moneyers seems to have an Anglo-Saxon name, Ælfsie,[3] just as the moneyer at Rhuddlan in William's reign was one Ælfwine?[4]

Thirdly, a small amount of evidence for professional mobility

[1] Dolley, *Numismatic Circular*, lxxi (1963), 227.

[2] D. F. Allen, *A Catalogue of English Coins in the British Museum: the Cross-and-Crosslets ('Tealby') Type of Henry II* (London 1951), clix.

[3] G. C. Brooke, *A Catalogue of English Coins in the British Museum: the Norman Kings* (London 1916), i, clxv–clxvi; ii, nos. 582–4.

[4] *Ibid.*, i, clxxix; ii, no. 869.

among moneyers can be gleaned from these coins. The Gillys who struck Hywel Dda's coin was later employed by the English kings at Chester and apparently at Hereford. Gillopatric, a moneyer to whom payment is recorded on the sole surviving pipe roll of Henry I's reign, was responsible for a penny attributed to the Pembroke mint.[1] The identification of dies can point to complex relationships between centres and personnel, but the difficulties involved in analysing die-movements require more expertise than the average historian is likely to muster. Attractive theories must be disciplined. Carlyon-Britton talked persuasively of the coiner Godesbrand of Shrewsbury going off to St David's at the invitation of Roger of Montgomery, bearing with him in his saddle-bag his reverse die, and he discussed how Godesbrand taught bishop Sulien's moneyer to make an obverse die which was then used in conjunction with the reverse from Shrewsbury. G. C. Brooke accepted this likelihood in the British Museum catalogue,[2] but Elmore Jones now claims that 'there is no doubt that Brooke subsequently changed his views on this and came to the conclusion that the "Shrewsbury" coin with its barbarous work on *both* sides was probably an irregular product of the "Devitun" mint', and Jones concludes that 'as such it is presumably a subtle piece of downright forgery'.[3] If it is forged, why and by whom was it forged? Was the reverse die copied from a coin or a die? What evidence for unquestioned die-movements in Wales exists? Who were the moneyers? Why did Rhuddlan coiners in the time of Richard I and John produce more elegant work than in the 1240s? To what extent can the interchange of expertise among philologists, topographers, political historians and numismatists improve the present unsatisfactory state of knowledge about the significance of Norman and Plantagenet coinage in Wales? These are some of the questions

[1] *Ibid.*, i, clxxviii; Carlyon-Britton, *Brit. Num. J.*, orig. series, ii (1905), 55; *The Pipe Roll of 31 Henry I* (London 1929 facsimile of 1833 ed. by J. Hunter), 136.

[2] Carlyon-Britton, *Brit. Num. J.*, orig. series, ii (1905), 52; Brooke, *Catalogue: Norman Kings*, i, clxxx; ii, nos. 883, 938.

[3] F. E. Jones, *Brit. Num. J.*, xxviii (1955–57), 194.

which come to mind, and to which at present there is little response.

Unlike the Norman and Angevin kings, who seem to have retained responsibility for coining in Wales, King Stephen was unable to do so. It is clear that a number of the rare Stephen pieces derive from the personal initiative of lords of the march.[1] The 'anarchy' of Stephen's reign has been the subject of three substantial books in recent years, two analytical, by Mr R. H. C. Davis and Professor Cronne, the third a chronicle by Mr Appleby.[2] Of these, only Professor Cronne uses the numismatic evidence, and he does not develop much discussion.[3] The significance of the baronial pieces should not be over-rated, nor should the virtual absence of such specimens in other reigns necessarily be more than fortuitous, but the strong likelihood is that in the civil conflict of Stephen's reign alone were the lords marcher in a position to coin independently. One of the strengths which the Norman conquerors inherited from the Anglo-Saxon kings was the mint-monopoly, in striking contrast to the position of most continental rulers.[4] If the lack of Stephen's governance was such as to allow private mints, the fact is an element in the history of Wales. The interpretation of these facts is another matter, of course: I am concerned only with reminding students of medieval Wales what sources can be utilised.

As I have already emphasised, an argument from silence is particularly dangerous when evidence is scanty. In circumstances of abundant hoards and well-documented series, some tentative conclusions can be drawn from lacunae: these circumstances never obtain in Wales. Any remarks which a historian makes, therefore, about the absence of coins must be very guarded; nonetheless, such absences are evidence of a sort. The very paucity of Welsh

---

[1] Brooke, *Catalogue: Norman Kings*, i, lxxi–cxxxiii; ii, 377–99.

[2] R. H. C. Davis, *The Reign of King Stephen* (London 1965); J. Appleby, *The Troubled Reign of King Stephen* (London 1969); H. C. Cronne, *The Reign of Stephen: Anarchy in England, 1135–1154* (London 1970).

[3] Cronne, *Reign of Stephen*, 240–1.

[4] Cf. R. R. Darlington, *The Norman Conquest* (Creighton Lecture 1962, London 1963), 8–9.

coinage is an evidential fact. The historian should consider the economic consequences of this scarcity. How well does it accord with the general view of the Welsh economy? How does it compare with the Hiberno-Scandinavian coinage of independent Ireland in the eleventh century or with the eighty-four native Irish coins found in the Bantry hoard of 1260–70?[1] Is a concept of self-subsistence and barter compatible with the evidence of the laws? The tribute of 926 or 927 consisting of gold and silver as well as cattle, dogs and hawks, raises general questions, not simply for the purpose of the Hywel Dda penny. Was the three hundred pounds of silver unminted? Or did English silver pennies circulate in Wales for certain purposes? And if so, at how early a date?

This is the sort of totality of evidence which is required. By combining the less familiar sources with the more conventional written evidence, some new insights may be gained. Among these less familiar sources are coin-hoards.

Hoards have, of course, produced most of the medieval coins which survive today. But a hoard has its own evidential quality as a hoard, not just as a store of individual coins. Coins were hidden deliberately in time of war or civil disturbance, or from apprehension in a time of economic or political crisis, or simply as savings in an age when few men had access to any sort of banking facility.[2] Mr Thompson has catalogued nearly four hundred hoards laid down in British earth between 600 and 1500, and the interleaved copy of his book in the British Museum's Department of Coins and Medals is kept up to date with additional information about hoards, old and new. There are strikingly few found in Wales. When Thompson's inventory and the museum's additions are tabulated, the Welsh hoards show a shallow scatter over a long period, with one predictable concentration in the reign of Edward I.

[1] J. D. A. Thompson, *Inventory of British Coin Hoards, A.D. 600–1500* (Royal Numismatic Society, Special Publications i, London 1956), xxv, xxxv, 11.
[2] Cf. Thompson, *Inventory of Hoards*, xvi.

| Date | Number of Welsh hoards | Reference no. in Thompson |
|------|:---:|------|
| 870–1000 | 3 | 10, 32, 305 |
| 1000–1066 | 2 | 131, 306 |
| 1066–1135 | 1 | Llantrithyd (1962–3) |
| 1135–1180 | – | – |
| 1180–1247 | 1 | Pembroke (1829) |
| 1247–1280 | 2 | 39, 237 |
| 1280–1307 | 4 | 78, 307, 343, 348 |
| 1307–1330 | – | – |
| 1330–1377 | 1 | 121 |
| 1377–1399 | 1 | 274 |
| 1400–1461 | 2 | 48, 238 |
| 1461–1500 | 3 | 219, 236, Haverfordwest (1825) |

The most striking feature of the geographical location of these twenty hoards is the predominance of coastal finds. If one adds the six Chester hoards, it is clear that coins were put away in the ground or otherwise hidden for reasons connected with sea-travel. The corollary is that most of the hoards found in Wales were probably not left by Welshmen at all. In the tenth century Chester was 'a meeting place for northern and southern currency and silver bullion . . . and a clearing-house for the Viking kings of Dublin':[1] it is in this context of Irish Sea trade and piracy that the four earliest medieval Welsh hoards should be seen. The two Caernarvonshire hoards of Cnut pennies point to the same context. During the period of Norman settlement in South Wales up to 1135, there is only one hoard. As Thompson commented, either the process of colonisation which created the mints of 'Cairdi', Cardiff and 'Devitun' was more peaceful than one might expect, so that no one buried his treasure, or Wales was so poor that 'little money was available for hoarding'.[2]

For over eighty years no hoard which has been found was laid down in Wales: the only short-cross period hoard dates from Henry III's reign. In the long-cross period of Henry III (1247 to 1280) there are two more deposits, including one of the few inland

[1] Cf. Thompson, *Inventory of Hoards*, xxiii.    [2] *Ibid.*, xxv.

hoards, hidden at Beddgellert between *c.* 1248 and 1260, possibly resulting from Henry's expedition into Wales in 1257.[1]

With the Edwardian Conquest, however, a small concentration of hoards, four in a quarter-century, was secreted, one each in Anglesey (at Castellor near Ty Croes), Carmarthen (at Pencarreg), Glamorgan (at Swansea) and Radnor (at Stow Hill). The relative rapidity of the conquest of Wales, compared to Scotland, coupled with the poverty of the country, accounts for the very much higher figure from Scotland and the north of England. Ireland, however, although much troubled too in the reigns of Edward I and Edward II, has few recorded hoards, ascribed by Thompson to a failure to keep records of finds and a very high level of native dishonesty.[2] These distributions are historical evidence, not only for medieval, but also very modern history. The contrast, however, between the Scottish experience on the one hand and the Welsh and Irish on the other, is striking and deserves investigation.

The Edwardian hoards in Wales include one very odd collection indeed. The Castellor hoard, found in Anglesey in the course of amateur excavations in the second quarter of the nineteenth century, contained leather coins.[3] In 'a small recess or stone cupboard in the wall of a hut' the workmen found 'a supposed leather money, often spoken of in this county as having been in circulation at some early period'. This 'large quantity' of coin was distributed by the excavators and, since the leather tended to crumble when exposed to the air, it is most unlikely that any survives. But the record of these 'well-formed circular pieces of leather, with bits of silver neatly inserted and riveted in their centres without any impressions or characters' is precise and puzzling enough.[4] Mr Thompson accepted a date round the build-

---

[1] Thompson, *Inventory of Hoards*, xxxv, 14 no. 39.    [2] *Ibid.*, xxxvii.

[3] Thompson was mistaken in giving 1871 as the date of discovery (24 no. 78). Mr Pritchard is quite specific that the excavation was principally done by a local farmer, Robert Williams, 'at the commencement of his tenancy some forty-five years ago' (H. Pritchard, 'Copper Cakes, etc. Castellor, Anglesey', *Arch. Camb.*, 4th series, ii (1871), 52).

[4] Pritchard, *ibid.*, 57.

ing of Beaumaris Castle, but he was unable to make up his mind whether foreign workmen brought this curious collection of small change or whether the fact that Castellor is on the other side of Anglesey from Beaumaris showed that they might be 'tokens' common to the whole area.[1]

Now this would be of purely speculative interest were it not for a series of other references to leather coins. The anonymous author of a history of Alchester (in Oxfordshire), writing in 1622, remarked, quite gratuitously, that 'King Edward the First his leathern money, bearing his name, stamp, and picture, which he used in the building [of Caernarvon, Beaumaris and Conway] to spare better bullion, were, since I can remember, preserved and kept in one of the towers of Carnarvon castle'.[2] This is a very firm, sober account of the author's own observation in Caernarvon and, although the source is unique and unexpected, there seems no *prima facie* reason to doubt that he and others believed these objects to be Edward I leather pennies. Nor is this all. Edward Lhuyd, in his hunt for parochial antiquities, recorded no fewer than five other hoards of leather coins: at Rhuddlan (inside the castle itself and in an acre of land adjacent belonging to the vicarage), in Mold and at Estyn, while in a turbary on the common of Capel Garmon there was found an 'oxe's horn almost full of Leather money'.[3]

Now all this concentration of leather money in North Wales begins to look more than coincidence. The ox-horn, too, should be put beside the only other hoards known to have been found in such a container: they come, not from England, but from Dornock and the Lochar Moss in Dumfriesshire, Caldale in Orkney, Castle Lenigan in Armagh and Kirk Maughold on the Isle of Man: the Kirk Maughold deposit was hoarded in the tenth

[1] Thompson, *Inventory of Hoards*, xlii–xliii.

[2] White Kennett, *Parochial Antiquities* (Oxford 1818 ed.), ii, 434: cited in *Inventory of . . . Anglesey*, cxviii.

[3] *Parochialia*, ed. R. H. Morris, i (1909), 50, 51, 92, 97; iii (1911), 113. The two Rhuddlan hoards may be different versions of the same one, but the wording is unambiguous.

century, the Caldale around 1030–35, the Castle Lenigan and Dornock early in Edward III's reign.[1]

No doubt there are more data available somewhere, but this question first of horns in the Celtic fringe, then, more significantly, of leather in North Wales, seems to have some meat already, and it is surprising that no one has written on the topic. Leather currency itself is found at different periods in widely scattered parts of the world: in Sparta and Carthage, in Rome, according to Seneca and Eusebius, certainly in China, in France in the time of Philip I, St Louis and John the Good (when his ransom from Edward III caused financial distress), in Italy in 1122 and again as siege-pieces by Frederick II in 1237 and 1248, and so on through sixteenth-century Leiden to seventeenth-century America and Russia. Of these, many, probably all save the Chinese, were irregular issues in some emergency.[2] But the only English leather coin known is in a tradition reported by William Camden that such money was issued during the civil wars of John's reign, and no other information about medieval English currency seems to have been produced. Probably leather money generally requires re-investigation: Welsh scholarship could play an important part in this reappraisal.

After the Conquest, the Welsh hoards peter out gently. There is only one each from the reigns of Edward III and Richard II: the only concentration anywhere in Britain in these years was in southern England around the time of the Peasants' Revolt. In the fifteenth century, Owain Glyndŵr's rebellion may have persuaded a Llangynllo gentleman that his eighty-odd gold nobles would be safer buried in a 'black crock . . . on the bank of a little stream',[3] while probably another Radnorshire hoard, from

---

[1] Thompson, *Inventory of Hoards, sub nomine*; D. M. Wilson, 'Some Archaeological Additions and Corrections to J. D. A. Thompson, *Inventory of British Coin Hoards*', *Medieval Archaeology*, ii (1958), 169. No date is known for the Lochar Moss hoard, which is recorded in the interleaved Thompson at the British Museum.

[2] W. Charlton, 'Leather Currency', *Brit. Num. J.*, orig. series, iii (1906), 312–21.

[3] Thompson, *Inventory of Hoards*, xlv, 85, no. 238.

Kinsley Wood, and possibly also the Llanarmon hoard in Denbighshire and the gold coins found at Haverfordwest in Pembrokeshire, were the result of the resurgence of civil war in
1471.[1]

The difficulty of dealing with these hoards is increased by the
disappearance of most of them. All the fifteenth-century hoards
found in the last century have been lost: that leaves only the
Borth hoard of thirty-one nobles deposited around 1423–25. At
least six of the earlier hoards have largely vanished. Mr Thompson's strictures on Irish honesty might perhaps be applied elsewhere with equal justice. But these losses mean that numismatists
and historians are wholly dependent for at least half of the Welsh
hoards on the inadequate records kept at the time of discovery or
dispersal. Nonetheless, to fit Wales into the early world of the
Irish Sea, to discuss the impact of the Norman adventurers, to
compare the Edwardian campaigns in Wales with those in
Scotland and Ireland, to assess the reaction to the Glyndŵr revolt
and the wars between fifteenth-century factions, the evidence of
hoards is an insufficiently exploited element, and numismatic
evidence in general could profitably assist discussion of a still
wider range of questions.

[1] Thompson, *Inventory of Hoards*, 80, no. 219, 85, no. 236.

# CHAPTER 8

## *Cartography and Place-Names*

A historian neglects geography at his peril. Communications, boundaries, farming, prosperity, war, all, especially in the Middle Ages, are directly affected by geography. The influence may be perverse. All boundaries are not natural ones, lines of communication may not in fact be those which a geographer might postulate in abstract: inherent geographical probability is just as dangerous a piece of evidence as Colonel Burne's inherent military probability. But the problems of interpretation merely emphasise the need for an understanding of what geography can offer. It is fashionable nowadays to use social sciences to illumine dark historical places, and anthropology in particular is vouched to warranty rather often: anthropology is a large discipline, and probably many historians' assertions based on Gluckman would barely satisfy in a first-year undergraduate's anthropology essay, but local topographical knowledge and understanding of maps are sufficient geographical understanding for the average historian and are beset with fewer perils than a comparison of Frederick Barbarossa with a Zulu chief.

The historian's interest in maps ought not to begin with the modern Ordnance Survey. Old maps, as well as being decorative, contain essential information about conditions before the Economic Revolution. But the very oldest maps are not particularly helpful. The medieval world-maps are valuable testimonies to current cosmographical ideas, but they have little to offer the Welsh historian. Nor have the celebrated itinerary maps or British maps drawn by Matthew Paris, the St Albans chronicler. The four Paris maps which show Wales give little detail and his description of South Wales as 'a hilly and marshy land, breeding nimble and warlike men descended from Brutus' does not significantly add to our knowledge.[1]

[1] *Four Maps of Great Britain designed by Matthew Paris about A.D. 1250*

But the mid-fourteenth-century map of Britain which Richard Gough, the last editor of Camden's *Britannia*, bought at an auction sale in 1774 for half a crown, has interest, not just for its unique place in British cartography. It shows, as well as a number of Welsh places, certain select roads, clearly roads known personally to the compiler: the absence of roads proves nothing, but the five principal lines radiating from London are clearly authentic and one road shown leads into Wales. This single road, from Gloucester, Newent, Hereford and Hay through Brecon to Trecastell, then diverging from the modern line of road, going instead by Llangatwg, where only a mountain road survives, and then to St David's via Llandeilo, Carmarthen and Haverfordwest, shows why Edward I in 1295 travelled from Llangatwg to Llanddeusant and Llywel:[1] it was the main road in the high Middle Ages. On the other hand, like many maps, the Gough Map contains out-of-date information. Bardsey Island is marked 'Bardsey ubi sunt britonum vaticinatores', although the bards had been dealt with in 1284: or is it out of date? Is this evidence of bards still on the island?[2]

The Gough Map stands alone, however. Had the map which Gerald of Wales drew for his *Descriptio Kambriae* survived the position might have been different. This map, drawn with 'a wealth of detail and craftsmanship' on a single piece of parchment showed castles and ecclesiastical buildings as well as physical details. Henry Wharton saw the map at Westminster Abbey and described it for posterity shortly before it was destroyed in the fire of 1694. In some ways ignorance of the map's existence would be preferable to the tantalising account given by Wharton, for no copy was made and speculation about what information addi-

reproduced from three Manuscripts in the British Museum and one at Corpus Christi College, Cambridge, ed. J. P. Gilson (London 1928); cf. R. Vaughan, *Matthew Paris* (Cambridge 1958), 235-44.

[1] J. E. Morris, *The Welsh Wars of Edward I* (Oxford 1901), 264-5.
[2] E. J. S. Parsons, *The Map of Great Britain circa A.D. 1360 known as The Gough Map: an Introduction to the Facsimile* (Oxford 1958). This also contains a discussion of the roads by Sir Frank Stenton.

tional to Gerald's writings has been lost is merely frustrating.[1]

Although Wales continues to figure on late medieval maps, only one sort of map provides source material. The names of Welsh ports on the manuscript maritime charts known as portolan charts, viewed over a period of two hundred years from the mid-fourteenth century, deserve more examination than they have received, for these charts are practical documents of seaborne commerce.[2] They do not include unnecessary detail and continued in use long after the invention of printing in the west had revolutionised map production. Cognate with the portolans were the various written manuals. For Welsh purposes, the interesting one is the *Briefe Summe of Geographie* written by Roger Barlow, a merchant of Bristol, whose brother William was bishop successively of St Asaph in 1536 and St David's from 1536 until his translation to Bath and Wells in 1548. Although Barlow, whose trading connections had been principally Spanish, based his *Briefe Summe* on a Spanish model, he added to Enciso's text one folio of original Welsh material. By the time of writing, in 1540–41, he had established an estate and family in Pembrokeshire and this, coupled with his episcopal connections, explains the Welsh section.[3] Although the basis of Enciso's Spanish work had been academic rather than portolan, Barlow's additions were first-hand, practical accounts. But they are very brief and so much is left unsaid. Like all merchants, he had a disproportionate interest in islands and is less informative about Milford Haven than about Skalney, 'which is but a smal iland and not enhabited, but ther bredys plentie of conyes and shepe'.[4]

While the portolan maps were still current, maps printed first from wood-blocks, then from engraved copper plates, became

[1] H. Wharton, *Anglia Sacra* (London 1691), ii, xxii–xxiii; J. C. Davies, 'The Kambriae Mappa of Giraldus Cambrensis', *Journal of Historical Society of Church in Wales*, ii (1950), 46–60.

[2] See the interesting diagrams based on six portolan maps in F. J. North, 'The Map of Wales', *Arch. Camb.*, xc (1935), 22.

[3] R. Barlow, *A Briefe Summe of Geographie*, ed. E. G. R. Taylor (Hakluyt Society, 2nd series, lxix, 1932), xi.

[4] *Ibid.*, 47–8. North, *Arch. Camb.*, xc (1935), 25, exaggerates Barlow's usefulness.

common. Wide dissemination, the emendation of errors and the insertion of new information became a reality. But most of the early sixteenth-century maps which include Wales are still very derivative productions, based on the official maps of which the Gough Map at Bodley is the only survivor. They are of the greatest interest to the historian of maps: their importance to the historian of Wales is slight.[1]

Even the great steps forward in accuracy of mapping Wales, which are observable in the manuscript map of Laurence Nowell, the map in Mercator's atlas from 1564 onwards and Humphrey Llwyd's two celebrated maps published posthumously in Ortelius' *Theatrum Orbis Terrarum* in 1573, are interesting as source material principally because they made generally available for the first time a tolerable view of Wales. All three map-makers distorted the Lleyn peninsula and south-west Pembrokeshire, but the improvement on early sixteenth-century maps is substantial.[2]

The real revolution comes, however, with the appearance of the county atlases of Great Britain from 1579 onwards. The relatively large scale of the individual maps made possible a wealth of topographical detail. The earliest, by Christopher Saxton, were in some ways never surpassed for sheer elegance and their pioneering quality of personal surveying: Saxton had his seven Welsh maps engraved in 1577 and 1578 and in the following year included them with the twenty-seven English county maps and a general view of England in the first *Atlas of England and Wales*. The scale of the maps was far from constant, varying (for the Welsh counties) from Monmouth at 1·8 miles to the inch to the combined map of Radnor, Brecknock, Cardigan and Carmarthen at 3·3 miles, in contrast to Llwyd's general map of Wales where the scale fluctuated internally between 11·2 and 9·7 miles to the inch.[3]

[1] Cf. North, 37–50.

[2] Cf. *ibid.*, 37–61 and North, 'Humphrey Lluyd's Maps of England and of Wales', *Arch. Camb.*, xcii (1937), 11–63.

[3] For Saxton, see R. A. Skelton, *County Atlases of the British Isles, 1579–1703* (London 1970), 7–16; for Llwyd's scales, see North, *Arch. Camb.*, xcii (1937), 36.

From Saxton's time onwards, there is available to the scholar the extraordinary richness of the atlases of Britain. But before using any single map, those unfamiliar with the habits of publishers (who re-used, amended and added to the copper plates), and with the habits of cartographers (who, like historians, unscrupulously pirate their predecessors' labours), would do well to acquaint themselves first with the late Dr Skelton's bibliographical survey of English county maps down to 1703. The state of the plates and the date of the information shown is of more critical significance to a student of Elizabethan or Stuart Wales than to a medievalist, but a proper grasp of the nature of the data which he wishes to use is no less desirable.

Saxton's maps are pure decorative topography: they lack roads and boundaries of divisions within the counties. John Norden, the greatest surveyor contemporary with Saxton, produced for his *Speculum Britanniae* maps of much greater detail, including roads, but financial problems stopped his project after only five English counties had been surveyed, although two more counties in England were subsequently mapped. The wealth of symbol for various kinds of buildings employed by Norden in his large-scale map of Sussex would have been invaluable applied to Welsh counties. Instead, the next major atlas to include Wales is the 1607 edition of Camden's *Britannia*, which contained George Owen's map of Pembrokeshire alongside forty-one Saxton's, six Norden's and nine anonymous maps. All the other Welsh counties, now treated individually in all cases, are Saxton's. None of the maps, even the Norden's, shows roads. The importance of the *Britannia* as an antiquarian exemplar has already been demonstrated in chapter 6: its history as an atlas is equally significant, first with the largely Saxton maps, then after 1695 with Robert Morden's maps, and finally in Gough's edition with John Cary's maps. A great deal of history can be learnt simply from comparing the many editions of the *Britannia*.

But one very important feature would not be found there, for town plans were never included in the *Britannia*, although John Speed pioneered this additional information in the corners or borders of his maps in 1611-12. Speed's *Theatre of the Empire of Great Britaine* contained no fewer than seventy-three townplans. The plans of Pembroke, St David's and Cardigan are all signed by Speed himself and almost certainly the others are also his own work. The other Welsh towns in plan are Carmarthen, Cardiff, Llandaff, Monmouth, Brecon, Radnor, Montgomery, Harlech, Denbigh, Flint, St Asaph, Caernarvon, Bangor and Beaumaris. All these seventeen plans (with the exception of Monmouth) are also shown in the border of Speed's general map of Wales. The practical value of these Jacobean town-plans is very great. Speed's are the earliest known ground plans of most British towns: the only rival is Braun and Hogenberg's city-atlas, *Civitates Orbis Terrarum*, which appeared between 1572 and 1618 and contained no Welsh towns. Most of Speed's plans have the additional value of a key to street names and the principal buildings. They are an essential part of the source-material for any student of medieval or Tudor boroughs.[1]

Blaeu's sumptuous atlases after 1645 contained a volume devoted to England and Wales: Scotland and Ireland did not appear until 1654. The Blaeu maps are rightly valued by collectors because of the delicacy of the engraving and tastefulness of ornament, but they cannot be said to add much to topographical knowledge. Like earlier maps, they do not show roads, although both Blaeu and Speed show internal divisions within counties. Blaeu, while relying heavily on Speed, particularly Speed's plates in their post-1623 state, dispensed with the town plans.[2] On all counts, Speed is more useful as a source than Blaeu after him and Saxton before him.

The next important innovation in map-making which has historical significance is the road-guide. Although strip itineraries had existed for pilgrims and other travellers in the Middle Ages, no such useful publication was attempted in print until John

---

[1] Skelton, 30-44, and cf. also subsequent editions described there.

[2] *Ibid.*, 72-9. An excellent short statement about Blaeu, and other mapmakers, is to be found in A. G. Hodgkiss, *Discovering Antique Maps* (Tring 1971), esp. 21-50.

Ogilby about 1669 commenced a new atlas project with a survey of English and Welsh roads. The atlas never materialised, but the roads, engraved on narrow strips, six or seven to a folio page, reading from bottom upwards in each successive strip, left to right, appeared as *Britannia, Volume the First* in 1675. The old concept was brilliantly successful and Ogilby's route-maps were utilised in many subsequent general atlases, the first being Morden's county playing-cards in 1676: the counties of England and Wales numbered by a happy chance fifty-two, as an entrepreneur had noticed as early as 1590 when Saxton's maps were converted to a pack of cards. Although Ogilby's folio weighing four and a half pounds proved rather clumsy for the average traveller, it remains the most valuable source for a historian. The pocket versions produced by John Senex in 1719 and Emanuel Bowen in 1720 are important for eighteenth-century topography, but do not add to Ogilby for earlier studies. Ogilby is not impeccable, of course: Morden's maps for Gibson's edition of the *Britannia* in 1695 incorporate, as part of the ordinary map, not as a strip, most of Ogilby's roads, but add others which he omitted.[1]

First natural topography, then town-plans, finally roads: this sequence is capped by the appearance of maps drawn to a more ample scale. These maps of one inch to the mile or larger have the fullness of information which is often necessary to elucidate the meaning of documents. In Wales, the earliest is Williams's map of Denbighshire and Flint engraved on four sheets and compiled around 1720. A copy survives only in Flintshire Record Office at Hawarden, but photographic reproductions can be seen at Aberystwyth and Oxford. Thereafter there is Yates's 1799 map of Glamorgan, Singer's 1803 Cardiganshire, both on the same one-inch scale, and Evans's 1795 North Wales, covering nine sheets at three-quarters of an inch to a mile.[2] But with the creation of the Ordnance Survey in 1791 everything becomes much more systematic and satisfactory. Based on military survey-

---

[1] Skelton, 151–2, 247; Hodgkiss, 30, 49–52.

[2] See E. M. Rodger, *The Large Scale County Maps of the British Isles, 1596–1850: a Union List* (Oxford 1960), 27–9.

ing both in Scotland after the '45 and throughout the Empire after 1750, and based also on the general civilian interest fostered by the commercial atlases and after 1759 by the Society of Arts, as well as the privately surveyed estate maps, the Board of Ordnance's coverage of Britain county by county, at one inch to the mile, from 1815 onwards is a fundamental tool for all topographical studies. This 'old series' took about seventy years to complete, but Wales and southern England had all been mapped by 1841.[1] The history of these maps and their revisions has complications too, but Mr Harley, Dr Harvey and Mr Thorpe have made rough places plain.[2] Although many will use the current editions, the original series, reflecting still a less industrialised country, retain a special value: their recent reprinting is very welcome.

The very large-scale Ordnance Survey maps too are indispensable. After experiences in Ireland, the Board decided in 1840 that a national map on the scale of six inches to the mile was necessary and in 1856 a twenty-five inch series was inaugurated. Wales came rather late to this dual series, but was completed by 1888. As with the one-inch maps, there have been subsequent revisions: the historian must balance against improved techniques and greater accuracy in recent editions the preservation on the original editions of features since lost.[3] As well as these grid maps, separate town-plans were also issued: in nineteenth-century Wales these include Merthyr Tydfil at ten feet to a mile and all the county towns at 10·56 feet.[4]

The special maps of Monastic Britain and Dark Age Britain issued by the Ordnance Survey are, like Professor William Rees's indispensable map of South Wales in the fourteenth century and his *Historical Atlas of Wales*, secondary works of reference and fall outside the scope of this book.

---

[1] J. B. Harley, introduction to C. Close, *The Early Years of the Ordnance Survey* (Newton Abbot 1969 ed.), xx–xxiv; *The Historian's Guide to Ordnance Survey Maps* (Standing Conference for Local History, London 1964), 7–10.

[2] *Ibid.*; P. D. A. Harvey and H. Thorpe, *The Printed Maps of Warwickshire, 1576–1900* (Warwick County Occasional Series, i, 1959).

[3] Cf. Harley, *Historian's Guide*, 17–26.     [4] For a full list, see *ibid.*, 29–30.

As well as the Ordnance Survey, the activities of the Tithe Commissioners produced uniquely valuable maps. After the Tithe Act of 1836 Commissioners toured England and Wales discovering how much commutation of tithes had already taken place in each parish: since for most parishes there was no large-scale map then available (even parish boundaries might be a matter for debate), the Commissioners arranged for a map to be made to accompany their apportionment of remaining tithes. Although many parishes did not in fact require formal apportionment, the great majority did, and the documents prepared by the Commissioners are of immense topographical interest. The apportionment gives the names of the landlords, the tenants, the rural property field by field, wood by wood (keyed by number to the map), the current agrarian usage of the land, its area down to the last pole, the rent and tithe-holders. This in conjunction with the map gives information systematically which would otherwise survive only very spasmodically in private estate archives. All apportionments are not so detailed, and only about 1,900 out of the 11,800 maps were sealed as accurate by the Commissioners.[1] Their evidence is reliable, whereas the others are a very various collection, from rough sketches to almost first-class maps. These second-class maps are very numerous and they may not even key accurately with the apportionment. They are better than nothing, but the user must beware.

These tithe records survive relatively intact, for three copies of each were made, one for the diocesan registry, one for the parish chest and one for the Commissioners. The diocesan copies for Wales are in the National Library, and the Tithe Redemption Office copies have recently been deposited in the Public Record Office (as I.R. 29 and I.R. 30), so the failure of many parishes to keep them safe is not a matter of great moment, except inasmuch as it is only one aspect of the neglect of parochial records.

[1] *The Records of the Tithe Redemption Office* (Board of Inland Revenue, London 1957).

In addition to these commercial or official maps, there are a great many private maps in existence, maps and plans which were made for the administrative convenience and information of the landowner and his officials. Like other maps, few of these are medieval. Despite the detail often given about boundaries in conveyances and the necessity of keeping a record of tenants' holdings in extents and rentals, the earliest estate maps to survive anywhere in Britain are fourteenth-century and the earliest Welsh example in the Public Record Office is the Henrician map of the parishes of St Brides Major, Wick and Ewenny in Glamorganshire.[1] Such maps (this one measures 3' 9" by 2' 6") are of uncommon value to the historian: presumably other Tudor or Stuart private maps exist in the National Library, the British Museum and local record offices. Later maps, both of estates and of townships, are also useful and they exist in rather larger quantity. A union list of Welsh estate maps would be yet another worth-while project, perhaps under the auspices of the National Library.

All these different kinds of maps call for careful handling, both physically and intellectually. In particular when, as so often happens, the tithe map seems to be the earliest available large-scale map, it is too easy to use its evidence indiscriminately for an earlier period. The late maps have to be used for identifying places, for clarifying manorial or urban topography, for testing theories about nucleated settlements or hamlet development, and so forth, but boundaries change, farms and houses disappear, new buildings, new groupings are created, forests and woods contract, marshes are drained, rivers even change their course. Maps can only show what has become of the medieval landscape, and all available earlier documentary and archaeological evidence has to be marshalled before a convincing interpretation of cartographic evidence can be made.

Anyone contemplating even localised use of maps should read

---

[1] *Maps and Plans in the Public Record Office*, i, *British Isles, c. 1410–1860* (London 1967), no. 4147. The call-mark is MR 6.

carefully the work of Miss Sylvester and Mr Glanville Jones as a preliminary.[1] But, as Professor Jones Pierce said, 'a Welshman who would write the history of his native parish cannot afford to neglect the tithe map and its explanatory schedule, for in them alone will he find a detailed ground-plan of his subject . . . a record near enough to our own day to be intelligible without overstraining the imagination, and yet sufficiently remote for us to perceive in it much that was characteristic of earlier landscapes and social settings'.[2] And if for purposes of agrarian research, not only a ground-plan but also an underground plan is required, then there are the maps produced by the Geological Survey and the Soil Survey, with their accompanying memoirs published over the years by Her Majesty's Stationery Office.

One of the many uses to which maps are put is the identification of place-names. Place-names are, however, sources in their own right. The interpretation of place-name evidence depends on a reasonable corpus of agreed information, covering a wide geographical area. Scandinavian scholars, with government assistance, made comprehensive surveys of their native place-names more than a generation ago. England has had its Place-Name Society publishing since 1924. Professor Mawer's complaint that he could not do justice to the place-names of Northumberland and Durham in 1920 because 'no single county can be dealt with satisfactorily apart from a survey of the field of English place-nomenclatures as a whole'[3] would not be made today after the appearance of the forty-fifth volume of the Society's surveys. The organised effort 'in which the historian, the student of records, and the man or woman possessed of local knowledge co-operate

[1] D. Sylvester, *The Rural Landscape of the Welsh Borderland* (London 1969); G. R. J. Jones, 'Some Medieval Rural Settlements in North Wales', *Trans. Institute of British Geographers* (1953), 'The Distribution of Medieval Settlement in Anglesey', *Trans. Anglesey Antiquarian Society and Field Club* (1955) and elsewhere.

[2] T. Jones Pierce, introduction to 'The Tithe Schedule for the Parish of Garn Dolbenmaen', *Trans. Caernarvonshire Historical Society*, xiii (1952), 77.

[3] A. Mawer, *The Place-Names of Northumberland and Durham* (Cambridge 1920), vii.

with the philologist and check or supplement his conclusions'[1] has been made and sustained in England, although there is still work enough to do. As a result of the first stage of this co-operative effort, Sir Frank Stenton could deliver five successive presidential addresses to the Royal Historical Society on 'The Historical Bearing of Place-Name Studies'[2] and post-war English scholars have made use of place-names for a wide range of historical argument.

The position in Wales is very different. The Board of Celtic Studies ignored not only the antiquaries who made Welsh studies possible but also the study of place-names when it organised the survey of *Celtic Studies in Wales* in 1963. Its only activity in this field of publishing has been the *Gazetteer*, edited by Elwyn Davies, giving a guide to the vexed question of the correct spelling of Welsh place-names in their Welsh form. English alternatives are ignored and the utility of the list for historical purposes is far less than Professor Melville Richards's *Welsh Administrative and Territorial Units, Medieval and Modern*, which appeared in 1969, twelve years after the first edition of the *Gazetteer*. Professor Richards's work is, however, only an off-shoot of his grander project to supply Wales with what an entire society has been supplying to England over forty-five years. Although Professor Lloyd-Jones, Sir Ifor Williams and R. J. Thomas published valuable work, the only areas recently covered in any systematic way are Flintshire and Dinas Powys: and Canon Ellis Davies made no use of the absolutely essential collections of estate documents for his Flintshire compilation. Only with Mr Gwynedd Pierce's *Place-Names of Dinas Powys Hundred* did Welsh onomastic studies draw level with English or Scandinavian, even in a restricted field. Mr Pierce's survey of the names in these twenty parishes is masterly, but it needs companions.[3]

[1] F. M. Stenton, 'The Study of English Place-Names', *History*, vi (1921–22), 201.

[2] *Trans. Royal Historical Society*, 4th series, xxi (1939) to xxv (1943), reprinted in *Preparatory to Anglo-Saxon England, being the Collected Papers of Frank Merry Stenton*, ed. D. M. Stenton (Oxford 1970), 253–324.

[3] Cf. Melville Richards' reviews of Davies and Pierce in *Arch. Camb.*, cix (1960), 183–5 and cxviii (1969), 161–2.

Already, however, there are studies of certain elements in Welsh names. Dr B. G. Charles gave a preliminary important survey of *Non-Celtic Place-Names in Wales* in 1938 and Professor Melville Richards's series of studies in local transactions and philological journals is already impressive. But until Professor Richards's own immense labours amid the estate collections finally take the published form of his 'historical dictionary of Welsh place-names',[1] the authoritative discussion of onomastic evidence for settlement, foreign influence (Scandinavian, Norman, Flemish, English), topographical detail, agricultural organisation, industrial development and so forth cannot be achieved. By contrast, a local historian in two dozen English counties has at his elbow the equivalent of Mr Pierce's *Dinas Powys*. No one, least of all Professor Richards, can be happy with the present record of printed materials on Welsh place-names.

[1] Melville Richards, *Welsh Administrative and Territorial Units* (Cardiff 1969), vii.

# CHAPTER 9

*Conclusion*

In 1808 Sir Samuel Meyrick published *The History and Antiquities of the County of Cardigan collected from the Few Remaining Documents which have Escaped the Destructive Ravages of Time, as well as from Actual Observation*. I have tried, from my actual observation, to collect some information about these scattered evidences of Wales's past. The documents, taken by and large, are not as few as Meyrick feared, but they do survive very unevenly. The outstanding feature of the archival remains is that one topic and one only can be explored in reasonable depth and that topic is the financial administration of the Principality. Everything else survives only in fragments and unsystematic transcripts, but the records of the chamberlains and their officials, and their relations with the English government, survive, poorly enough by the standards of the English Exchequer, but well enough to promote more studies like those of Mr Waters and Mrs Fryde.

This by no means limits, however, the useful and necessary work waiting to be done. I have tried to emphasise throughout this book how studies of charter-forms, of episcopal administration, of marcher lordships, of land-holding and *gwelyau*, of place-names, of masons' marks, of books owned by Welsh monasteries, of comparisons with Scotland and Ireland and so on, are needed before students of Welsh history have a proper base. And before these secondary studies are done, there is an urgent need for guides and indexes and calendars and union-lists from many repositories. They are dull enough things to compile, but they have been achieved for England on a scale unknown to Wales. This is attributable partly to the breadth of vision shown by English historians and archivists throughout this century, partly to the achievements of the Public Record Office and the omni-purpose county record offices, partly to the Historical Manuscripts Commission. The increasing centralisation of Welsh historical records in Aberystwyth and the consequent emasculation of the Welsh county record offices have, it might well be argued, done more harm than good. Glamorgan County Record Office supplies copies of its few estate lists to the National Register of Archives with minimum delay; the National Library supplies nothing. Local historians are increasingly prevented from any archival research without the inconvenient journey to Aberystwyth, in the strongest contrast to the activities of local societies and secondary schools in most English county towns and metropolitan boroughs. The Welsh counties are, it is true, really too small and too poor to support a viable record office apiece. An outsider without involvement in local rivalries can, however, argue that an archive service created on a regional basis might have supplied some satisfactory compromise between inefficient morcelation and the present over-centralisation. The re-creation of Gwynedd, Dyfed and Powys in the proposed reform of Welsh local government is precisely what the archival services of Wales needed decades ago. But even if local government reform brings archival reorganisation, the fact of the National Library's holdings will remain, and the problems of locating and reaching materials cannot be solved by any decentralisation or reversal of the present trends.

Finding-aids remain and will remain just as necessary, and because of their absence Welsh historians have achieved less than their potential. There are too many obstacles in their path, and these same obstacles seem to deter post-graduate students, even native Welsh ones, from working on Welsh history. The obstacles are fundamentally created by the inadequacy of the guides to record materials, by the failure to produce workable texts of sufficient archival, narrative and poetic sources, by a general preoccupation with prehistoric and Roman archaeology in preference to medieval, by an indifference to medieval numismatics, by a lack of co-operative enterprise in place-name studies, by a general lack of encouragement to the outsider, but most of all by the failure of any national body to make a comprehensive assessment of what needs to be done in Welsh historical scholarship, to publicise this for discussion and then to do something about it. Too little is being done too late by too few.

As a result, Welsh history, particularly late medieval history, is particularly hard to teach. A lecturer in Welsh history remarked to me once that he had perforce to treat the thirteenth century as a dialogue between himself and Sir John Lloyd. Now there is an element of personal involvement in this, and the students in such a seminar come into contact with the historical process at work, but can one contemplate teaching the thirteenth century in England as a dialogue between oneself and Powicke? Whereas it is becoming increasingly hard to advise a student from one's own knowledge which of an array of possibilities, both books and articles, he should read on any given English topic, medieval Welsh historiography remains dominated by Lloyd and Rees. Only Glanmor Williams has produced any comparable work of synthesis, and some antidote to Lloyd and Rees is urgently required.

A programme for reform is essential. Too much is left entirely to the uncertain chance of a supervisor's knowledge and interest. Recently graduated students, even within Wales, have little comprehensive guidance to the potential range of research topics. Yet, whereas English history is increasingly driving its postgraduates into cramped corners of archival experience, Welsh history still offers topics of wide interest and relevance, texts of major importance still unedited, fundamental work still to be undertaken.

# Index

*Authors cited in the book appear in the Index in italics*